10-17-77

THEODOR FONTANE

THE FRONTISPIECE

THEODOR FONTANE

THEODOR FONTANE

An Introduction to the Man and his Work

by

A. R. ROBINSON

CARDIFF
UNIVERSITY OF WALES PRESS
1976

Printed by The Cambrian News (Aberystwyth) Ltd.

PREFACE

Twenty years ago Theodor Fontane was little known outside his own country except in university departments of German. Today his work is frequently studied in our schools, thanks to the existence of annotated texts, and it is available to a wider reading public through English translations. Far beyond the frontiers of Germany his status as a novelist of European rank is belatedly acknowledged.

The purpose of this monograph is to fill a gap left by the various studies in German, written mainly for the specialist. It is designed for all those likely to come into contact with Fontane's creative writings, whether they be students at universities and colleges, sixth-form pupils or general readers. An account is given of the man and his spiritual development. His travel books and poetry are examined as well as the later novels and *Novellen*, each of which is surveyed individually before general conclusions are drawn and an attempt made to view Fontane in a European perspective.

I should like to express my warmest thanks to the following for their valuable suggestions and unfailing help during the preparation of this book : Emeritus Professor C. P. Magill and Miss Eiluned Rees from the National Library of Wales.

Aberystwyth, May 1975   A. R. ROBINSON.

CONTENTS

Chapter 1

EARLY DAYS

In the summer of 1867 two men were strolling in the little hamlet of Schiffmühle by the Oder, talking of the past. The elder of them, Louis Henri Fontane, was 71 years old, frail and asthmatic, but still lively in spirit; the younger, his son Theodor, a man of 47, was known to a modest but growing circle of readers as a writer of ballads, travel books and war histories. Together they recalled the days of forty years earlier when the father had enjoyed a brief spell of freedom from financial worries and spent several happy months travelling about North Germany, seeking in his leisurely manner for a new place in which to settle and practise his profession as a pharmacist.

The foregoing years had been difficult ones for Louis Fontane. He was born on March 24, 1796, as the son of an art teacher, Pierre Barthélemy Fontane, a man of Huguenot descent and at one time a private secretary to Queen Luise of Prussia. In 1809 he became an apprentice at the Elefanten-Apotheke in Berlin. He took part as a volunteer in the War of Liberation against the French, seeing active service at Groß-Görschen near Leipzig in 1813 and elsewhere, and then worked as an assistant pharmacist in both Danzig and Berlin until obtaining his state diploma in 1818. Married early in the following year, on March 24, 1819, he was already a father by the end of that same year at the age of 23. Since Easter 1819 Louis Fontane and his young wife, Emilie (née Labry), had been settled in the Löwen-Apotheke, Neuruppin, where their eldest son, Theodor, was born on December 30, and there they were to remain until Easter 1826, by which time their family had increased to four. But Louis Fontane's love of gambling and consequent habit of living above his income had already cast its shadow over the domestic circle. Debts were mounting and creditors pressing for payment, foremost among them being Louis Fontane's own father. Domestic scenes and reproaches grew as the orderly-minded Emilie supported her father-in-law in his attempt to curb the recklessness of his spendthrift son.

In an effort to break out of this painful situation, Louis Fontane sold the Löwen-Apotheke at a good price, appeased his creditors, and enjoyed a fifteen months' interlude as a gentleman of leisure during his none-too-rigorous search for another pharmacy—preferably one which lay well out of the reach of his own parents and their supervision of his affairs. If he had had his way, his son Theodor believed, this interim period would have lasted for a lifetime, since Louis Fontane loved horses and travel even more than he loved playing cards. " Sein Lebenlang in der Welt herumzukutschieren, immer auf der Suche nach einer Apotheke, ohne diese je finden zu können, wäre wohl eigentlich sein Ideal gewesen."[1] Finally common sense prevailed and Louis Fontane became the new owner of a small pharmacy in the little Pomeranian seaside resort of Swinemünde, to which the family moved on Midsummer Day, 1827.

Theodor Fontane has left us a vivid description[2] of his first impression of Swinemünde, the North Sea watering place which exerted such a strong influence on his formative years. Initial disappointment at the somewhat rural, unsophisticated nature of the little town soon gave way to lively pleasure as the eight-year-old boy explored their new home with its series of mysterious lofts, one above the other, in the steep gabled roof, listened to the gruesome tales and local lore of the old coachman Ehm in an unfamiliar *Plattdeutsch* and discovered for the first time the joys of living by the sea—the new world of ships and harbours. Just as Swinemünde seemed to present glaring contrasts of the ugly and the attractive in its architecture and layout, so also did the quality of its social life appear to be one of sharply differentiated characteristics. Looking back on it in later years, Fontane tells us[3] that local society was mercifully free of many of those narrow philistine values which were typical of the inland provincial towns, thanks to its international character. Seafaring Swedes, Danes, Dutch, Scots and other foreigners had settled there over the years, quite apart from a floating population of visiting seamen and merchants from all over Europe. Contrasting with this free and easy social scene of the waterfront, public life and its social ramifications were almost exclusively in the hands of twenty families, forming the 'Honoratiorenschaft' of Swinemünde. From one point of view the town might have been, in the early nineteenth century, "ein unschönes Nest" as Fontane later admitted,[4] but its harbour life had a charm of its own, a lively atmosphere of comings and goings, a continual bustle of trade and shipping. "It was a truly wonderful life in this little town," he was to write in 1894, "of which even now I think with the liveliest emotions, as indeed of my whole colourful and varied childhood existence."[5]

Here the youthful eye of the future novelist surveyed a far wider social spectrum than would have been possible away from the ' Waterkante '. The harbour, too, provided an ideal playground for boys ; in his autobiographical work *Meine Kinderjahre*, Fontane recalls in some detail and with much gusto a youthful adventure there on one April Sunday of 1831.[6] On that day their games nearly ended in disaster, as one of the group lost his footing on the slippery deck of a moored ship and plunged into the icy waters below.

The boyhood years at Swinemünde were a time not only for play but also for discipline and learning. His formal education had been very scanty. During the eight years spent at Neuruppin (1819-27) he had attended for a brief period the local infants' school, and, on arrival at Swinemünde in June 1827, went for a few weeks to the *Stadtschule*, from which he was summarily removed when his mother, returning after a period of illness, discovered the conditions prevailing there. Until 1832 he relied mainly on his father's teaching to provide him with some sort of educational background, occasionally supplemented by the help of a tutor shared with other boys. Louis Fontane's educational theories were distinctly unorthodox, but, thanks to his lively imagination and passion for detail and data, he appears to have succeeded in stimulating the boy's interest in a way which later earned his lasting gratitude. During his early years the young Theodor was closer to his father than to his mother, and the personal influence of Louis upon his son was considerable. They shared a similar impressionable nature, the same zest for life, and the ability to find much happiness in its simpler joys. Fontane has described his father as " a tall, distinguished-looking Gascon, good-natured, full of imagination and humour, and an accomplished raconteur . . . "[7] The latter qualities were found in equal or greater measure in his son. His manner of educating the boy

was, to say the least of it, highly original. He laid greater
stress on ' bon sens ' and ' savoir faire ' than on book learning,
and his teaching was based on a system of continuous question
and answer, his so-called ' Socratic method '. In this process
much emphasis was placed on historical reminiscence. This
helped to stimulate in the boy that outstanding sense of history
which was not only to lend colour to his ballads, travel books
and early prose tales, but was to appear again and again in
the later works for which Theodor Fontane is best remembered
today. In these the historical element is sometimes closely
woven into the fabric of the plot, occasionally inserted as a
frank digression. Fontane's mother clearly disapproved of her
husband's methods of teaching the boy, but he himself has
stated : " I owe to these lessons, as also to the accompanying
conversations of a similar nature, all the best, or at any rate
all the most useful items of my knowledge."[8] The 'Anekdoten-
reichtum ' (as he calls it) acquired from his father and from
their joint perusal of journals and encyclopedias he rated more
highly than all he later learned from his high school teachers.
Their combined dramatization of historical scenes (e.g. the
ceremony of Latour d'Auvergne, ' le premier grenadier de
France '[9]) remained vividly in his memory throughout the
later years. " If I were to be asked," he writes, " to which one
of my teachers I felt truly indebted, then I should have to
answer: my father."[10] Time and time again during his long
life the mature Theodor Fontane was to recognise these un-
conventional hours of home teaching as the source of his early
interest in topics which served him well both in his social life
and as a writer. He is most explicit about this—" auch bei
meinen Schreibereien waren sie mir immer wie ein Schatz-
kästlein zur Hand."[11]

Louis Fontane, however, could not claim equal distinction
as a *moral* tutor to his son. He was oddly boyish in outlook for a
man of mature years, was easily deflected from his aims, and
he tended to be irresponsible in money matters, preferring
cards and gambling to his daily round of duties. When bank-
ruptcy threatened the household, Louis Fontane continued to
give elaborate weekly dinner parties which, in retrospect,
reminded his son of the feast of Belshazzar " insoweit . . . als
eine Geisterhand schon den Bankrott des Gastgebers an die

Wand schrieb."[12] But in one respect he was a model husband and father ; despite his good looks and the obvious attraction he had for women, Louis Fontane was, as his son puts it, " das absolute Gegenteil von einem Don Juan, auch stolz auf seine Tugend."[13] On the other hand he enjoyed the company of attractive women and, like his son in later years, possessed a profound insight into the feminine psyche. He also had the ability to broach highly personal topics in conversation with them without causing the least embarrassment. In *Meine Kinderjahre* we read : " Ich habe diese Neigung, in scherzhaftem Tone mit Damen in diffizile Debatten einzutreten, von ihm geerbt, ja, diese Neigung sogar in meiner Schreibweise mit herubergenommen, und wenn ich entsprechende Szenen in meinen Romanen und kleinen Erzählungen lese, so ist es mir mitunter, als hörte ich meinen Vater sprechen."[14] Despite these similarities, however, their paths were later to diverge. Fontane's father lacked the more balanced qualities of his son and ended his life in an atmosphere of Micawber-like unreality, his famous ' Plaudertalent ' degenerating at times into mere garrulity.

Theodor Fontane's mother was virtually a complete contrast to her husband. Also a descendant of the French ' colony ' in Berlin, she was—on the surface at least—a strong, energetic personality, unselfish in her devotion to duty, reliable in all the practical emergencies of everyday life, sparing of words and austere to the verge of harshness. The young boy felt nothing of the close link with her that he enjoyed with his father, and only later in life did he fully realise the superiority of her moral fibre and acknowledge his personal indebtedness to it. Thus, in his adult years, a new bond of affection was forged between Theodor Fontane and his mother, as their correspondence in the *Familienbriefe* has shown. In an autobiographical account, *Von Zwanzig bis Dreißig*, he refers to two characteristics he possesses : " . . . a longing for work and steady devotion to duty, the best qualities which I inherited from my mother."[15]

Unlike her husband, Emilie Fontane, Theodor's mother, had but scant respect for scholarship, and the highest academic honours counted but little in her eyes when compared to the more tangible success of the rich business-man or banker. Her values were essentially of a practical nature, and her ideal of happiness was viewed in terms of property and income. In bringing up her children, therefore, she laid great stress on the social virtues of a smart appearance and good manners. At times she tended towards that ' Sinn für Repräsentation" which her son was later to portray satirically in *Frau Jenny Treibel*. On the positive side, however, she also represented at her best those ' bürgerlich ' (as distinct from merely ' bourgeois ') qualities—the distinction is Fontane's—of the German middle classes for which he had a genuine respect and which are treated in his prose tales with a slightly reluctant admiration.

The price of the intense self-discipline practised by Fontane's mother was a tendency towards nervous hypersensitivity, and this weakness was to some extent passed on to her son. In middle and later life Theodor Fontane suffered acutely at times from nervous depression and inner conflicts. These he further projected, as we shall later see, on to a considerable number of his novel-characters. The conflicting aspects of his personality appear to be closely linked with the divergent traits inherited from his parents, and he refers quite frankly to " die Gedoppeltheit meiner Natur ".[16] This caused prolonged and difficult struggles between the rival claims of reason and emotion—struggles which are frequently reflected in the characters of his novels, for whom they often have tragic results.

Perhaps the most unexpected trait in the character of Fontane's mother was her generosity, often dangerously liberal for a family of slender means. Fontane later remarked ironically " es gab Zeiten, wo wir, schon erwachsen, uns die Frage vorlegten, welche Passion eigentlich bedrohlicher für uns sei, die Spielpassion des Vaters oder die Schenk- und Gebepassion der Mutter ".[17] But there was a fundamental difference; these acts of generosity were selfless and achieved a positive result, whereas Louis Fontane's gambling fever brought pleasure to nobody—neither to his well-off card-playing circle nor even to himself, as he later admitted. As father and son strolled together in Schiffmühle, forty years after these events, Louis Fontane talked of those far-off days. Clearly his conscience troubled him in old age that he should have left his wife and family without any financial security, allowed his love of gambling to break up his marriage, and yet have done all this, as he later realised, mainly through boredom and the assumption of family responsibilities at too early an age. Sadly he concludes :

"Aber wenn ich mich dann den ganzen Tag über gelangweilt hatte, wollte ich am Abend wenigstens einen Wechsel verspüren, und dabei bin ich mein Geld losgeworden und sitze nun hier einsam, und deine Mutter erschrickt vor dem Gedanken, ich könnte mich wieder bei ihr einfinden. Es sind nun beinahe fünfzig Jahre, daß wir uns verlobten, und sie schrieb mir damals zärtliche Briefe, denn sie liebte mich. Und das ist nun der Ausgang. Zuneigung allein ist nicht genug zum Heiraten ; Heiraten ist eine Sache für vernünftige Menschen. Ich hatte noch nicht die Jahre, vernünftig zu sein."[18]

This was in fact to be the last conversation between old Louis Fontane and his son. A few weeks later, in October 1867, Theodor Fontane returned to Schiffmühle, but his father's restless spirit had departed for ever.

The influence of one other personality during this Swinemünde period of Theodor Fontane's boyhood must not be overlooked. From Easter 1828 until the late autumn of 1830 Fontane was allowed to share the services of a house tutor employed to teach his young friend Wilhelm Krause. This earnest, scholarly man, about thirty years of age, also possessed those qualities of imagination and sincerity which could make a direct appeal to the mind of youth. Fontane writes : " Dr. Lau, so hieß der neue Hauslehrer, war ein vorzüglicher Pädagog, weil er ein vorzüglicher Mensch war, und wenn ich oben gesagt habe, daß ich eigentlich alles den Anekdoten meines Vaters zu verdanken hätte, so muß ich doch den guten Doktor Lau ausnehmen."[19] His special contribution was the addition of method and order to the teaching begun by Fontane's father. "Das bißchen Rückgrat, das mein Wissen hat, verdanke ich ihm,"[20] concludes his former pupil. Despite his unenviable position, almost akin to that of a domestic servant in the Krause family as far as the ' good society ' of Swinemünde was concerned, Dr. Lau somehow contrived to give the impression of inner freedom and superiority, while in the Krause home he earned both esteem and affection, above all from his young charges.

The comparative freedom and the open-air life of Swinemünde were, however, gradually drawing to a close. Looking
back on them, Fontane recalled these years as a time of play,
exercise and make-believe rather than of schooling and discipline. And so indeed it was for the most part. His autobiography, *Meine Kinderjahre*, tells us about trials of strength with
the local boys, risky acrobatic adventures, antics on stilts,
modelling, hide-and-seek, tree-climbing, amateur firework-
making, the firing of model cannon and dangerous home-made
guns, playing 'robbers and travellers' amongst the quays
and boats, and getting into risky situations in drifting dinghys
at the harbour mouth. Noteworthy, too, are the accounts of
Louis Fontane's tolerant understanding when his son occasionally ran into trouble through trespassing on board tied-up ships
or falling from forbidden chestnut trees. The last few months
of all this carefree life, in 1831-32, were to some extent overshadowed by personal problems and conflicts. His long-
standing leadership of a small private 'army' of youngsters
from Swinemünde's 'better' families was threatened by
defeats at the hands of his old enemies, the 'Schiffsjungen',
while the sense of impending departure from home filled him
with a mixture of uneasy anticipation and diminished self-
confidence in the face of the unknown. No more would he be
the proud leader of a troop of devoted followers, practising
elaborate manœuvres in the fields and on the shores outside
the familiar little town, never again could he identify himself
with the heroic adventures of Klaus Störtebeker, the 15th
century pirate, as he threatened the whole of Swinemünde
with bombardment. Henceforth he would merely be an
unknown boy of twelve at a strange school in a far-off town.
Even the final Christmas and New Year with his family were a
disappointment and filled with minor humiliations and inner
disharmony. When the time came for him to receive the
traditional homily on upright living and good behaviour in
the world away from home, the result was a disaster. Both he
and his father were equally embarrassed by the occasion, and
he was obliged to fight an exhausting and not altogether
successful battle against hysterical laughter.

It had been decided that Theodor Fontane should attend
the Ruppiner Gymnasium, where friends and relatives would

be on hand to watch over his welfare, so, in April 1832, he set out for the town of his birth, accompanied by his mother—for Louis Fontane felt unequal to this stern task, involving as it did interviews with the headmaster and with a minister at whose home his young son was to stay. Looking back upon this end of an era, Fontane was later to write :

"Es war, trotz des letzten Halbjahres mit seinen vielen kleinen Ärgernissen, eine glückliche Zeit gewesen ; später—den Spätabend meines Lebens ausgenommen—hatt' ich immer nur vereinzelte glückliche Stunden. Damals aber, als ich in Haus und Hof umherspielte und draußen meine Schlachten schlug, damals war ich unschuldigen Herzens und geweckten Geistes gewesen, voll Anlauf und Aufschwung, ein richtiger Junge, guter Leute Kind. Alles war Poesie. Die Prosa kam bald nach, in allen möglichen Gestalten, oft auch durch eigene Schuld."[21]

Theodor Fontane's first year away from his parents' roof and spent in the ' Quarta ' of the Ruppiner Gymnasium, under its choleric headmaster, ' der alte Thormeyer ' (described as " eine Kolossalfigur mit Löwenkopf und Löwenstimme " and as " der Schulmonarch, wie er im Buche steht "),[22] does not appear to have done very much to fill the many gaps in his formal education—a situation about which Fontane was somewhat sensitive in later years. " Einige Lücken wurden wohl zugestopft, aber alles blieb zufällig und ungeordnet, und das berühmte Wort vom ' Stückwerk ' traf auf Lebenszeit buchstäblich und in besonderer Hochgradigkeit bei mir zu."[23] Nor did Fontane react favourably to the heavily authoritarian atmosphere of the school, and it is probably from this date that his lifelong aversion to the Prussian educational system began.

He was taken away from Ruppin in the autumn of 1833 at his parents' wish and transferred to the Klödensche Gewerbeschule, a technical school in Berlin. He arrived in the Prussian capital at the age of fourteen, and thereafter it remained the focal point of his life and work until his death there in 1898 at the age of seventy-nine.

The technical school interlude was to last for three and a half years, during which time he stayed at the home of his Uncle August and Aunt ' Pinchen ' (Philippine). If Fontane's father had shown signs of frivolity in his attitude towards life's responsibilities, he was but a tyro in comparison with Onkel August. Where the money came from (when there was any) remained for a long time a mystery to Theodor Fontane, but the only concern of his jovial uncle and his well-matched spouse, a former actress, was to spend it with the maximum of enjoyment. The atmosphere of this new home was congenial though hardly calculated to provide the minimal amount of discipline and supervision needed by a boy of tender years. Finding his movements almost totally unchecked and dis-covering at the same time ingenious ways of absenting himself unnoticed from the large classes, often taught by outside teachers, at the technical school, Fontane began to prefer the exploration of Berlin and its environs to the mixed bag of subjects thrust at him by the Klödensche Gewerbeschule. He became in fact a skilful truant on a large scale, and spent morning after morning at attractive places outside the city, such as Grunewald, Jungfernheide and Tegel, referred to later as his " travels through the Mark of Brandenburg long before their legitimate beginning."[24] Then, during the afternoons, he would explore the historic centre of Berlin or sit in one of the smaller cafés, such as Anthieny's, where he was least likely to be discovered, and browse through a pile of newspapers and literary periodicals provided for the customers. He was later to observe drily that, if he had spent those afternoons dutifully at school, his conscience might have been better but his know-ledge poorer ; " so wäre mein Gewissen zwar reiner geblieben, aber mein Wissen auch."[25]

The Berlin idyll was shattered abruptly. One afternoon he came home from school—attended in fact, not in fiction, on this particular occasion—to discover a great domestic drama in progress.

Onkel August had been unmasked as a petty swindler who had embezzled the funds of relatives, children, and even the lifetime savings of the crippled old maid-servant. Theodor Fontane's final memory of life with Onkel August in Berlin was his uncle, the last shreds of his bonhomie and dignity destroyed, being heaped with curses and abuse by the old woman.

If the humour and ' Plaudertalent ' of Onkel August had earlier made a strong impact upon the impressionable boy, the eventual catastrophe was to serve as a lifelong warning. In the final appearance of his uncle, Fontane saw the extreme expression of something he had sensed in his father and which lurked deep down within himself. It was a lesson he never forgot. Three days later his schooldays, such as they had been, were ended, and he began his apprenticeship as a pharmaceutical chemist—his father's profession. From a strictly academic viewpoint Fontane's boyhood years had provided a totally defective and fragmentary background ; for the future writer, on the other hand, they provided a rich storehouse of varied impressions, memories and social experiences granted to few of his contemporaries. Writing as a mature novelist in 1892 he could say in all sincerity : " Wie wurden wir erzogen ? Gar nicht und—ausgezeichnet !"[26]

Chapter 2

APPRENTICESHIP TO LIFE

THE four-year period spent as a pharmaceutical apprentice began at Easter 1836, when Fontane entered the business of Wilhelm Rose in the Spandauer Straße, and his first employer was in many ways a historical prototype of the future bourgeois characters in his novels. Fontane deals with him harshly in his autobiography, defining for us that quality of ' Geldsackgesinnung ' masked by apparent idealism, which he was later to attack ruthlessly in his prose works, especially in *Frau Jenny Treibel*. " Alle geben sie vor, Ideale zu haben ; in einem fort quasseln sie vom ' Schönen, Guten, Wahren ' und knicksen doch nur vor dem Goldnen Kalb."[1] They also possess the second disagreeable characteristic of self-praise, as did Rose ; Fontane recalls his habit : " alles, was von ihm ausging oder ihm zugehörte, gründlich zu bewundern."[2] As a part of his pretension to ' das Schöne ', Wilhelm Rose subscribed to a reading circle and received in return frequent packages of books—books which he never read, but which were seized upon gratefully by his apprentice.

It was during these early years in Berlin, too, that Fontane first tried his hand at literary composition—much of it thought out while performing routine duties in the dispensary, he tells us. By the end of the summer of 1840 he had completed two substantial works : a verse epic entitled *Heinrichs IV. erste Liebe* (inspired by a *Novelle* of Zschokke's) and a novel called *Du hast recht getan!* (based on a contemporary court action for murder in Mark Brandenburg). He also, in this period, became a member of two literary circles, the Lenau-Verein and Platen-Verein, about whose members he has left us some lively reminiscences.

In the autumn of 1840 Fontane left Berlin for Burg, near Magdeburg, but remained there for only three months, finding the town insufferably dull. On the 30th December (" es war mein Geburtstag, den ich dadurch feierte "[3]) he left Burg thankfully and returned to Berlin. But his sense of well-being was short-lived, for on the evening of the 3rd January he collapsed and was found to be suffering from typhus. Recovery was a long process, and it was seven weeks before he was even fit enough to be moved to his parents' home in the country to convalesce. By 31st March 1841, however, he was able to assume his duties at the new post he had just accepted before his illness, namely in Leipzig at the Neubertsche Apotheke.

Fontane's first impressions of Leipzig were nearly all favourable ones, as he recalls in *Von Zwanzig bis Dreißig*, and he recognized with the eye of an artist that this city possessed the very element which Berlin lacked—architectural individuality. Even the somewhat spartan quarters assigned to him at the Neubertsche Haus in the Hainstraße failed to dampen his spirits, thanks to their ' interesting ' quality. He has described for us in some detail his daily routine at Leipzig, particularly in the summer months when, by dint of very early rising, he could enjoy the morning sunshine for two hours or more before work began, following up his walk or bathe with an open-air breakfast at Kintschy's to an accompaniment of bird-song. Back in the Neubertsche Apotheke, the next milestone of the day's activities was the visit of the local doctors for their pharmaceutical needs and the exchange of gossip, always a welcome, almost social occasion before the more routine duties which followed.

Later in the year, when autumn days were shorter and cooler, his excursions took on a different character, and Fontane's steps turned towards the famous battlefields of the War of Liberation (1813). " Historischen Grund und Boden zu betreten, hatte zu jeder Zeit einen besonderen Zauber für mich," he recalls.[4] On the exact anniversary of the battle fought at Wachau-Markkleeberg, on 18 October, he tramped over the historic area, and, combining his interest in the past with his hopes for the future, he was inspired to create an early cycle of poems on the subject of German political freedom. But by and large these Leipzig days, as he admits, were mainly occupied with hard work in his daily routine at the Neubertsche Apotheke—a fact about which he has no complaints in later years : " Ich setzte meine Ehre darein, alles Dahingehörige nach bestem Vermögen zu tun, und segnete die Tage, wo's soviel Arbeit gab, daß ich an andere Dinge gar nicht denken konnte."[5] Mindful of the dilettante shiftlessness and unstable streak in his father and uncle, Theodor Fontane records for later generations the link which he felt existed in those days between the intense enjoyment of his leisure hours and the conscientious fulfilment of his day's routine work ; in this way a dangerous clash between profession and inner inclinations had been totally avoided.

However, his personal interests were by no means completely neglected while at Leipzig. As the result of a short satirical poem, *Shakespeares Strumpf*, in the widely-read ' Leipziger Tageblatt ', Fontane's name became known in local literary circles. The circumstances were as follows : the ' Leipziger Schillerverein ' had come into possession of a waistcoat which had belonged to Schiller himself and, with much ceremony, had presented it to the local Schiller Museum. Inclined, as always, to an ironical view of formalities, Fontane found this slightly absurd and responded with a five-stanza lampoon which began :

> Laut gesungen, hoch gesprungen,
> ob verschimmelt auch und dumpf,
> Seht, wir haben ihn errungen,
> William Shakespeares wollnen Strumpf.[6]

This led to an invitation from the Leipzig publisher, Robert Binder, to visit him shortly afterwards, and through him Fontane was also to meet other members of Leipzig intellectual society, principally Hermann Schauenburg (a medical student with poetic talents), Hermann Kriege (a young radical, who later emigrated to America) and Georg Günther (Binder's energetic, able young editor). Connection with this group led to other, wider contacts, including the poetic circle which Fontane has dubbed the ' Herwegh-Klub ', inspired as it was by the revolutionary poet Georg Herwegh (1817-1875). Here began Fontane's acquaintance with a circle of young student intellectuals, nearly all of whom were later to make a name for themselves to a greater or lesser degree in the outside world, in particular Wilhelm Wolfsohn and Max Müller. The former, well-read in the literature of Germany, France and Russia, first introduced Fontane to the works of Dershavin, Karamsin, Shukovsky, Pushkin, Lermontov, Pavlov and Gogol—in translation, it is true, since Wolfsohn's attempts to teach

Fontane Russian were quickly doomed to failure.

All his life Theodor Fontane deeply regretted the fact that he had as little ear for foreign languages as he had for music ; " so ist es mir mit einem halben Dutzend Sprachen ergangen," he remarks sadly : " Italienisch, Dänisch, Flämisch, Wendisch —immer wenn ich mir ein Lexikon und eine Grammatik gekauft hatte, war es wieder vorbei."[7] The only real exception seems to have been English, as we shall later see. Max Müller, son of the poet Wilhelm Müller, and later to become a Sanskrit scholar and mythologist of international reputation at Oxford, was at this time only eighteen years old, but the friendship was to develop and be resumed later both in Berlin and in England. All in all, this Leipzig phase represented for Fontane a sharpening of his critical and aesthetic senses. His personality, too, underwent considerable development, and, with his genial manner and obvious sincerity, he was able to break down the traditional barriers between Prussian and Saxon.

These happy days, lasting almost a year, came to an abrupt end when Fontane was suddenly stricken with rheumatoid arthritis, a consequence of his earlier typhus, so he believed. From the middle of February 1842 he lay immobilized in his alcove-like room at the Neubertsche Apotheke, shared by four in all, his only diversion being an occasional visit from his young Tante Pinchen, of Berlin memory, now living in Leipzig. Shortly after his Berlin débâcle Onkel August had somehow managed to find his feet again and make a fresh start at Leipzig, working for an art dealer. Such was his personal charm and good-will that Theodor Fontane had no hesitation in once again accepting his hospitality during his weeks as a convalescent patient. As he explains : " Ich war unter Verhältissen großgezogen, in denen überhaupt nie etwas stimmte. Sonderbare Geschäftsführungen und dementsprechende Geldverhältnisse waren an der Tagesordnung."[8] So at Easter, 1842, he moved into Onkel August's home in Leipzig and has recorded his happy memories of the weeks that followed. Everything seemed as it had been before the catastrophe six years earlier ; the pleasurable way of life went on as formerly and his uncle appeared unchanged—except that the adaptable rascal now spoke in fluent Saxon dialect when appropriate ! They visited Bonorand's and Kintschy's, just as they once

made expeditions to Liesens in Berlin, enjoyed the best of good
food, and chatted together in easy, good-humoured reminiscence. The effect on Fontane of the transition from the brooding loneliness of the Hainstraße attic was remarkable, and he
was soon well enough to join his aunt and uncle on a convalescent holiday in the ' Sächsische Schweiz ' before commencing
on the 1st July, 1842, a new post at the Struvesche Apotheke in
Dresden, an establishment which enjoyed a very high reputation throughout Germany.   Fontane remained there for one
pleasant if undistinguished year, which was followed by several
months of uncertainty about his future plans.   A scheme to
publish some early verses written in Dresden came to naught,
despite much patient negotiation back in Leipzig, and a spell
at his parents' home led to a determined, if rather hopeless,
effort to make good the gaps in his formal education by private
study in order to enter a university.   However, studies of a
sterner nature were to intervene, since at Easter 1844 Fontane
was called on to serve his obligatory year in the army, which
brought him into the ranks of the Prussian Guards regiment,
' Kaiser Franz '.

The second battalion, commanded by Major von Wnuck,
an old campaigner from the 1813 battles, was quartered in the
Neue Friedrichstraße, Berlin, and here the young recruit,
Fontane, was assigned to the 6th Company under another
seasoned veteran, who had fought at Leipzig and Waterloo.
Serving alongside regular troops, the one-year civilian-soldiers
were expected, after initial training, to carry out the same tasks
as their more professional comrades, including ceremonial
guard-duties in the capital.   It was during one such spell of
duty that a totally unexpected diversion occurred in Fontane's
military life.   Standing on the guard-room steps at the Neue
Wache just before resuming his duties as sentry in the Ober-
wallstraße, he was suddenly hailed by an old friend, Hermann
Scherz from Ruppin, who had come with the almost incredible
suggestion that Fontane might like to accompany him to
England in two days' time as a guest !   Improbable though
this idea might seem to be, Fontane felt that nothing would be
lost in approaching his Company Commander who, presumably taken aback by this unlikely request for fourteen days'
leave, not only allowed him to go to the colonel with his plea

but even advised him on how to present his case. The leave was granted.

So Theodor Fontane in July 1844 set off for his first visit to England. Arriving at seven in the morning at the Potsdamer Bahnhof with a modest parcel in lieu of luggage, he left on what was in fact to be the first of many journeys across the North Sea to Great Britain. From Magdeburg, which was the point of departure for the tourist group to which Hermann Scherz belonged, they proceeded slowly by river-steamer down the Elbe, past the old town of Tangermünde (later to figure prominently in one of Fontane's early prose tales), to Hamburg. Here they transferred to an elderly paddle steamer, the 'Monarch', which had formerly seen better days as an elegant passenger vessel but in recent years had been used principally as a cattle boat.

Despite the less than luxurious transport Fontane later recalled the feeling of intense happiness as he sat on deck, dressed in his makeshift civilian clothes (a brown jacket and grey uniform trousers). The one gnawing problem was that of money; apart from a few coins in his trouser pockets he was reliant on the generosity of his friend, which caused him some misgiving. On the following day they dropped anchor in the Thames near London Bridge, and were taken ashore in small boats. Fontane, 'von Jugend an ein abgeschworener Feind aller Ellbogenmanöver',[9] held back from the general scramble for the gangway, with the result that he became separated from his friend and host, Scherz, and even found himself accommodated in a different hotel, the 'Adelaide' near London Bridge, thus being threatened by grave financial problems right from the start. But there was no time to reflect on this at the moment, for the energetic organizers of the expedition whisked away the newly-landed German visitors to see Greenwich Fair as a sample of English folk life. Scherz had in fact been quartered in the London Coffee House, an old city inn not far away on Ludgate Hill, and this was duly discovered. Fortunately his financial assistance was not needed after all during the visit.

In the mornings the party toured the City of London and Westminster, in the afternoons they went on group excursions to places such as Kew, Richmond, Hampton Court, Eton and

Windsor. In Windsor they not only saw the castle, which made an instant and lasting impression on Fontane, but also—by chance—had a close view of Prince Albert and the Duke of Cambridge escorting the Czar of Russia from a parade of the Guards. At Hampton Court Fontane's most lasting impressions were of two portraits, side by side, of Queen Elizabeth and Mary Queen of Scots. In London itself Fontane's chief memories in later years were of the Tower, with its grim associations, and Westminster Abbey—less for its architectural interest than for its rich historical undertones: ' ganz unmittelbar wirkt der historische Zauber, der in diesen Steinen verkörpert ist ', says Fontane in his memoirs.[10]

Less formal in nature but equally vividly remembered were two visits of a different kind : one was to the home of a chance English acquaintance, Mr. Burford, where he had his first insight into the informal hospitality of a middle-class English household. He admired the superb sang-froid with which the housewife met this totally unexpected invasion, and saw something of the other side of life in that country of contrasts. The second was to the vast wine cellars of the East India Docks, where they were regaled with vintage port and sherry in liberal measure. Amazed by their own sobriety, the members of the German group ascended the stairway once again with dignity and confidence. ' Aber nun kam es. Kaum draußen in frischer Luft, so waren wir unserem Schicksal verfallen und mußten froh sein, einen Cab zu finden, der uns in unserem Adelaide-Hotel leidlich heil ablieferte.'[11]

On this convivial note the London visit ended. The next morning the party boarded the ' Monarch ', and two days later Fontane was in uniform again and on duty in Berlin. Soon afterwards he was promoted to the rank of ' Unteroffizier ', and as such experienced his one and only moment of minor glory when, as guard-commander, he arrested a riotous drunken civilian, who turned out to be a notorious character known to the police. Any satisfaction he may have felt was subsequently diminished when he was privately visited by three civilian friends of the accused, seeking assurances as to the nature of the charges to be laid against their boon companion ! By Easter 1845 Fontane himself was again a civilian, his year of service completed. The special significance of this year lies in the manifold contacts he made with military personalities, both commissioned and in the ranks, their jargon, values and ways of thinking. He met all types—kind, fatherly officers (such as the veteran Hauptmann, so charmingly sketched in his memoirs), stern but just Prussian officers of the old school, fashionable young lieutenants, his fellow NCO's and all kinds of private soldiers. They were to make their reappearance with great frequency in his later Berlin novels.

One of the incidental events of the year 1844-5 had been his first contact with the literary group known as the ' Tunnel über der Spree ', founded in 1827 by M. G. Saphir and of which Fontane was to remain a loyal member for many years. It was not in any sense a Berlin ' Dichterschule ' ; no manifestos were issued and there was no profession of a common literary aim. It was first and foremost a meeting place of poets and those interested in poetry, where members' work might be read and discussed. Its members were varied in social background—lawyers, teachers, lecturers and professors, army officers, also professional artists and writers. For the sake of anonymity and the ironing-out of social differences, the statutes insisted that each member be known by a pseudonym, concealing military rank and professional status. It was also forbidden to discuss politics. Fontane received the nickname of ' Lafontaine ', when he joined in May 1844 during his year with the colours. Other members since known to literary history include Moritz Graf Strachwitz ('Götz von Berlichingen' to the ' Tunnel '), Emanuel Geibel (' Bertran de Born '), Theodor Storm (' Tannhäuser '), C. F. Scherenberg (' Cook '), Paul Heyse (' Hölty ') and Heinrich Seidel (' Frauenlob '). The proceedings had a certain formality ; after the reading and acceptance of the minutes from the previous meeting, the chairman—or ' Haupt ', as he was called—would enquire whether any poetic offerings were available for discussion, whereupon aspiring young poets were expected to test their abilities before this frank if friendly company by reading out their works and subjecting them to oral criticism then and there —an ordeal of some magnitude. These were then graded by common consent into ' sehr gut ', ' gut ', ' schlecht ' and ' verfehlt '. ' Letzteres war besonders beliebt ', Fontane adds drily ; ' Von fünf Sachen waren immer vier verfehlt.'[12]

At first the young poet Fontane gained as little success with his contributions to the ' Tunnel ' as he had just before leaving Leipzig, and the style and content remained within the sphere he called ' das Herweghsche ', his verse dealing mainly with the ideal of political freedom. But it was not because of a clash with the club's rule about politics that he failed—others risked similar themes and were successful—but because Fontane had not yet found a field and style suited to his poetic temperament. This became apparent, both to him and to his audience, when he hit upon the topic of *Der alte Derfflinger*, which not only succeeded but established his position within the club. Following on the heels of this initial success came a whole series of similar poems on patriotic themes and written in the style of the 'Volkslied'. Of these, *Der alte Zieten* aroused the greatest enthusiasm, both within the club circle and out-side, though Fontane later maintained his own preference for the original prototype, *Der alte Derfflinger*, adding character-istically : ' Der erste Wurf ist immer der beste '.[13]

The ' Tunnel ' flourished until some time after 1890, when it finally began to disintegrate despite all efforts to hold it together. Fontane's active connection with it covered a period of over ten years, including one year (1854) as co-editor of its journal, *Argo*. Then he left Berlin for some time and, on his return, found himself something of a stranger : not only had its membership changed, but so had his own values and out-look. He thereafter attended its sessions only on rare occasions. His participation in its activities had led to numerous friend-ships which lasted for many years or indeed, in some cases, a lifetime. As we have seen, this was not the first literary circle of which Fontane had been a member. He had been associ-ated with the Platen and Lenau Clubs in Berlin and, later, the ' Herwegh ' group in Leipzig. But the special importance of the ' Tunnel über der Spree ' lay partly in the literary ex-perience he had gained there, together with the criticism of new work which he had both to give and to receive, and partly in the variety of social contacts to be found amongst the members. In the ' Tunnel ' he met on a familiar footing not only writers by calling but amateur *littérateurs* from the highest levels of Berlin society, military and civil, academic and admin-istrative, many of whose portraits later appear in part or in combination within his ' Berlin ' novels. The proceedings of the ' Tunnel ' increased his knowledge of and interest in English and Scottish literature (most of his free translations and adaptations of Anglo-Scottish ballads date from this period), and here, too, his interest in Shakespeare and Shakespearean translation received a new stimulus. Perhaps the factor of greatest importance, in assessing the literary and social value of the ' Tunnel ' for Fontane, was the unique opportunity it gave him of meeting the aristocracy of Mark Brandenburg, not as legendary names but as human personalities.

Returning to civilian life after a year with the ' Franzern ', Fontane faced the question of a career once more. Early attempts to be self-supporting as a poet had failed, and he was by now convinced that the hopes he had entertained of reaching a university were misguided. So it came down to the resumption of his old job as pharmacist. Having previously served in establishments which were reckoned to be amongst the best in Germany, he was hesitant to commit himself now, and it was not until midsummer 1845 that he entered the ' Polnische Apotheke ' in the Friedrichstraße, where the main attraction seems to have been the agreeable personality of his new employer, Medizinalrat Schacht, and his gifted wife, a woman of French refugee ancestry. The other members of the staff do not appear to have inspired Fontane greatly.

At the same time as Fontane had come back to Berlin from Leipzig, in 1844, almost (as he remarks) as though they belonged together, Onkel August had also returned to the Prussian capital. This was to have indirect consequences a year later which were to be of lifelong importance for his nephew. On 8 December, 1845, Onkel August celebrated his birthday, an event which Fontane was unable to attend owing to his hours of duty. But one who did attend was Emilie Rouanet-Kummer, whom he had known since she was a little girl. Whether by accident or design, it was arranged that Fontane's brother should afterwards accompany her as far as the ' Polnische Apotheke ', where Theodor would then be free to see her safely on the rest of her way home. They met outside the shop at 10 p.m. By the time Emilie reached her home she was engaged to be married. Fontane describes the event as follows : ' Es war wenige Schritte vor der Weidendammer Brücke, daß mir dieser glücklichste Gedanke meines Lebens kam, und als ich die Brücke wieder um ebensoviele Schritte hinter mir hatte, war ich denn auch verlobt.'[14]   The betrothal happened in an instant, but the engagement was a long one, lasting five years, principally for financial reasons.

Emilie Rouanet-Kummer was an orphan of French extraction, adopted by the Kummer family in her early years and brought up in the Große Hamburgerstraße next door to Onkel August's home at the time when Fontane was attending the Klödensche Gewerbeschule.   When they first met he was fifteen, and she ten years old.   Her striking, southern appearance, and particularly the dark and glowing quality of her expression had fascinated Theodor Fontane even in those days, and there had been a certain degree of rivalry between him and his friend Hermann Scherz to win the friendship of this unusual, lonely child.   But their ways had soon parted and he had seen little of the girl for nine years until he returned to Berlin for his year of military service.   He then found the somewhat *gamine* child of yesteryear transformed into an elegant young lady of nineteen, no longer withdrawn or alien in appearance, but a laughing, industrious young woman who was in many ways typical of Berlin.   When she was presented to Fontane's mother as her future daughter-in-law, that sharp-eyed lady, who normally laid so much stress on wealth and status, remarked with unusual discernment of real values : ' Du hast Glück gehabt ; sie hat genau *die* Eigenschaften, die für dich passen '.[15]   How often was this theme of ' Zueinanderpassen ' to be debated and extolled in the author's later works !

With the prospect of marriage and its responsibilities ahead, Theodor Fontane now began to think in earnest about his qualifying examinations in pharmacy.   Leaving his paid employment, he rented a room in the Dorotheenstraße, his landlord being none other than the ever-present Onkel August, and once again life in his company proved most agreeable. While funds lasted he received tuition in analytical chemistry from a Professor Sonnenschein.   Later he contented himself with private study at his parents' home in the country.   By the early spring of 1847 Fontane felt the time had come to try the examination, for good or for ill, and—thanks partly to some inspired last-minute revision of notes in Raehmels Weinhand-lung, where he sought Dutch courage on his way to the oral test—he passed. So there he was, armed with paper qualifications but without a job again. *Faute de mieux* he returned in the late autumn of 1847 to the old, well-known routine, this time at the Jungsche Apotheke by the corner of the Neue Königs-straße and the Georgenkirchstraße. This had a somewhat more suburban, even proletarian character than his previous places of work, and Fontane relates with some irony that the vast quantities of free cod-liver oil issued to the undernourished children of the poor usually ended up by being used for lamp-oil by their parents.

Here, in 1848, he was to experience at close quarters the March Revolution, was indeed even suspected by the management of being a disguised revolutionary or police spy himself. Men who published articles and verses in liberal newspapers could, it seemed, be capable of anything, so he was regarded with some awe, even fear. Writing with unusual cynicism, he was later to comment : 'Wer glaubt, speziell hierlandes, sich ausschließlich mit "Liebe" durchschlagen zu können, der tut mir leid'.[16] Recalling the political situation of that time, Fontane gives us some idea of the basis of his own political philosophy ; he asserts that it is not the task of rulers to distinguish between the old conception of the state and the new constitutional demands on a purely academic or ethical basis, but simply to express the popular will, even if this is faulty. He then goes on to compare Friedrich Wilhelm IV, who in 1848 did not recognize this truth, with Bismarck who later did and thus was able to harness the energies of the German people in the service of his ideas.

In his autobiographical work, *Von Zwanzig bis Dreißig*, we find a moving description of the casual mischance which finally sparked off the March Revolution in Berlin. After four tense days of minor incidents, the city was swept by the news early on the 18th that the King had granted all the popular demands. Crowds gathered in the Schloß-Platz to celebrate and to cheer the king who appeared on the balcony. But the number of people in the square, ever increasing, began to cause alarm, and finally at about 1.30 p.m. the king authorized troops to clear the Schloß-Platz. The dragoons, under General von Prittwitz, advanced slowly in extended order, but the mood of the crowd changed suddenly. The troopers were resisted and attempts made to pull them from their horses. At this critical moment other troops, infantry, began to intervene and a few shots were fired. This had the effect of clearing the square, but the popular mood had swung completely from celebration to revolution. Barricades were thrown up throughout the centre of Berlin and hitherto sober and responsible citizens were affected by the heady atmosphere of the moment —among them Theodor Fontane. With vague poetic memories of historical revolutions, he felt that these occasions traditionally began with a tocsin on the local church bells and raced to the nearby Georgenkirche in order to have this honour in Berlin's historic hour. Alas, the church was firmly bolted and barred—' protestantische Kirchen sind immer zu '[17]—and his attempts at uprooting a nearby post to use as a battering ram merely wore him out. ' Mit meinem Debüt als Sturmläuter war ich also gescheitert, soviel stand fest. Aber ach, es folgten noch viele weitere Scheiterungen.'[18] Joining a mob ransacking the Königstädter Theater for arms used in stage performances, Fontane was handed an ancient carbine. Gunpowder was procured from a nearby shop (Fontane offering to pay for his share), and the mob then manned the barricade, which by now had taken on a picturesque hue, thanks to the addition of landscape stage-sets commandeered from the theatre. Feverishly pouring gunpowder into the barrel of his ancient weapon, Fontane finally came to his senses when an onlooker, noticing the rusty, precarious state of the carbine, exclaimed with typical Berlin irony : ' Na, hören Sie . . . !'

The spell was broken. The absurdity of all these heroic but futile gestures struck him forcefully—the rusty old guns, more dangerous to their users than to any enemy, the suicidal folly of opposing a trained Guards unit with such playthings, and he, a trained soldier, behaving in this way. Crushed and embarrassed, he slunk off to his room to brood on the irony of this whole situation which had infected Berlin with such hysterical violence. But curiosity became stronger than shame. What was happening outside in Berlin ? He had to know. Over the city hung an ominous calm. Here and there workers had occupied the roof-tops and assembled great heaps of tiles to rain down upon the expected troops. Modern weapons against roof-tiles ! Beyond the Friedrichsbrücke were the Dragoons, waiting for orders, the expressions of both officers and NCOs suggesting hearty dislike of the task ahead as being below their soldierly dignity. ' Unsere Leute sind nicht darauf eingerichtet, sich untereinander zu massakrieren ' is his comment.[19] Both then and later the signs of effective preparations by the insurgents struck Fontane as pathetically inadequate. Sounds of shooting and gunfire could be heard sporadically, but nothing seemed to be happening in the areas Fontane visited. After exchanging views with his cousin, Hermann Müller, in the Friedrichstraße, he walked back with him through the moonlit night towards his own abode. Not a sound was heard nor a single combatant to be seen. ' Das Ganze glich einer ausgegrabenen Stadt, in der das Mondlicht spazierenging. Wenn vielleicht wirklich Verteidiger dagewesen waren, so hatten sie sich etwas früh zur Ruhe begeben. Mein Elendsgefühl über das, was eine Revolution sein wollte, war in einem beständigen Wachsen.'[20] Ironically, the only action he encountered was near his own home, shortly after returning. The Fusilier Battalion of the Life Guards had been ordered to clear a way through to the Schloß-Platz by midnight and the Königstraße came under a hail of bullets. One improbable ricochet even penetrated Fontane's own room, which appeared fully protected, and he found his bedroom floor littered with broken glass. ' Wenn die Gewehre erst losgehen, weiß man nie, wie die Kugeln fliegen,' he records.[21]

On the following morning, 19 March, the dispensary was full, and Fontane, assuming that the prescriptions would be for bandages and medicine for the civilian wounded, hastened to snatch them from the waiting women's hands. But no, they were the usual requests for free cod-liver oil ! ' Freiheit konnte sein, Lebertran mußte sein,' he commented with a sad smile at human frailty ![22] His deepest irony was reserved for those cautious middle-class citizens, ' die spießbürgerlichen Elemente,'[23] who had been conspicuous by their absence during the actual fighting but who now came out to celebrate the ' victory ' and congratulate one another. But this so-called ' victory ' did not convince Fontane ; he called it ' ein bloßes königliches Gnadengeschenk, das jeden Augenblick zurückgenommen werden konnte,'[24] and rightly foresaw the moment seven months later when the same regiments returned and calmly disarmed the 'Bürgerwehr' at their leisure. His conclusion concerning the whole affair was that even the bravest civil population is doomed to defeat at the hands of well-trained regular troops. This view he held for forty years, but in the evening of his life, in 1891, he considered the matter afresh in the light of a revelation that General Prittwitz had frankly admitted the precarious nature of the military situation at that time. With that remarkable transition towards newer, more radical viewpoints which accompanied Fontane's old age, he admits he was probably wrong in his earlier assessment, and that a popular cause, if widely supported and deeply felt, is bound to prevail in the long run.

On the 21st Fontane saw the King make his famous tour of the city on horseback, promising everything asked of him, including Prussian royal leadership in all-German affairs. Louis Fontane, his father, who had rushed to the capital as soon as news of the revolt had arrived from his son, pondered on this unusual and somewhat enforced royal tour and found it vaguely disturbing : ' Es hat doch ein bißchen was Sonderbares, . . . so rumreiten . . . ich weiß nicht . . . ,'[25] a sentiment which his son secretly shared. Even stranger was the scene a few weeks later when elections were to take place under the then existing ' indirect ' system by which the electors (*Urwähler*) chose a *Wahlmann* from amongst their number, who would then, in his turn, vote for the actual parliamentary representative. Few, if any, of the thirty or so people who turned up had the least idea of what they were expected to do, so that Fontane, thanks to his articulate explanations, ended up— against his wishes and intentions—as the *Wahlmann* himself !

An interim employment of an unusual kind occurred at this point, when Fontane was asked by Pastor Schultz of the Bethanien Foundation if he would undertake the task of training two Protestant nursing sisters in pharmacy, and this he agreed to do in June 1848. The experience proved a pleasant one ; if the male element (consisting of doctors and a superintendent) was disappointing and the residence governed by petty rules—Fontane got into trouble about driving a nail into the wall—at least the two pupils were competent and socially delightful persons. To his pleasure, they both passed their qualifying examinations a year later, one of them brilliantly. Their instructor, while modestly ascribing this principally to their own native ability, claims at least a part of the credit on the grounds that he knew just about enough of the subjects taught and no more. ' Je weniger man weiß, je leichter ist es, das, was man zu sagen hat, in Ordnung und Übersichtlichkeit zu sagen. Und darauf allein kommt es an.'[26]

But the Bethanien idyll could not last permanently. After a year and a quarter his task there was done, and he had to think again of the future. To return to his old style of work was repugnant, especially as he had already experienced several of the top-level establishments in Germany, so that the next post was likely to prove a disappointment. Fully realizing the risks involved, he decided to try to live by his pen, and rented a modest room in the Luisenstraße, where the attic-dwellers above him almost invariably seemed to choose the moment when he was settling down to work as being the most suitable for chopping their firewood. Here he remained for a year, and in retrospect he does not find it an unhappy one despite everything. His income was very small indeed, especially as he insisted on concentrating upon verse rather than speculative articles or tales in prose which might have been easier to sell to publishers. He reasons thus : ' Wenn du jetzt ein Gedicht machst, das dir nichts einbringt, so hast du wenigstens ein Gedicht. Das Gedicht ist dein Besitz, und wenn es nur leidlich gut ist, kann es immerhin für etwas gelten. Wenn du aber einen Aufsatz schreibst, den niemand haben will . . . so hast du rein gar nichts.'[27] Indeed he succeeded after initial setbacks in publishing the first volume of his verse at this time. The end of the Luisenstraße interlude was abrupt ; Fontane had been a passionate supporter of the revolt in the duchies of Schleswig and Holstein against Danish overlordship, and the decisive defeat of the rebel army at Idstedt on 24-5 July, 1850, was a shattering blow to his hopes. In despair he set off to join the ranks of the hopelessly outnumbered Schleswig-Holstein forces, but was brought to his senses by the timely receipt in Altona of an official letter, forwarded from Berlin, offering him a regular position in the so-called ' Literarisches Kabinett ' of the Prussian Ministry of the Interior. Prudence and his

responsibilities to the patient Emilie won the day. He wrote
two letters, one accepting the post and the other to Emilie,
suggesting marriage in the autumn. It took place on 16
October, 1850, at the French Reformed Church in the Kloster-
straße, Berlin, and Fontane's father distinguished himself on
the occasion by arriving half an hour late for the ceremony.
This union was to last for nearly fifty years, whereas the post
in the ' literary bureau ', which had helped to expedite it,
survived for only another two months.

Chapter 3

THE STRUGGLE FOR MASTERY

THE first five years of his married life were to prove difficult
and challenging ones in many respects. Materially they were
marked by constantly recurring financial need and insecurity.
The 'Literary Bureau' suffered from political changes and was
dissolved at the end of 1850, soon after Fontane had entered it.
A period of real poverty followed. Much of his literary work
was still honorary; articles and book reviews brought in next to
nothing, even poems accepted for publication were paid for at
derisory rates. At the same time he had acquired the responsibilities of a married man. Depression and bitterness character-
ize many of the utterances of 1850-51, a severe testing-time for
the new marriage. Then in November 1851, he succeeded in
obtaining part-time employment writing articles for the
Preußische Zeitung, issued by the *Zentralstelle für Presseangele-
genheiten*, successor to the former *Literarisches Kabinett*. This
journal was also known as the *Adler-Zeitung* in order to distinguish it from the *Neue Preußische Zeitung* (popularly called the
Kreuzzeitung because of the large Maltese cross on its title-
page).

April 1852 saw him once again setting off for England's
shores, commissioned by the *Preußische (Adler-) Zeitung* to study
conditions in Britain which he was to describe in articles ' from
our correspondent '. The paper even guaranteed him a small
regular salary as well, thus providing some sort of income for
his wife and child left behind in Berlin, though friends and
relatives also helped in this difficult time. Despite his limited
means in a land where money counted for a great deal, Fontane
appears to have enjoyed his second stay in England. He saw a
fair amount of the country outside London, and was able to
gain a deeper and more balanced impression of English life
than during his first brief visit as an inexperienced twenty-five-
year old. He has left us a record of his stay in *Ein Sommer in
London* (1854), which was based on his personal observations
and experiences. This was sent to Germany as *feuilleton*

contributions and later reprinted in book form. Owing to their original journalistic character, the chapters read in a somewhat episodic fashion, but are nevertheless fascinating as the account of an intelligent, sensitive German visitor's reactions to the England of 1852. The topics range over a wide field—the approach to London via the Thames, the city's public monuments, streets, bridges, parks and famous buildings, its commercial life, the Englishman at home, his values (both public and private), attitudes towards foreigners, excursions outside London, e.g. Richmond and Hampton Court, and further afield to Waltham Abbey and Hastings. The essays, though uneven in quality and depth, reveal a remarkable degree of psychological insight and penetration, and they provide lively and vivid impressions of the mid-Victorian scene.

The end of September saw the end of Fontane's second, five-month sojourn in England and his recall to Berlin. He returned to a winter of domestic problems, culminating in a period of quite serious illness, but this, too, was overcome, and work resumed at the *Preußische (Adler-) Zeitung*, first in charge of the English news, then of proof-reading the paper. This latter duty involved evening work and, by way of compensation, left him free during the day to increase his modest income through private tutoring and free-lance journalism. But all this was to be but an interlude, for in the autumn of 1855 he was again destined to set sail for England, this time for a period of over three years (September 1855 to January 1859). The Prussian Government, under Manteuffel, had decided to support a permanent German-English column in the pro-Government press, and Fontane seemed the obvious choice as their London correspondent, not on account of his political views but rather because of his previous journalistic experience. When this experiment ended in March 1856, he stayed on as a semi-official press agent. His earlier impressions of the country were now to be supplemented by knowledge in depth, by contact with the current of everyday life that flowed behind the façade presented to the casual traveller. In July 1857 he was joined by his wife and family.

The culmination for Fontane of this third and longest stay in Britain was the two-week tour of Scotland undertaken in the summer of 1858. The resultant account of his experiences, presented in *Jenseits des Tweed* (1859), has a distinct advantage over its English counterpart ; it was intended from the start to appear as a book, not in individual newspaper articles, and thus possesses greater coherence of form. Moreover it was the work of an independent author, whereas the essays contained in *Ein Sommer in London* were commissioned work. Fontane is therefore more relaxed, more himself as readers of his later works know him. The historical element can be lingered over in greater and more loving detail, personal adventures may be included, the elements of humour and irony increased. With Fontane we are able to experience travel as it was in the late 1850s partly akin to that of the twentieth century, with its railway network and steamer routes, partly harking back to the days of the stage-coach and the horse and carriage. We share the rigours of a long mid-Victorian rail journey from London to Edinburgh, with its many changes en route, have a lively vignette of hotel life in the Scottish capital, take an informed historical tour around the city, its castle and Holyrood Palace, see the life of the ' auld toon ' and its inhabitants before moving on to Linlithgow, Stirling and Perth, then deep into the Highlands at Inverness. There is a visit to the historic battlefield of Culloden, and a trip by steamer down through the lochs and waterways of the Caledonian Canal to Oban. Here Fontane inserts a delightful sketch of Scottish thrift in the scene where he and his companion are deliberately allowed to oversleep and, in the morning panic, relieved of more than the advertised overnight charges on the excuse of ' no change available ' ! His well-informed and sensitive account of the traditional sea-trip to Staffa and Fingal's Cave is matched by his subsequent appreciation of the silent majesty of Loch Lomond seen from the deck of a lake steamer. Abbotsford, the former home of his beloved Sir Walter Scott, is visited, while the old castle of Loch Leven, near Kinross, conjures up for him not only memories of Scottish history but the first conscious urge to visit systematically the castles and historic sites of the Mark of Brandenburg so that they too may tell their story to the nation and the world.

The fall of the Manteuffel ministry brought Fontane's post to an end, and he returned to Berlin again in January 1859.

This was in fact to be his last direct connection with Britain, although contact by letter continued, and its influence remained in a variety of ways for the rest of his life. What had these three visits achieved ? Personally, they had provided him with a broader basis of social comparison, as had the Leipzig and Dresden sojourns of an earlier period, and sharpened his sense of aesthetic judgement. Politically he had acquired a sympathy for the evolving system of democracy as he saw it in the British Isles. His talent as a *causeur* of a high order developed during this period and appears most noticeably in the pages of the more successful chapters of *Ein Sommer in London* and *Jenseits des Tweed*. The skill acquired in achieving this unique blend of travel diary, social commentary and historical reminiscence led him subsequently to a parallel achievement on German soil in his *Wanderungen durch die Mark Brandenburg*, themselves but a stepping-stone to the whole series of later social novels on which his fame rests today. In these works we still find, twenty or more years after his last English visit, vivid traces of its influence ; English phrases and allusions occur frequently, references to English literature or social customs are made again and again, while many characters of British origin appear in these pages, either as visitors to Germany or as coachmen, grooms and servants who have settled there. It was with some considerable foresight that, in 1857, Theodor Fontane had written to his mother from London : " I am firmly convinced that the schooling and apprenticeship which I am undergoing here are absolutely essential for my later life at home.'[1]

The first year and a quarter back in the Prussian capital, however, was not particularly promising. He again attempted to live as an independent writer and supplement his meagre earnings by writing freelance articles for the newspapers and giving private tuition, especially in English. A visit to the Bavarian Court, arranged by Heyse, led to no practical results —and, indeed, how could it have, for Fontane in Munich would have been a plant uprooted from its native soil ! Finally, however, another friend, George Hesekiel, succeeded in obtaining for him a post as editor of the English column in the *Neue Preußische Zeitung (Kreuzzeitung)*, and he held the position for ten years, from 1 June, 1860 to early 1870. Despite private political qualms about the policy of this paper, he found an unexpectedly tolerant atmosphere amongst its staff and later recalled the period with considerable affection. His duties were comparatively light, thus leaving him with a good deal of time to devote to his own writing, and it was in this period that he began his travels through the Mark and composed the *Wanderungen*.

For almost forty years, to the very end of his days, Fontane was now to remain in Berlin and Mark Brandenburg, the heart of his life's work, leaving it only briefly for occasional holidays in Silesia, the Harz, on the North Sea coast, or at Karlsbad, for the two brief visits to Italy in 1874 and 1875, and his three professional journeys as war-historian to the battlefields of 1864, 1866 and 1870-1. Within a year or two he settled permanently in the capital, first in the Hirschelstraße (No. 14) and later, from 3 October, 1872, in the well-known Potsdamerstraße 134c.

By 1863 the first two books of the *Wanderungen durch die Mark Brandenburg* had appeared, and the remaining volumes were to occupy him intermittently for many years. By the end of the 1860's we can note once again a sense of restlessness and dissatisfaction in Fontane's correspondence, which led, in 1870, to his giving up the position held for the last ten years with the *Kreuzzeitung*, and to the beginning of his long period as theatre critic for the *Vossische Zeitung*. This sudden decision to leave a safe job on the staff of the *Kreuzzeitung*, which was to bring considerable domestic tension in its wake, was not the result of a momentary whim or of a particular crisis, but rather an awareness that he was getting mentally stale and needed a new, challenging stimulus if he were to progress along his chosen path as a creative writer. The new duties on behalf of the *Vossische Zeitung* (a liberal paper holding political views far different from those of his former employers) brought him into continuous and intimate contact with the world of the theatre. From this point began the long series of lively and sometimes controversial theatrical reviews ' von meinem Eckplatz 23 ', usually signed ' TH. F. ', an abbreviation which led to the caustic comment on the part of an offended dramatist that it stood for ' *Theaterfremdling* ' ! But his sense of what was effective on the stage and his instinctive feeling for what was real and convincing in characterization and dialogue soon established a healthy respect for his judgement on the part of dramatists, actors and the theatre-going public. His daily life became more closely identified with the life of Berlin, where he moved on close terms with diverse representatives of society— actors and playwrights, journalists and poets, scholars and teachers, officers and civil servants, businessmen and employees. He grew to love the city, despite the vast expansion and changes which it underwent after 1870, and came to know its local history and topography intimately. To the end of his life he explored it ceaselessly, mainly on foot, and finally became for the younger generation a kind of patriarchal symbol of its spiritual life.

Three breaks in the increasingly fixed Berlin routine, apart from holidays in the country or by the sea, deserve special mention, namely his visits to the battlefields of Bismarck's three wars during the process of German unification under Prussian leadership. The first of these occurred in May 1864, while he was still with the *Kreuzzeitung*. An armistice had been agreed between Denmark and Prussia-cum-Austria following the successful storming of the Danish fortifications at Düppel, and during this period Fontane travelled with a colleague to the scene of the recent battle in order to describe it graphically to his readers, thus adding a new dimension to his abilities, that of war-reporter and contemporary historian. In September, after further fighting had resulted in the complete defeat of Denmark by late July, he re-visited the scenes of the recent clashes on a similar mission. The result was a careful study of the whole campaign and the publication in late 1865 of a 374-page illustrated account of the war, entitled *Der Schleswig-Holsteinsche Krieg im Jahre 1864*. Again, in 1866, when the victorious allies of only two years ago—Prussia and Austria— were locked in mortal combat to settle the issue of supremacy in German affairs, Fontane visited the scene of the brief seven-weeks war, arriving in Bohemia well before the temporary armistice had been followed on 23 August by the Peace Treaty of Prague. He collated his observations in book form, and this work appeared in 1870, as a 1100-page war history entitled : *Der deutsche Krieg von 1866*.

The third episode was of a more hazardous nature. Once

more resuming his rôle of *Schlachtenbummler*, as he ironically called it, he set out on the 27 September, 1870, for France, where Prussian—indeed, this time German—armies were engaged in a prolonged and serious campaign, making the previous wars of 1864 and '66 resemble mere skirmishes. French resistance, though ineffectual in the long run, was determined and persistent, while casualties on both sides were high by the standards of the period. On 3 October Fontane was in Toul, then held by Prussian forces. Here the poet and historian in him temporarily won the upper hand, and he decided to risk an unofficial visit to Domrémy, birthplace of Joan of Arc, which lay about twenty-five miles away in unoccupied territory between the opposing armies. Hiring a horse and carriage, he set off on 5 October with a French driver, was promptly arrested while examining a statue on the square of Domrémy and handed over as a suspected spy to the nearest French sous-préfecture at Neufchateau. Although he himself later treated the whole affair lightly and ironically, both informally and in print, the incident involved a very real danger of execution. It was only after repeated interrogations, detailed statements in writing, and long uncomfortable periods of uncertainty in various French prisons that his innocence was accepted, and he was then transferred to a camp for civilian internees on the island of Oléron in the Atlantic off the west coast of France. His release was procured by the intervention of none other than Bismarck himself, with whom friends had interceded, though this was not realised by Fontane. Using the good offices of the Protecting Power concerned, in this case the United States, Bismarck requested American help to secure the release of this ' well-known historian, Dr. (*sic*) Fontane ' and hinted characteristically at draconian measures against French civilians if he remained in custody ! The gesture succeeded, and Theodor Fontane was expelled from the land of his forefathers, returning through Switzerland to Berlin, where he arrived on 5 December.

The literary outcome of this remarkable interlude was two-fold. The official war-history, *Der Krieg gegen Frankreich, 1870-71*, duly appeared in 1876 (volume 1 in 1873), but of more immediate interest for the reader of today is the informal work *Kriegsgefangen* (1871), which represented the personal account of his adventure. The tone of this autobiographical essay was so mild and objective that it displeased Prussian government and army circles, who would have preferred to see the enemy portrayed in somewhat more lurid colours. However, it soon achieved international repute, its literary merit being appreciated even in France, and has since withstood the test of time. For the future development of Fontane's prose, moreover, it clearly indicated certain typical features, notably the avoidance of anything suggestive of sensationalism, and a tendency to 'play down' even genuinely dramatic occurrences and crises.

Undeterred by the experiences of his first trip to France, Fontane voluntarily embarked on a second in April-May 1871, this time under the safer guise of a German entering German-occupied territory. This visit included Alsace and Lorraine, now the new 'Reichsland' Elsaß-Lothringen, and he attempts an unbiased and objective assessment of the chances of winning over its population. These and other impressions are given in another informal work which appeared early in 1872, namely *Aus den Tagen der Okkupation*.

At the same time, during the 1870s, the travel-cum-historical works, *Wanderungen durch die Mark Brandenburg*, were continuing to appear, one volume following another until the completion of the series in 1882, with a supplement, *Fünf Schlösser*, to follow as late as 1889. The mounting total of published work was by now providing the author with a modest but rising income, freeing him and his wife for the first time from nagging financial worries. But artistic satisfaction still lay in the future. The present was a distinct advance on the era of his daily English column, written to order for a newspaper, while poems of distinction were accepted grudgingly or ignored. At the same time he realised that it was merely a halfway house, a stylistic schooling for something better, namely the complete fulfilment of himself as a creative writer. But by now he was over fifty and at times despaired of such fulfilment. Perhaps he had reached his goal and the rest was a daydream? Cynically he commented at this time that only two further major events remained to look forward to—conferment of the title *Geheimrat* ... and death. 'Des einen bin ich sicher, auf den andern verzicht' ich allenfalls.'[2]

One ' honour ' which was to come his way in March 1876
proved to be more of a halter around his neck than a distinction. He was offered the position of First Secretary at the Royal
Academy of Arts in Berlin and accepted it, knowing that the
duties would be modest in scope and the status and security
involved very considerable—factors always yearned for in vain
by his wife, Emilie. This proved to be a disaster, for the entire
tone of its civil service routine was anathema to the new
Secretary and the personalities involved highly uncongenial,
while the work was both tedious and superficial. His own
attitude turned the permanent officials on the staff into op-
ponents, and he was glad to seize upon an excuse for escape
from this bureaucratic strait jacket, resigning on 2 August of
the same year. For him this meant freedom to be himself
again, to think and write as he really felt ; to his wife, however,
it was almost the last straw in a partnership which had brought
none of the outward signs of success and security by which she
judged human happiness, and the twenty-six year old marriage
was shaken to its foundations. Fontane remained confident
that he was doing the right thing, and, guided by his inner
sense of direction, turned once again to his creative writing.
' Ich muß durch Taten beweisen, daß ich nicht leichtsinnig
gehandelt habe,' he wrote.[3] And at this point he takes up anew
a work begun probably as early as 1864, *Vor dem Sturm*.

So far Fontane's writing had consisted of his early lyrics
and ballads—some adapted or imitated from Anglo-Scottish
sources, some a transference of this tradition to the history of
Brandenburg—day-to-day journalistic contributions, mainly of
a *feuilleton* nature, theatrical and book reviews, lengthy war-
histories of the 1864, '66 and '70-71 battles, the two incidental
books of personal reminiscence arising from the Franco-
Prussian war, and a series of travel books combined with local
history dealing with Mark Brandenburg. Now, as a natural
step forward, he proceeds cautiously from the familiar to the
untried in a work of fiction which has a close affinity with his
Wanderungen. *Vor dem Sturm, ein Roman aus dem Winter 1812 auf
'13* was begun as early as the winter of 1863-4, but the following
years of journalism and work in the historical field forced him
to postpone its completion. In July 1875 he referred to it as
' meinen Roman, der nicht leben und nicht sterben kann ',[4]
but still planned to complete it for publication. Not until

April 1878 was it in fact ready for the press. The appearance of this long *Roman* was crucial : Fontane realized that his real métier lay in the field of prose fiction, and from this point there was no turning back. At an age when most writers are already set in a particular pattern, Theodor Fontane in his sixtieth year had proved that he was capable of embarking on an entirely new adventure in creative writing.   Swiftly there followed the whole series of *Romane* and *Novellen* on which his later fame was to rest, as he moved ever more decisively into the field of contemporary social problems.   The public image of him as a writer of patriotic ballads and historical prose-works began to alter.   On the heels of two 'balladeske Novellen', *Grete Minde* (1880) and *Ellernklipp* (1881), came *L'Adultera* (1882), his first major venture on to the thorny path of problematic marriages in the Berlin of his own day. *Schach von Wuthenow* (1883) represented a slight retreat from this newly-won ground, inasmuch as it deals with events set at the beginning of the nineteenth century, while *Graf Petöfy* (1884), though in a contemporary era, moved away from the familiar setting of Berlin and the Mark to Hungary, even though returning afresh to the problem of love and marriage which so greatly interested the author.   The following year—and we note with astonishment the rapid succession of these titles—saw an experiment (not repeated) in the field of the mystery story with the publication of *Unterm Birnbaum* (1885).   But two years after this in *Cécile* (1887) Fontane returned decisively to the themes and settings first introduced in 1882 and these were now to remain his special sphere.   The eight years 1888-1895 witness the appearance of the best-known titles of all ; *Irrungen, Wirrungen* (1888) and its 'pendant', *Stine* (1890), *Frau Jenny Treibel* (1892) and *Effi Briest* (1895), as well as the more modest but significant novel *Unwiederbringlich* (1892), the less successful *Quitt* (1891) and a most attractive autobiographical work, *Meine Kinderjahre* (1894).   His final years saw the publication of *Die Poggenpuhls* (1896) and the second volume of autobiography, *Von Zwanzig bis Dreißig* (1898).   His last completed work of fiction, *Der Stechlin*, came out in 1899, shortly after the author's death.   In the early years of the twentieth century a few further items were published, notably *Mathilde Möhring* (1907), the *Kritische Causerien über Theater* (1904) and a combined volume of his earlier Anglo-Scottish impressions.

Such was the harvest of the last twenty amazing years of Theodor Fontane's life, years largely devoid of major outward events and journeys, a time of increasing simplicity in his daily routine.

Having found his real sphere, the novel, when he was nearly sixty—indeed, over sixty by the time he had established his favourite themes—he sensed that he had no time to waste if he was going to achieve the aims of a lifetime in his remaining years. Excursions from Berlin became fewer and were restricted mainly to quiet country holidays, usually in Silesia or the Harz, occasionally by the sea. Berlin, now the Reich capital, remained his greatest love, despite sweeping alterations in its outward appearance, the rapid expansion of its boundaries, and changes in its population. He knew it intimately and followed its progress with deep personal interest, if not always with unqualified approval. Contemporaries have recorded their impressions of him, in later years, taking his daily constitutional in the streets and parks he knew in such detail, pausing here and there to note a change, observing men and places with his keen blue eyes. Dressed in his habitual manner, with the inevitable woollen scarf flung over one shoulder whatever the weather, he became a local institution, a part of the life of Berlin. Social contacts were cut to a minimum and even his beloved correspondence was pruned ruthlessly so that he might devote the maximum amount of his time and energy to creative work. During these later years, too, he had to face increasing illness and periods of nervous exhaustion, when it seemed to him that he would never be able to resume his writing, never fulfil his plans. Time and time again his correspondence has recorded his fear, his despair that he is ' finished ' . . . and each time the succeeding months showed a dramatic contradiction in the form of a sudden upsurge of creative energy, the completion of a fresh major work. Even the illness of 1892, which caused not only Fontane but those around him to feel serious concern, was finally overcome.

Public recognition came but slowly to Fontane during these years. His earlier modest reputation had depended upon such a different image—that of the *balladier,* the factual historian, the interpreter of countryside and people in the Mark. It took both critics and readers some time to adjust to the new Fontane, and they were at a loss to know what to make of this unusual phenomenon of a man who, from the age of sixty, had begun to write on themes suggestive rather of the younger generation of Naturalists than the spirit of his own age-group. But the appearance of *Irrungen, Wirrungen* in 1888 made it clear to all that this was no aberration of old age. Then, in his seventies, he showed himself capable of producing works of the quality and significance of *Frau Jenny Treibel* (1892) and *Effi Briest* (1895), and no one could doubt any longer that this was the real Fontane at the height of his creative powers. Though it was not until the middle of the twentieth century that his work was to attain truly international standing, his fame within Germany—and especially Prussia—was now secure in his own lifetime, though by no means on a scale worthy of his talents. His seventieth birthday, in 1889, was publicly celebrated—though not by those for whom he originally wrote, the aristocracy of the Mark—and he was awarded the Schiller Prize in 1891. His seventy-fifth anniversary, in 1894, was marked by the conferment of an honorary doctorate from the University of Berlin. He received these belated honours with a certain gentle scepticism, though this was not unmixed with genuine pleasure and never resembled the bitterness and despair of the ageing Grillparzer in similar circumstances, for Fontane realised that : ' vor strenger Kritik kann überhaupt nichts bestehen '.[5] He had his devoted circle of readers, if not perhaps amongst those old families whose way of life he had so often celebrated in poetry and prose, and this circle was moreover growing steadily. He had fought his battles alone and gone in many respects against the trend of current fashions and contemporary public taste, but had finally won.

In the last few years the scope of his activities narrowed still more. Old holiday haunts farther afield were abandoned and resorts within easier reach of Berlin were preferred ; even the sophisticated Karlsbad in Bohemia now claimed him amongst its distinguished elderly visitors. But his heart was in his beloved Berlin. Though the arduous walks of earlier years were no longer within his powers, he remained faithful to familiar places near at hand . . . a daily stroll in the Tiergarten, to the Leipziger Platz, or by the Spree ; this he could still accomplish without overstraining his energies or depriving himself of the freshness needed for the work awaiting him in his study. An afternoon nap was no longer to be scorned, if this, too, could prolong his creative powers.

The end came gently but suddenly in the evening of 20 September, 1898. Alone, in the familiar setting of his home at Potsdamerstraße, 134c, surrounded by plans and drafts for new work, he passed quietly on without prior illness and apparently without pain or prolonged struggles. So lively had his mind and spirit been, but four days earlier, at a small party given in honour of his daughter's engagement, that all those who had witnessed him on that occasion were stunned and grief-stricken by the unexpected loss. He was buried in the unpretentious Huguenot cemetery in North Berlin.

Chapter 4

FONTANE'S EARLIER ACHIEVEMENTS
IN POETRY AND PROSE

Ballad, Lyric and Aphoristic Verse

THE period from about 1840-60 is very often quoted as though it covered Fontane's whole contribution to the field of the ballad, but this is only a half-truth. During these years the ballad was predominant in his work, but it did not cease to claim his attention when his interests broadened into a new sphere, namely that of his travel-books entitled *Wanderungen durch die Mark Brandenburg*, in the following twenty years, from 1860-80. Still less was this the case between 1880 and 1898, during the final flowering of his genius as a writer of *Romane* and *Novellen*. His development as a poet continued simultaneously with each successive widening of his creative powers, beginning with the youthful effusions of a fifteen-year-old and ending only with his death at the age of seventy-eight. Fontane was very much aware of his earlier mastery of the ballad rather than prose forms and referred to the apparent cycle in his creative life, which in old age led him right back to the poetic interests of his early youth, as : ' Die Schlange, die sich in den Schwanz beißt ; der Ring, der sich schließt '.[1] In later life he also found that he was able to re-read his early poems with genuine pleasure, whereas most of his prose-writings of the same era caused him acute embarrassment when viewed through the perspective of the intervening years. ' I acquired an ability in poetry thirty years earlier than in prose ', he wrote to his wife in 1882.

Much of his early verse was of a political and indeed radical character, written for the most part at Leipzig under the influence of the émigré revolutionary writer, Georg Herwegh (1817-75) and, to a lesser extent, the political poet, Ferdinand Freiligrath (1810-76). Even before this period, however, he had produced a number of youthful verses, starting with *Die Schlacht von Hochkirch* at the tender age of fifteen, and progressing to a verse epic, *Heinrich IV*, when he was seventeen. Neither was published. In 1840, during his apprenticeship in Berlin he was able to get some early poems (twelve in all) printed in the *Berliner Figaro*, among them *Pizarros Tod, Vergeltung* and *Simson im Tempel der Philister*. These all employed fairly conventional language and imagery, showing the influence of three writers in particular : Chamisso, Lenau and Heine. None of these attempts were included in his later collected verses, but they are of historical importance, since they represent his first attainment of some degree of mastery in the ballad technique, One of the poems from this period, however, namely *Frühlingsklage* of 1838, foreshadows his transition from conventional lyricism to political poetry with a *Leitmotiv* of ' freedom ', for here the Romantic tone and symbolism are blended with political undertones indicative of a new realism.

The political ideals of the Leipzig period and of Berlin during the *Vormärz* years, 1842-48, inspired Fontane to break the bonds of the conventional ballad altogether and write in a totally new vein, perhaps best summarized as *Herwegh-Dichtung*, with its outcry against the prevailing political state of Germany. Two manuscript volumes of poetry covering the years 1837-41 were compiled by the young author, entitled *Erstes Grünes Buch* and *Zweites Grünes Buch*, though neither of these appeared in print. He did make a determined attempt to arouse the interest of Julius Fröbel, a radical publisher living in Zürich as a political refugee, suggesting as his title : *Gedichte eines Berliner Taugenichts*. Unfortunately for him, the book-market was already flooded with works by idealistic young radical poets, and nothing came of the venture. A few of these poems later found a home in the periodical *Die Eisenbahn* in 1841-42, and fewer still were afterwards considered worthy of inclusion in his collected *Gedichte* of 1854. Even these were excluded from the second edition of 1875. Soon Fontane began to move away from the Herwegh style, with its alternating pathos and aggression, towards something more truly his own, namely a blend of radical, reforming zeal and detached irony. Henceforth he was to achieve his objects with a subtle mixture of assumed innocence and implicit criticism, expressed through the medium of well-directed satire. Little of this earlier radical verse is known to the average Fontane reader today. A good deal was suppressed by Fontane himself on mature reflection, mainly on aesthetic grounds, some has been lost in the passage of time, while much was deliberately ignored by those who wished to illustrate only one aspect of Fontane's social and political views, which always tended to be of a dualistic nature.

A turning-point in his development as a poet was represented by his entry into the writers' circle, *Der Tunnel über der Spree*, in July 1843. It could hardly have happened at a more auspicious moment. Fontane needed the discipline provided by outspoken criticism of his work by others with literary pretensions and experience. Although he later outgrew the *Tunnel* group and saw its limitations, it could and did perform this valuable service for him at a significant point in his poetic career. At first he continued to offer his fellow-members political verses in the old Herwegh style or translations and adaptations of poetry by English radical writers. But gradually, under the influence of frank but friendly criticism and the different viewpoints of other writers within the same circle, especially Bernhard Lepel, he began to modify, to blend and to discriminate. No longer did he regard everything in the existing social order and national tradition as outmoded and useless, while some of the outstanding political and military personalities in Prussian history began to fascinate him as people. To his artistic eye they appeared as potential sketches through the medium of words, a form of verse anecdote. He discovered the power of the past to regenerate the present and began to offer a picture of the simple Prussian virtues of yesteryear in order to achieve a revival of national self-respect. So we come to the famous *Feldherrenballaden*, starting with *Der alte Derffling* in October 1846, which was soon followed by six others in the subsequent year: *Der alte Dessauer, Der alte Zieten Seydlitz, Schwerin, Keith*, and the somewhat different theme represented by *Schill*. Fontane had also begun to develop his own individual style and technique in the treatment of the ballad form, and this was emphasised a few years later when he turned to Anglo-Scottish themes.

Fontane had chosen an English ballad theme as early as December 1844, when he read out to the *Tunnel* group his poem *Der Towerbrand*, based on the story of a great fire at the Tower of London, and this ballad had enjoyed an instant success and marked his début as a master in this sphere. A factor of major importance was his discovery in 1848 of both Percy's *Reliques of Ancient English Poetry* and Scott's *Minstrelsy of the Scottish Border*, which stimulated translations, adaptations and frank imitations. However, his deeper understanding of English and Scottish themes was closely linked with his experience of the countries themselves during the longer visits of 1852 and 1855-59. First-hand acquaintance with the countryside and people, combined with his intuitive feeling for historical atmosphere in buildings and landscapes, brought the ancient lays to life for him and spurred him on to express them anew through the German tongue. Amongst the best-known today of Fontane's Anglo-Scottish ballads are such examples as : *Johanna Gray* (1852), the well-loved *Archibald Douglas* of 1853, and his *Lied des James Monmouth* (1854). Not only were these appreciated by his contemporaries, but Fontane felt strongly at this stage that he had discovered within himself a special skill given to few others in this type of ballad composition. He was hurt and perplexed by the cooler views of the critics who, while acknowledging his powerful and effective presentation of the subject-matter and central characters, also noticed certain limitations. They drew attention to a tendency towards imprecision in his adaptations, mainly because of a typically Fontane desire to ' tone down ' the more rugged and barbaric features.

On the whole, therefore, Fontane's greatest and most sustained success in the ballad was probably in a German, indeed specifically Prussian setting, especially the Prussia of Frederick the Great. Here the identification between poet and subject-matter is closer and more intense, though without undue pathos or conventional postures. As a result, the figures he presents are credible, living personalities, not just symbols or myths. There is, too, a happy blend of stylistic traditions taken from both German and Anglo-Scottish ballad techniques. His style is terse and the tone a distinctive one. Driven onward by the intensity of personal feeling in the poet's mind, his verse is more flowing and effortless, so that the reader is not aware of details of construction and technique.

This bold experimentation in the sphere of the ballad achieved that which his earlier efforts in pure lyric poetry could never have gained for him at the present stage of his artistic maturity—assured public recognition, even though still within the comparatively limited sphere of Berlin and the

State of Prussia. His poems, which first appeared in the *Morgenblatt für gebildete Leser,* a respected journal, were later published as a book in 1851 (*Gedichte* : Miniaturausgabe) and in an enlarged edition in 1860 (*Balladen*). A second enlargement appeared in 1875, entitled *Gedichte,* in which only very little of the original material was missing. Fontane's poetry remained in popular demand throughout his lifetime, even when his earlier reputation in this field had long since been overshadowed by his wider fame as a novelist.

At the time when he achieved his later successes in the field of prose fiction, Fontane also increased the range and depth of his poetry. He showed a greater interest in contemporary events and personalities as suitable subjects for poetic treatment. In a sense, he became, as it were, a social balladist as well as a social novelist, for his heroes were now often ordinary people of his own time, such as the American helmsman, John Maynard, and his subject-matter was drawn from events recently in the news, such as the Tay Bridge disaster in Scotland. This process has been termed ' the secularisation of the ballad ' and signifies the evolution of a new form of the *Kunstballade.* Here the flamboyant heroism of kings, princes or knights is replaced by the smaller-scale heroism of everyday life. Sometimes the bravery is of an unseen, inward kind—the heroism of silent suffering . . . that ' stilles Heldentum ' found so often in the later prose works. With increasing age came also further detachment from the human scene, though with an undiminished interest in all that went on within it. Often we find that the action involved in the later poetry and the background against which it takes place are smaller and more ' local ' in character. Personalities, speech and environment frequently assume a regional quality. Berlin and the Mark of Brandenburg predominate as favourite settings. But never did Fontane permit the detachment of old age to deteriorate into emotional indifference. His irony deepened, but so did his humour and his underlying kindliness. During these later years Fontane at last embarks on personal themes and autobiographical subjects, long held in reserve, sometimes treating them openly, as in *An meinem Fünfundsiebzigsten* (1895), sometimes thinly disguised, as in *Fritz Katzfuß* (1888), with its echoes of the young Fontane in his apprentice days. There is a late flowering of the personal lyric, so long denied to him, which reaches its culmination in such poems as *Lebenswege*, *Was mir gefällt*, or *Mein Leben*, a moving tribute to placid old age. The final period, then, concentrates on the *Lied*, the *Spruch* and the *Epigramm*. Even the thought of death itself is not shirked, and a reconciliation with the remorseless cycle of nature is implicit in a poem such as *Herr von Ribbeck auf Ribbeck im Havelland*. The simple and unpretentious tone in much of Fontane's final poetry is at first glance misleading, for this verse contains a great deal of his matured wisdom and personal philosophy. In the *Spruchdichtung* especially we can discover a good measure of hard-hitting social criticism in forms even more direct than those found in his prose work. Notable examples are *Aus der Gesellschaft* and *Neueste Väterweisheit*.

One problem arising from the poetry written in his later years is presented by the tone and substance of what might be called his 'political occasional poetry' dealing with major events and personalities in the Second Reich. Too much a man of his own time to ignore these in verse, he nevertheless sometimes betrays an inner uncertainty in his attitude towards them, and this reflects itself in the uneven quality of some of these poems. Here we may think particularly of the *Einzugsgedichte*, commemorating the victorious conclusions of Bismarck's wars. They seem to lack much of the depth and life of Fontane's genuine ballad poetry. He was aware of this himself, and recognised the dangers inherent in the poetic treatment of contemporary political subjects. A happier adaptation of the occasional poem by Fontane may be found in a work such as *Auf der Treppe von Sanssouci* (1885), with its relaxed, almost casual tribute to his friend Adolph von Menzel.

What does Fontane's poetry mean for the present-day reader, who sees it within the context of his work as a whole ? Certainly it will not occupy the place of major importance that it did for his contemporaries. Many of them bitterly resented the new image of Fontane as a controversial social novelist and would have preferred him to remain a successful but innocuous ballad-writer. As Paul Schlenther has remarked: 'Man wollte ihn ins Großpapatum hineinphilistern.'[2] With the change of aesthetic taste since Fontane's day, too, it seems likely that our contemporary selection of his best work in this field will differ noticeably from that of the nineteenth century reading public. Nevertheless Fontane can still claim a place of undoubted merit for his verse, seen in historical perspective, despite the over-whelming modern preference for his work in the *Roman* and *Novelle*. Time cannot touch the direct appeal of such verses as *Archibald Douglas*, with the old knight's moving lament:

> Ich hab es getragen sieben Jahr,
> Und ich kann es nicht tragen mehr,

or the harsh and bitter reply of the King :

> Ich seh dich nicht, Graf Archibald,
> Ich hör deine Stimme nicht,
> Mir ist, als ob ein Rauschen im Wald
> Von alten Zeiten spricht.

Nor will the modern reader fail to respond to the delicate charm of the ghostly *Herr Ribbeck auf Ribbeck im Havelland*, who in death as in life stands for kindness to the young.

Though the changes in the map of Germany and in our attitude towards national mythology since 1945 have removed some of the immediate appeal made by the Prussian-Branden-burg historical subjects, the human qualities of Fontane's portraits of these great personalities from the past still arouse our sympathy without difficulty. The rise to rank and fame of Field Marshal Derffling, the one-time tailor's apprentice, and his lifelong loyalty to the values and terminology of his original calling—such things are not affected by the political changes, however drastic these may seem. We still recognise and enjoy the typically Fontane quality of the old warrior's dry humour when speaking on his death-bed:

> Er sprach: Als alter Schneider
> Weiß ich seit langer Zeit,
> Man wechselt seine Kleider—
> Auch hab ich des nicht leid.[3]

Nor have we any difficulty today in conjuring up the scene at the court of Frederick the Great, when another ageing warrior, Joachim Hans von Zieten, Husarengeneral, nods off at the dinner-table as the old campaigns are fought anew over the wine, and the King rebukes the anxious courtier who would awaken him :

Laßt schlafen mir den Alten,
Er hat in mancher Nacht
Für uns sich wach gehalten,
Der hat genug gewacht.[4]

Probably for us today, however, the most direct appeal of all is made by the more personal poems of Fontane's old age. In them we find the essential Fontane and a compendium of the wisdom he had gathered over the years. In *Überlaß es der Zeit* there is his concept of Time the Healer as a solution to many of life's problems :

Erscheint dir etwas unerhört,
Bist du tiefsten Herzens empört,
Bäume nicht auf, versuch's nicht mit Streit,
Berühr es nicht, überlaß es der Zeit.

He has learned, as we see in this poem, that it is sometimes better to do nothing in the heat of the moment and to wait until the dust of conflict has settled, for ' Alles ist wichtig nur auf Stunden '.

In *Lebenswege* he contrasts, with an ironical smile, his modest achievements in life with those of his former associates in the *Tunnel über der Spree*, who have made a name for themselves in the army, the public service or big business. From time to time he chances to meet them during one of his strolls in the Tiergarten and, as he receives their friendly but slightly condescending greetings, he wonders without bitterness why they have achieved many of life's outward marks of success while he appears to have stood still. The answer to his question is suggested in *Was mir fehlte*, with its concluding lines :

Suche nicht weiter. Man bringt es nicht weit
Bei fehlendem Sinn für Feierlichkeit.

So, like the Chinaman in *Aber wir lassen es andere machen*, he stands quietly to one side while others join in the wild dance of life and the frenzied search for happiness :

... All derlei Sachen,
Ich lasse sie längst durch andere machen.

His is the quiet happiness of the observer who contents himself with the small pleasures of life—' das Kleine '. He gives examples of this in *Was mir gefällt*, ranging from the first signs of spring in the Tiergarten and the cherry trees in blossom at

Werder to a stroll along the ' Läster- (i.e. Sieges-) Allee ' and,
surprisingly, ' ein Backfisch mit einem Mozartzopf '. He has
long since done with the major hopes and ambitions of this
life, but a few small wishes still remain, as we see in : *Ja, das
möcht ich noch erleben.*   The ultimate in resignation finds its
expression in *Ausgang* :

> Immer enger, leise, leise
> Ziehen sich die Lebenskreise,
> Schwindet hin, was prahlt und prunkt,
> Schwindet Hoffen, Hassen, Lieben,
> Und ist nichts in Sicht geblieben
> Als der letzte dunkle Punkt.

Outside the main categories of his ballad, lyric and aphoristic
poetry there are various areas of poetic experimentation, some
successful and others less so.   In the former group one may
perhaps think of *John Maynard*, a partly historical and partly
invented tale of the brave steersman who sacrificed his own life
in order to save the passengers on board the burning vessel.
(It is sad to note that ruthless modern research has uncovered
the disagreeable fact that, in the incident on which the poem
is probably based, the helmsman survived while no less than
249 passengers perished !) Here the strict form of the ballad is
blended subtly with rhythms from the North American folk-
song, as we see at the very beginning, where the name is
repeated rhythmically as a kind of refrain :

> John Maynard !
>   ' Wer ist John Maynard ?'
> John Maynard war unser Steuermann,
> Aushielt er, bis er das Ufer gewann,
> Er hat uns gerettet, er trägt die Kron,
> Er starb für uns, unsre Liebe sein Lohn.
>   John Maynard.

He also makes effective use here of semi-repetition in the last
line of four stanzas, emphasising the gradual approach of the
burning ship to the shore and salvation, e.g.

> Und noch zwanzig Minuten bis Buffalo.

The knife-edge between effective experimentation and
banality which he is treading here had been attempted six
years before this in a modern ballad based on the then con-

temporary Tay Bridge disaster. Here, however, Fontane's step is somewhat less sure. The account of the railway accident is enclosed within a mythical framework strongly reminiscent of the witches' scene in *Macbeth*. A fatalistic element is thus introduced right at the start, contrasting with the heroic struggle between man and the elements in *John Maynard*. The bridge is shown as doomed in advance and the frailty of man and all his works is emphasised by the final lines, spoken by one of the witches after the disaster :

Tand, Tand
Ist das Gebilde von Menschenhand.

But, alas, the poem slips from time to time into the realms of bathos, including even the author's brave attempt at railway onomatopoeia in the lines :

Ich komme, trotz Nacht und Sturmesflug,
Ich, der Edinburger Zug.

Franz Servaes has compared the more traditional ballads written by Fontane to ' dichterisch angeschaute Geschichts-anekdoten '[5]—historical anecdotes seen through the eye of a poet. In this definition we discover two elements which indicate the connection between Fontane's ballad poetry and his later prose. Firstly, the ballads are inspired by *history*, whether recent or remote, and this historical thread continues through the prose works. It is found again in the travel books known as the *Wanderungen durch die Mark Brandenburg*, in the early *Romane* and *Novellen*, such as *Vor dem Sturm, Grete Minde, Ellern-klipp* and *Schach von Wuthenow*, and it reappears in the numerous historical discussions and digressions of the major novels. Secondly, Fontane's approach to the ballad is an ' anecdotal ' one, a trait which is passed on right down to the last and most anecdotal of all his novels, *Der Stechlin*.

The ballad poetry dealing with Brandenburg-Prussia, tinged though it is with a romanticism which is alien to the later verse and prose, does demonstrate the deep inner attachment which the poet felt for his native Brandenburg. At first this feeling was largely based on historical sentiment, to which the *Wanderungen durch die Mark Brandenburg* were to add the deeper affection born of intimate personal contact with both country-side and people. From this point on, the province remained

the background of all his greatest works. The style and construction of the novels and *Novellen* were also to stand indebted
to the ballad-era. Gustav Roethe speaks of their ' sprunghaft '
qualities and their ' anschauungsschweren Vordeutungen '.[6]
In some respects Fontane, the mature novelist, remained at
heart a ballad-writer, even though operating through the
medium of prose. However, the gap between Fontane the
ballad-poet and Fontane the novelist of contemporary society
and its problems was a considerable one, despite certain
underlying affinities. It could only be bridged gradually, but
an important span in this process is represented by the *Wanderungen*.

Wanderungen durch die Mark Brandenburg

When Fontane began his journeys through the Mark of
Brandenburg it is probable that he felt interest rather than
enthusiasm. The travels themselves brought out and developed
his latent affection for the province. These essays were not an
attempt to provide an exhaustive handbook for travellers or a
treatise for scholars and historians. It was primarily the *people*
of Mark Brandenburg that interested him, together with their
social customs and natural background. The result was, as
Harry Maync has aptly called it, ' a charming collection of
human documents ',[7] in particular of the old landowning
families. Another pleasing definition of the *Wanderungen* is
that given by Paul Schlenther, who points out that Fontane
' aimed neither at being a Baedeker nor a Ranke for his native
province ', achieving instead ' a combination of landscape-
painting and historical reminiscence, a blending of social and
human studies with nature-poetry expressed in prose, of
general observation with personal experience.'[8] He, too, feels
that the novels and *Novellen* owe their existence to the inspiration of these *Wanderungen*.

In his preface to the work, Fontane tells us about the in-
ception of this project and the aims he had in view during its
compilation. It was on the occasion of a visit to the old castle
at Loch Leven in Kinross during his Scottish tour of 1858
that he was reminded of an earlier visit to the Rheinsberger
Schloß, in a similar lakeland setting, and asked himself the
question : was the German experience any less memorable or
attractive ? He concluded that it was not, and from that

moment there began his determination to make known to the German-speaking world the quiet charms of his native Branden-burg. His approach to this task was a casual one : ' Sorglos hab ich es gesammelt, nicht wie einer, der mit der Sichel zur Ernte geht, sondern wie ein Spaziergänger, der einzelne Ähren aus dem reichen Feld zieht.'[9] He stresses the need for a histori-cal sense, for without it the traveller might go heedlessly by an old but unpretentious castle, where momentous deeds had been done, or cross a flat and featureless stretch of landscape without realising that here the destiny of Prussia was settled in the battle of Fehrbellin. Above all, he counselled those who would follow in his footsteps, one must find contact with the ordinary men and women of the countryside.

> Verschmähe nicht den Strohsack neben dem Kutscher, laß dir erzählen von ihm, von seinem Haus und Hof, von seiner Stadt oder seinem Dorf, von seiner Soldaten- oder seiner Wanderzeit, und sein Geplauder wird dich mit dem Zauber des Natürlichen und Lebendigen umspinnen. Du wirst, wenn du heimkehrst, nichts Auswendiggelerntes gehört haben wie auf den großen Touren, wo alles seine Taxe hat ; der Mensch selber aber wird sich vor dir erschlossen haben. Und das bleibt doch immer das Beste.[10]

Basically there were four volumes of *Wanderungen durch die Mark Brandenburg* : *Die Grafschaft Ruppin* (1862), *Das Oderland* (1863), *Das Havelland* (1872) and *Das Spreeland* (1882), to which a supplementary volume entitled *Fünf Schlösser* was added in 1889. The journeys through the Mark, which gave rise to them, began in the summer of 1859. By 1860 Fontane had some idea of the scope of the written work that would result from them and wrote to Theodor Storm that it might well occupy him for ten years and fill twenty volumes. In fact the period of time involved (though interrupted by other works) extended over no less than thirty years, but the number of volumes produced was condensed to five, including the later addition. As a genre it was not new, of course, and it has strong affinities with the prose descriptions of land and people found in the works of the Romantics or their more realistic successors, *Das junge Deutschland*. Goethe, Heine, Annette von Droste-Hülshoff, Stifter and Storm had, amongst others, contributed in their varying ways to the tradition. Closest in spirit to the *Wanderungen* of Theodor Fontane, however, was W. H. Riehl's *Naturgeschichte des Volkes*, consisting of four parts : *Die bürgerliche Gesellschaft* (1851), *Land und Leute* (1854), *Die Familie* (1855) and *Wanderbuch* (1869). Fontane specifically acknowledged[11] his indebtedness to Riehl on five counts : his advice to precede the actual journeys by careful study, then to experience the places and historic material by walking in the area, to gain personal contact with the local people, to keep a travel diary, and to enliven the work with anecdotes from the journey.   This last-named item was particularly close to Fontane's own inclinations.

Aided by his innate sense of history and his years of journalistic experience, Fontane proved to be a master in this field. According to a letter of 31 October, 1861, to his publisher, Wilhelm Hertz, he hoped not only to describe the natural beauty and architecture of the province, but also to familiarize his readers with its historical personalities and thereby encourage greater popular affection for their memories.   It is perhaps difficult for us today to understand fully what this involved in terms of personal effort in the nineteenth century—the miles of walking, climbing, searching in graveyards for tombstones and inscriptions, detailed inspections of old churches, castles, manor-houses, the endless conversations with local personages (including some who were more garrulous than informative) and the continual taking of notes, to be followed by the sifting through of countless memories and the careful interpretation of all that was seen and heard.

The literary harvest is as varied in style as the original material.   Werner Lincke distinguishes four main stylistic categories in the *Wanderungen*—the Feuilleton, the Novelle (e.g. in the account of the Katte tragedy), the essay in the history of art (the Schinkel chapter), and the specialised treatise, as in *Fünf Schlösser*.[12] After beginning with a somewhat generalised, ' touristic ' approach in volume one, Fontane then places historical events and personalities increasingly in the foreground, though he comes back to nature description and items of local interest in the later volumes. All in all, therefore, we have a combination of topography with local and provincial history (of persons and families as well as of events), forming a work of art worthy of serving later generations as an abiding monument to a vanished era. Having been written down either on the spot or soon afterwards, Fontane's impressions have a lively spontaneity which has assured their survival where more scholarly tomes might have perished.

As three contrasting examples of Fontane's style in these travel essays, we might suggest *Die Menzer Forst und der große Stechlin, Die Katte-Tragödie* and *Eine Landpartie.* The first appears in the volume *Die Grafschaft Ruppin,* the second in *Das Oderland,* and the remaining one in *Das Havelland.* The description of the Menz Forest is linked with the unusual story of its history during the previous century, and this is related in the casual, anecdotal manner now associated with Fontane's prose. In the eighteenth century, apparently, nobody knew what to do with this large forest, the upkeep of which cost more than the revenue from it, despite the introduction of charcoal burning and glass-manufacturing. In desperation, therefore, it was decided to burn it—not on the spot, but through the chimneys of the growing capital, Berlin, in the form of firewood. At last it showed a profit, though of course the capital was used up in the process. Within thirty years the entire Menzer Forst had gone. The present forest, Fontane adds, is a subsequent regrowth. He then creates briefly for the reader an impression of the forest as he found it—the rough tracks, the dead branches crackling beneath the carriage wheels, the immense stillness and sense of oppression, culminating in the sudden, dramatic discovery of the Stechlin-See. This is the high-point of the whole essay and now dominates the scene. The drama and mystery associated with this forest lake is emphasised by the cry of the guide as its glittering surface is first espied through the branches : ' Das ist der Stechlin !' Here is a story after Fontane's own heart . . . a lake of measureless depth, surrounded by legend and superstition, feared even by the fishermen who make their living from it, and reputedly in league with dark, subterranean powers. So profound an impression did it make on the young Fontane of this period that, decades afterwards, he was to revive the theme in his last novel, *Der Stechlin,* and there make it into the dark symbol which pervades the story.

Subsequent descriptions of the glassworks near one arm of the lake are brief and factual, and it is only when the interest of Fontane, the storyteller, is aroused by the history of *Metas Ruh* that the essay again springs to life. Foreshadowing the style of the early *Novellen*, Fontane gives the reader the anecdote of Meta's burial in local dialect through the mouth of a country-man. The essay as a whole is brought to a comfortable con-clusion around the fireside of a village inn, not without a neat reversion to the point of original departure as Fontane reflects with quiet humour that the logs in the grate before them, like those which warmed Berlin for thirty years, are ' echte Kinder der Menzer Forst '.

Contrasting with the above in both theme and style, the tragic story of Leutnant von Katte springs naturally from the description of the fortress at Küstrin, where its culmination was reached. ' Auf Bastion " Brandenburg " oder in seiner unmittelbaren Nähe vollendete sich die Katte-Tragödie.' Again the physical description of the setting is comparatively brief, whereas the human aspect of Katte's sacrifice is dealt with at some length. Fontane refers to the event as a symbol of ' dieses Land, dieses gleich sehr zu hassende und zu liebende Preußen '—in itself a not untypical piece of Fontane dualism. It is also typical of him that he views the occurrence, unlike other writers and historians, not through the eyes of the Crown Prince Friedrich, for whose sake Katte has to forfeit his life, but from the viewpoint of the humbler Katte himself, whose only crime was loyalty to his friend, the Prince, during his attempt to flee from a tyrannical father (King Friedrich Wilhelm I).

From the conscientious and detailed description of each stage of the events, including the subsequent court-martial of Katte and his rejected appeal, it is clear that Fontane is emotionally involved as a man and as a creative writer. His emphasis is always on the theme of simple human loyalty between friends, between the man of rank and his trusted subordinate. By contrast the portrait of the King is harsh and grim, and the extent of royal intervention in the course of justice in order to procure an exemplary sentence is empha-sised. The final scene of execution at Küstrin, on 6 November, 1730, is merciless in its realism, a trait found again in the two early *Novellen*, *Grete Minde* and *Ellernklipp*, though later modified in favour of more discreet and sparing indications of harsh reality.

The third example, *Eine Landpartie*, is probably the most revealing of all to students of Fontane's later work in the sphere of the novel and *Novelle*. It is presented in that easy-going *Plauderton* of the later Fontane, of whom we have here a kind of preview, as he describes himself at breakfast beneath a lime-tree, outside the inn, sharing his meal with a host of friendly, chirping sparrows. There follows a brief but effective ' still life ' of the village scene around him, an idyll which is then abruptly shattered by the arrival of a carriage full of trippers from Berlin—elegant, confident, outspoken and somewhat disconcerting once away from their normal urban setting. We shall later meet these Berlin ' Landpartien ' on many future occasions in the world of Fontane's novels, though seen from the viewpoint of the excursionists themselves. On this occasion, however, the author is in his rôle of observer, and he proceeds to analyse the nature of the country excursion as he sees it, expressing the view that there are basically two contrasting types : ' die heiteren Landpartien ' and ' die ernsten Landpartien ', though paradoxically he later adds, with renewed awareness of the duality in all things : ' Sonderbar. Auf den heitren Landpartien wird immer geweint, auf den ernsten wird immer nur gelacht.'

His ' heitere Landpartien ' are the family groups who come out from the big city with boisterous determination to have a merry time in the country They include large numbers of children, mainly little girls dressed in impeccable white. ' In dem Moment der Landung, wo immer es sei, scheint die Welt aus lauter weißgekleideten Mädchen mit rosa Schleifen zu bestehen.' But the picture, alas, is apt to change. An expedition into the woods for wild strawberries results in disaster.

> Martha I ist an einem Wacholderstrauch hängengeblieben, Martha II hat sich in die Blaubeeren gesetzt—wie Schneehühner gingen sie hinein, wie Perlhühner kommen sie wieder heraus. Der Sturm bricht los. Wer je Berliner Mütter in solchen Augenblicken gesehen, wird die kriegerische Haltung der gesamten Nation begreiflich finden. Die Väter suchen zu intervenieren. Unglückliche ! Jetzt ergießt sich der Strom in sein natürliches Bett.

The ' ernste Landpartien ', on the other hand, will be eminently recognisable to readers of the later novels, with their recollections of Hankels Ablage and similar resorts. He describes the tone of them thus :

> Man spricht in Pikanterien, in einer Art Geheimsprache, für die nur der Kreis der Eingeweihten den Schlüssel hat. Bowöe und Jeu lösen sich untereinander ab ; unglaubliche Toaste werden ausgebracht, und längst begrabene Gottheiten steigen triumphierend wieder auf.

His description of the ' Venus ' of this particular party recalls both the broad humour of his family correspondence and the more restrained and delicate variety of the later novels. The new era of industrial wealth and outward show is evoked by his summary of the men in the party : ' Fünfziger, mit großen melierten Backenbärten, Lebemänner aus der Schicht der allerneuesten Torf- und Ziegelaristokratie.' Their feminine companions are, for the most part, dismissed as ' Staffage, blosse Najaden und Tritonen, die als Beiwerk, auch wohl als Folie notwendig da sein müssen, wenn Venus aus den Wellen steigt.' Venus herself, the undoubted queen of the party, is attractive—but on a generous scale : ' Alles im Brunhildenstil; dieselbe weiße Hand, die jetzt auf der Laute ruhte, hätte auch jeden beliebigen Stein fünfzig Ellen weit geschleudert.'

The foregoing examples, which are in no sense isolated instances, indicate quite clearly that certain stylistic features of Fontane, the novelist, developed during the *Wanderungen* period. There is his love of the anecdote, his preference for the historical personality rather than the lifeless fact, a tendency to stray into paths which digress from the strict direction of the story, a sense of humour tinged with irony, his interest in the changing modes and values of society, and—perhaps most important—his growing skill at reproducing the casual conversation of all social classes, including dialect speech. Thanks to the prolonged discipline of the *Wanderungen*, with their wide variety of topics and treatment, Fontane's prose style was both broadened in range and refined in technique. While summing up his intentions in the *Schlußwort* of the series, he emphasised that it was not his ambition to become a famous historian.

> Ich habe " mein Stolz und Ehr ", und zwar mit vollem Bewußt-sein, auf etwas anderes gesetzt, aufs bloße Plaudernkönnen, und erkläre mich auch heute noch für vollkommen zufrieden-

gestellt, wenn mir *dies* als ein Erreichtes und Gelungenes zugestanden werden sollte.

There is little doubt concerning his success in that aspect of the *Wanderungen durch die Mark Brandenburg,* whatever other shortcomings the modern reader may care to find. This, too, was the soil from which there grew in easy, natural fashion his first work of prose fiction, *Vor dem Sturm,* in 1878.

Chapter 5

Vor dem Sturm (*Roman*, 1878) and the 'balladesque Novellen'
(*Grete Minde*, 1880 ; *Ellernklipp*, 1881)

Vor dem Sturm

IT would be idle to pretend that *Vor dem Sturm* is an unqualified
success, if regarded strictly as a novel. Fontane's contemporaries felt that it was a new species of *Wanderung* which had in-
advertently strayed into the realm of prose fiction and there
lost its way. The present-day reader tends to be critical of its
length and diffuseness, for it has no fewer than eighty-two
chapters. Other weaknesses become apparent as well. Some
of these may be due to the curious history of this work, the
earliest plans for which go back at least fourteen years, to
1864. According to Fontane himself, the original idea came
even earlier, around 1856, although his urgent commitments
as a journalist, theatre critic and war-historian forced a post-
ponement. Only in 1875 was he able to find the necessary
peace of mind and leisure to resume work on *Vor dem Sturm*.
In the following year, 1876, after giving up his position with the
Academy of Arts, he settled to the task in earnest and completed this lengthy novel two years later, in 1878. Because of
the period of domestic and financial stress during which it was
written, he referred to it as ' ein Schmerzenskind '.[1] Nevertheless it represented a tremendous act of self-fulfilment for him.
As early as November 1876 he wrote : ' Ich empfinde im
Arbeiten daran, daß ich nur Schriftsteller bin und nur in
diesem schönem Beruf mein Glück finden konnte.'[2]

However, the weaknesses of form which can be criticised in
Vor dem Sturm probably result mainly from its close relationship
with the *Wanderungen*, which continued to be published throughout this period. For years Fontane had accustomed himself to
make his prose work a compendium of everything that seemed
to him of historical, geographical and sociological interest in
the Mark of Brandenburg, spicing this information with humour
and anecdotes in order to sustain the reader's interest through-

out the lengthy series. Faced with the task of creating a *Roman*
set in the same province and amongst the same kind of people,
he tended almost inevitably towards a similar broad canvas
and to employ the same leisurely technique, unaccustomed as
he was to the formal requirements of the novel. So we have a
work overflowing with local detail, bursting with secondary
characters, sub-plots, peripheral episodes and digressions—
but without any real unity of form. The author himself is
quite frank about this :

> Ich habe mir nie die Frage vorgelegt : soll dies ein Roman
> werden ? Und, wenn es ein Roman werden soll, welche Regeln
> und Gesetze sind innezuhalten ? Ich habe mir vielmehr
> vorgenommen, die Arbeit ganz nach mir selbst, nach meiner
> Neigung und Individualität zu machen, ohne jegliches Vorbild.[3]

He then states the aim he had in view :

> Ich habe mir einfach vorgesetzt, eine große Anzahl märkischer
> Figuren aus dem Winter 1812 auf 1813 vorzuführen, Figuren,
> wie sie sich damals fanden und im wesentlichen auch noch
> jetzt finden. Es war mir nicht um Konflikte zu tun, sondern
> um Schilderung.[4]

The result was naturally a fragmentary and episodic work,
despite its many positive features. The casual progression of
personalities, historical incidents and landscape descriptions
which might be appropriate for a long series of travel books
just could not be made to fit in with the formal requirements
of the novel. Originally the sub-title was to have been :
Zeit- und Sittenbild aus dem Winter 1812 auf 1813, avoiding the
term *Roman*, and this would have been in many ways a more
accurate description of the contents. Although his lengthy
work purports to deal with Prussia on the eve of her liberation
from the yoke of Napoleon, this stirring issue remains discreetly
in the background until quite near the end of the book, when
we read of the abortive raid on Frankfurt an der Oder. True,
the situation is talked about, and it dominates the mind of
Berndt von Vitzewitz, but of direct action we find remarkably
little. Comparison is sometimes made with *Isegrimm* by Willibald Alexis, which has the same theme and setting. There,
however, the stress is entirely different, so that the political
events and struggles dominate the story and its characters,

and do not merely add colour to the tale. In that work, too, there is one major weakness ; the historical atmosphere has been achieved to some extent at the price of a more pallid characterisation, which cannot be said of Fontane's story.

Although the action of *Vor dem Sturm* is divided between rural Hohen-Vietz and Schloß Guse on the one hand and Berlin on the other, it is the countryside of the Mark which predominates, not the capital city. We are introduced to the area in detail, as indicated by the chapter headings, so that the reader is as well-informed as though he were accompanying Fontane on his travels through the Province. The church, the village inn at Hohen-Vietz or the castle at Guse, for instance, each occupies a separate chapter, while the principal characters are similarly introduced to the reader in individual sections bearing their names. As the total of these names continues to mount, the reader may be excused for wondering just how their functions could ever be made to unite in a common purpose. Whether in a town or country setting, the same tendency towards ' behagliche Breite ' can be observed. There is description for its own sake of both places and people, irrespective of any potential rôle in the story, and there are numerous digressions on topics of historical or geographical interest, genre scenes, anecdotes, and so forth. Meanwhile the ostensible theme of the work appears to make little progress. Milieu and character have taken over from the national issues involved.

The ' hero ' of the story, if such he may be called, is Lewin, the son of a country *Junker*, Berndt von Vitzewitz, though he might equally well be termed the story's ' co-ordinator ', for he is little more than a link between its various parts. There are obvious points of resemblance between him and the younger Fontane, especially through his literary interests and activities. The same may be said of the minor character, Hansen-Grell, who is later to lose his life in the futile assault on Frankfurt. Soon after the introduction of Lewin in chapter one, however, the reader's attention is diverted to a wider scene. The mood of the winter countryside of Brandenburg is skilfully evoked during Lewin's sleigh-ride from the capital to Hohen-Vietz, where he is to spend Christmas with his family, whom we then meet. His father, Berndt von Vitzewitz, quickly establishes his strong position in the novel, foreshadowing the part he is going to play in preparing for resistance against the occupation troops of the nominal ally, France. We learn about his bitter hatred of Napoleon, greatly increased by his wife's death following an incident involving French troops. In the exchanges between father and son some information is also given about the current military and political situation. Napoleon's armies have been defeated in Russia and are in headlong retreat through Poland and Germany. Clearly the liberation of Prussian territory from the French is now only a matter of time, and resistance groups are already beginning to spring up in the area. One of these is going to be organised by Lewin's father. ' Nicht viele werden den Njemen überschreiten,' he comments grimly, ' *Über die Oder darf keiner.*' It is indeed a scene ' Vor dem Sturm ' ! Lewin's viewpoint is a slightly different one, as befits an idealistic young man under the spell of the Romantic poets. ' Ich bin für offenen Kampf', he says, ' bei hellem Sonnenschein und schmetternden Trompeten.' He is worried, too, by the enforced alliance between Prussia and France, with its implied moral duty to succour the French armies in their hour of distress. Lacking the more robust and worldly qualities of his father, Lewin has to undergo the ordeals of battle and an unhappy love affair before attaining spiritual and emotional maturity.

The scene of action anticipated by this conversation is, however, still a long way off. At present we are concerned with the description of a family Christmas in the country, meeting all the relatives and friends, and getting to know the village and its inhabitants. We are given a detailed introduction to the church and its minister, Pastor Seidentopf, later being taken into his home and enjoying a leisurely account of his archaeological interests. The reader's attention is then claimed by Tante Schorlemmer, an ' adopted ' aunt from Herrnhut, who scatters her religious ' Sprüche ' around as though they were magic charms against all the dangers of life. The chapter entitled *Im Kruge* provides an opportunity for the collective introduction of various minor characters, but Hoppenmarieken, the dwarf woman who later helps to save Lewin's life, receives a separate chapter of her own. There is the village mayor, too, Schulze Kniehase, also his adopted daughter Marie, who is destined to grow in significance towards the end of the work.

In leisurely progression the list of persons confronting the reader continues to expand. The social scene shifts for a while to Schloß Guse and Tante Amelie, a prototype of Fontane's ' elderly aunts '. Amelie von Vitzewitz lives mainly in the past, with her memories of Prinz Heinrich and the faded glories of the court at Rheinsberg. A woman of intellect, wit and strongly francophile interests, she is an ' outsider ' in rural Brandenburg and serves largely as a foil to the traditional Junker of the Mark. In *Allerlei Freunde* Fontane creates a whole portrait gallery of additional friends and acquaintances, including the swashbuckling ex-Hussar, General Bamme, whose later performance as a commander at Frankfurt is considerably less impressive than the figure he cuts in society—though his speech to the volunteer troops before the battle is a masterpiece of verbal caricature.

More centrally placed in the action of the novel are the two *Geschwisterpaare*, Lewin and Renate on the one hand and Tubal and Kathinka on the other. The mutual feelings of love which link these two pairs (Lewin and Kathinka, Tubal and Renate) are doomed from the start for reasons of temperamental incompatibility which Fontane is to analyse more explicitly in his later works. But somehow this love-element remains lifeless and unconvincing, proving to be one of the least satisfactory features in the characterisation of this novel. Renate attracts attention, however, because of the unusual features in her temperament and character. Elsa Croner has called her ' die leidenschaftloseste von allen Fontaneschen Frauen.'[5] She is notable for her intense loyalty to family and friends, her instinctive insight into the character of others, her cool, objective judgment of issues, and an increasing tendency towards withdrawal from life, renunciation of its pleasures and the substitution of good works and inner piety.

When the persevering reader arrives at chapter 31 and sees the heading *Es geschieht etwas*, he may be forgiven for assuming that here, at last, he has reached the central incident of the story, the attack on the French garrison in Frankfurt. But no ; it is merely the account of a burglary at the Herrenhaus. The main action still lies no less than forty-two chapters away, and the path there leads through a tangled undergrowth of complicated description. We experience an evening of amateur theatricals at Schloß Guse, a visit to Berlin, a party in the capital given by Lewin's landlady, Frau Hulen (who plays no part whatever in the real action, but whom we should be most reluctant to miss), an attendance at a university lecture given by Fichte, a meeting of the literary club *Kastalia*, with its memories of Fontane's own days in the *Tunnel über der Spree*, and numerous other incidents as well.

Apart from hearing occasional rumblings in the background, we have to wait until chapter 67 before learning more about the plan to attack the garrison in Frankfurt on the Oder. Not until chapter 73 do we discover, to our surprise, the action itself. At this point the whole narrative seems to spring to life, not only during the battle scenes but afterwards, too, in Berndt's sad reflections on the defeat and on his own complicated motives in organising the attack, The same can be said about the capture and rescue of Lewin, or the quixotic bravery of Tubal, when he saves the wounded dog and pays for it with his life—all these chapters sparkle brilliantly. By and large, however, Fontane seems more concerned in this work with the psychological effects of these stirring events on the minds of his characters than with the events themselves, while the conclusion of the story by means of extracts from Renate's diary is both contrived and unsatisfying.

As a novel the work is a structural failure, but viewed as a loose collection of associated chapters it has much to recommend it, at least in parts. Here is the largely untapped source of much that delights the reader in the later Berlin social novels : the humour, the power of characterisation through conversation, the flair for depicting unusual human types, the ability to reproduce the atmosphere and topics of the aristocratic dinner-party and other social occasions, or to capture the essentials of the various professions—church, army or state. Here, for example, we find Pastor Seidentopf, the first of a long line of clerical figures distinguished by some highly individualised trait of character or by some unusual interest. In this case it is a love of archaeology, which has become a kind of mission in his life, far exceeding that of his official duties, as we see from the layer of dust which lies undisturbed over the theological tomes on his bookshelves. He has formed a special theory of his own about the history of the area—one that is bitterly opposed by his fellow-collector, Justizrat Turgany—and every object he collects is used to support his views. To quote Fontane, he is a ' Tendenzsammler ' of no mean order. ' Innerhalb der Kirche ... ein Halber, ein Lauwarmer, hatte er, sobald es sich um Urnen und Totentöpfe handelte, die Dogmenstrenge eines Großinquisitors.'

Two chapters stand out in this long first novel and fore-shadow much that is to come from the pen of Fontane—and that, moreover, quite soon, for it must not be forgotten that this transitional prose work was written by a man of nearly sixty, whose great achievements in the novel and *Novelle* lie immediately ahead of him. One chapter of especial promise is No. 28, entitled *Doktor Faulstich* and largely devoted to a portrait of this scholarly enthusiast for the works of Novalis. We meet him in his lodgings at the home of Frau Griepe, another Fontane ' original ' and a forerunner of many other landlady portraits. Her intimidating entry, when asked to serve refreshments, arouses the reader's keenest sympathy for her luckless lodger.

> Sie blieb in der Türe stehen, und mit einem Ausdruck äußerster Respektlosigkeit, der ihr im übrigen noch hübsches Gesicht geradezu verzerrte, auf den ängstlich dasitzenden Doktor blickend, faßte sie alles, was sie zu sagen hatte, in ein halb wie Frage und halb wie Drohung klingendes : ' Na ?' zusammen.

The room itself tells us less about Witwe Griepe than about its present inhabitant, Faulstich, whose books lie around on every available space, one particularly handsome volume sporting a teaspoon as a marker. Our initial impression of an insignificant personality is, however, quickly dispelled when we hear him discourse upon his favourite subject of Novalis and the German Romantics.

The other chapter which is rich in promise—indeed, in fulfilment if regarded as an independent social vignette and not in terms of its relevance to the main purpose of the novel—is chapter 40, *Bei Frau Hulen*. Here we are less concerned with one character than with a whole group gathered together on what is intended to be a festive occasion. In these circumstances Fontane excels, and he was to prove his mastery again and again in the later novels. Although Frau Hulen, Lewin's landlady in Berlin, serves as the kingpin of this chapter, we are also concerned with the private reactions of her dinner-guests, both to their hostess and to each other. In this account of a soirée which constantly teeters on the brink of disaster, Fontane demonstrates in brilliant fashion his skill as a social novelist. In many ways it fully bears comparison with similar examples in the later and better-known novels. We find here the same gentle mockery of human weakness and vanity, as for example in the guest who cannot help admiring his own reflection in the mirror on the dining-room wall, the second who ' putzte erst seine Brille, dann heimlich auch die Gabel am Tischtuchzipfel ab ', or the dinner-table strategist who provokes a heated discussion of the current military situation and almost brings the festivities to a violent end. Having survived this episode, the visitors are led away to enjoy the musical portion of the evening's entertainment, which proves to be a rare treat for the reader if not for the guests themselves, anticipating in its tone something of the musical soirées in *Frau Jenny Treibel*. We arc allowed to trace the complicated pattern of mistrust and jealousy underlying the whole evening's performance and wince on behalf of the luckless hostess as the guests discuss her, the refreshments and each other on their way home. ' So dachten auch die anderen,' Fontane concludes, ' Befriedigt war nur Frau Hulen selbst.' A delightful interlude for the reader but, alas, almost entirely irrelevant to the progress of the story as such.

There are, of course, numerous little idiosyncrasies to remind us that this is Fontane's first work of prose fiction. He is, for example, a little too fond of addressing his readers personally, which means that the figure of the author tends to come between them and the characters he is presenting. In chapter 6, for instance, when introducing Tante Schorlemmer, he does so in a manner which intrudes disconcertingly into the flow of the story :

> Da wir nun im langen Verlauf unserer Erzählung nirgends einen Punkt entdecken können, der Raum böte für eine biographische Skizze unter dem Titel ' Tante Schorlemmer ', so halten wir hier den Augenblick für gekommen, uns unserer Pflicht gegen diese treffliche Dame zu entledigen. Denn Tante Schorlemmer ist keine Nebenfigur in diesem Buche, und da wir

> ihr, nach flüchtiger Bekanntschaft in Flur und Kirche, an dieser Stelle bereits zum dritten Male begegnen, so hat der Leser ein gutes Recht, Aufschluß darüber zu verlangen, wer Tante Schorlemmer eigentlich ist.

Having satisfied the reader's curiosity, Fontane then concludes rather awkwardly: 'So war Tante Schorlemmer.' He uses the same unfortunate technique again in the following chapter about the local innkeeper : ' So war Krüger Scharwenka.'

In the chapter devoted to Tante Amelie and Schloß Guse the use of French words or phrases is perhaps a little heavy-handed at times. Apart from this, however, the conversational technique is most promising.   Another little trick, which occasionally jars, is the linking of author and reader by means of the confidential possessive adjective, as for example when Dr. Faulstich becomes ' unser Doktor '.

The chief weakness still lies in the diffuse nature of this work. But Fontane has the perfect defence inasmuch as he declared specifically and *within the text of the novel itself* (a remarkable breach of form indeed !) that he had no intention of following any particular rules of construction in telling his story, and— ' wenn dies ein Verstoß gegen die Gesetze guter Erzählung ist, so möge der Leser Nachsicht üben ', with more to this effect.

As well as looking back to the past, to the *Wanderungen durch die Mark Brandenburg* and to the influence of Scott and Alexis (in the choice of subject if not in detail), *Vor dem Sturm* also points ahead in many respects. We can find here, to a greater or lesser extent, almost every feature associated with Fontane's prose masterpieces, even though in some cases expressed more hesitantly than in the later works.   Already we notice, for example, the use of symbolism, especially in the selection of people's names, the employment of superstitions as a kind of *Leitmotiv*, the effective use of humour, the art of reproducing natural and convincing conversations, and, above all, the ability to create a wide variety of entirely credible and sharply differentiated characters.   It is true that in this first novel these characters tend to be presented to the reader in isolation, as closed studies, and not always with any particular function to perform.   This is where Scott's personages have a certain advantage over those of Fontane in *Vor dem Sturm* ; they seem to be more vitally concerned in the turbulent events around them, so cutting more of a dash than Fontane's patient, meditative figures in all but the last few chapters of this novel. With its diffusion of interest and wide range of social portraiture, the work has perhaps more points of contact with Dickens or Thackeray than with Scott. But the very fact that it can be, and has been, cut in length and issued in a shortened version without losing any vital element in the story implies that it is not sufficiently closely-knit to rate highly under the title of ' novel '. As H. H. Reuter has pointed out,[6] we cannot imagine shortening one of the later masterpieces such as *Irrungen, Wirrungen*.

The ending is particularly lame and unsatisfactory, both because of the re-emergence of the author's personality in the text and because of the irritating, awkward use of the diary extracts. Fontane was often to find some difficulty in rounding off a story neatly without falling into the conventional sentimentality of his era (always repugnant to him), but never again was the problem quite so obvious.

Grete Minde and *Ellernklipp*

Following this loosely-woven first novel came a whole series of *Romane* and *Novellen* in quick succession—a remarkable feat for an author of Fontane's years. He proved to an astonished public that not only was he capable of revealing a completely different facet of his creative gift at an age when the powers of some writers already show signs of declining, but that he was able to acquire a lasting reputation in the new field he had entered. At first the transition was a gradual one. The following two *Novellen*, *Grete Minde* (1880) and *Ellernklipp* (1881), while already indicating some of the problems which later came to predominate in the ' Berlin ' novels, preserve a historical distance between the events described and the social background of the late nineteenth century. Known to German critics as ' die balladesken Novellen ', both of these tales are modest in length, in striking contrast to their immediate predecessor, and retain something of the atmosphere found in the ballad despite the prose treatment of their subjects.

Grete Minde takes as its theme the tragic destruction of the little town of Tangermünde in Brandenburg not long after the

Reformation in the seventeenth century—an act of desperation by a young woman of beauty and sensitivity whose mind has given way beneath the weight of life and its injustice. The story is treated in loose chronicle style, and both construction and characterisation show increased confidence and a mastery of historical material. It bears a sub-title, *Nach einer altmär-kischen Chronik*, and is indeed based upon an incident recorded among the historical events of the Altmark by, *inter alia*, Caspar Helmreich and Andreas Ritner in the seventeenth century, Georg Gottfried Küster in the eighteenth, and August Wilhelm Pohlmann in the nineteenth century.[7]

While on holiday at Wernigerode in the Harz during the summer of 1878, Fontane paid a visit to Tangermünde, the setting of his new story. The remote little town in the Altmark, with its timeless atmosphere, appealed strongly to his sense of history, while the tragic story of Margarethe Minde touched a responsive chord in his poetic imagination He then picked out the main features of the town which play an important part in the story—Stephanskirche, castle and town hall—studied them with care, and made a sketch-map of the area. Next, with the experienced eye of the ' Wanderer ', he noted the chief characteristics of the countryside. The method of composition was more or less the same as in all his future prose works. First a rough draft of the story in outline was made and its key points established. This included the distribution of the principal events and the relative emphasis to be placed on various characters. Later he turned his attention to the details, key passages in the dialogue were worked out and then gradu-ally the other gaps were filled. The final process of stylistc revision often took him at least as long as all the previous phases put together. After three versions, completed between August 1878 and April 1879, Fontane was at last content. *Grete Minde* was printed in the periodical *Nord und Süd* in May 1879 and subsequently appeared as a book, published by W. Hertz of Berlin, in 1880. Fontane has recorded his satisfaction at the praise it received from both the critics and the reading public.

Though we know from the sub-title that the story was in-spired by the reading of old chronicles and that Grete Minde was a historical personage, much of the detail was invented by

Fontane himself. Only about one-fifth of the material available in the sources he used was actually adopted, and the tale was brought to an end after the outbreak of the great fire at Tangermünde, the subsequent trial and execution of the historical Grete being avoided altogether. From the reports in the chronicles it is known that a certain Margarethe Minde, believing that she had been wrongfully deprived of an inheritance (apparently by her uncle and not by her stepbrother as in Fontane's version), set fire to the town as an act of revenge on 13 September, 1617. It was alleged that she had been helped by her husband and another man, and, after a long trial and cruel tortures, all three were burned at the stake on the 22 March, 1619.

Fontane portrays the events somewhat differently. His Grete Minde is the daughter of a well-to-do local merchant and his Spanish wife, who had died soon after Grete was born. The girl was thus left mainly in the unsympathetic hands of her half-brother, Gerdt, born of an earlier marriage, and his wife Trud. After the death of her elderly father, Grete's loveless home life becomes intolerable, despite the affectionate devotion of her young neighbour, Valtin. When finally she runs away, Valtin goes with her, and nothing is heard of either of them for three years. By the time the reader meets them again, it is clear that their life together has been full of hardships and disappointments. Valtin is mortally sick, but before his death he persuades Grete to promise that she will return to her old home and ask Gerdt for forgiveness and a place at his hearth for their child and herself. But her brother shows stony indifference towards her plea and turns her away, denying moreover that she is entitled to any part of the inheritance from her father's estate. Determined to obtain her rights, Grete appeals to the Town Council for justice, but fails to convince them. In crazed despair the frenzied girl sets fire to her half-brother's home, then to the entire town. She completes the scene of horror by taking Gerdt's child, together with her own, to the top of the church tower, where she gloats upon the havoc she has created. Gerdt has to witness his own son being held aloft in vengeful glee by the demented Grete Minde just before the tower and its occupants collapse into the inferno beneath.

In Fontane's treatment of the material the figure of Grete dominates the scene. The author is primarily concerned with the problem of how a girl from a good family and obviously endowed with intelligence could be brought to such a desperate situation. Gradually the impression emerges that Grete is one of those unhappy souls whose temperament and social environment are in constant conflict and who are consequently doomed to unhappiness. There are also certain contradictions within Grete herself which further complicate the problem. Fontane shows how such personalities can also destroy those who love them, in this case Valtin. Had Grete not been placed in such an uncongenial home background, of course, much that happened need never have occurred. It is the harsh and unsympathetic treatment she receives that encourages the more dangerous aspects of her character—her tendency towards violent anger in the face of injustice, her romantic yearning for perfection and an escape from the realities of life, and above all her intense secret pride When Grete returns to Tangermünde seeking a reconciliation, it is clear that disaster will follow if her pride should be wounded in the process.

Grete clearly stood in need of a strong guiding hand in order to solve her problems in life, but Valtin was not the man to supply it. As the price of his submission to her will he has to share her tragic fate as well. He lacks the colour and vigour of Grete, though he is by no means without sterling qualities. His physical courage is shown beyond doubt when, as a fifteen-year-old youth, he rescues Grete from the panic-stricken crowds after the Town Hall explosion. His good nature and generosity earn for him the reader's respect and sympathy. Even on his death-bed Valtin's thoughts are for Grete and no word of complaint about his own hard lot crosses his lips. But in spite of all his fine qualities, Valtin is a weak character in his relationship with Grete and lets himself be governed by her to an extent which proves their undoing.

Usually Fontane's villainous characters have a number of redeeming features and win at least our grudging tolerance as likable rascals, but this cannot be said of Gerdt Minde or his wife Trud. Gerdt is portrayed as a cynical, miserly man with little spontaneous emotion left in him except when his possessions are threatened. Trud's hard, egoistic personality is further complicated by suppressed jealousy of Valtin's love for Grete.

The minor characters are drawn in sparing outline, mainly by means of Fontane's developing ' conversational technique ' whereby the reader forms his own picture of the persons concerned from the style and substance of their conversations. Successful examples of this are Pastor Gigas, the zealous Lutheran minister with his hatred of all forms of heresy but whose strictness is tempered by his essential kindness and human sympathy, the wise old Domina of Arendsee with her deep insight into human nature and her gift of accurate presentiment, Regine, the devoted old family servant, and Emrentz, Valtin's stepmother. Old Jakob Minde, on the other hand, is deliberately kept in the background during his brief appearance in the story and remains a somewhat shadowy figure.

In this short work the traces of Willibald Alexis in form and style, so noticeable in *Vor dem Sturm*, have become much fainter. Particularly divergent from the Alexis tradition is the concentration of interest upon a small range of persons and events. In the first chapter there is also an unusual idyllic note, contrasting effectively with the sombre tones at the end of the story and bringing it closer in spirit to a ' Stimmungs-novelle ' by Theodor Storm than is normally the case with Fontane's prose work.

Fontane himself referred to this tale as ' eine balladeske Novelle ' (or prose ballad), and indeed a good deal of the ballad technique has been preserved. . There is, for example, a considerable dramatic element involved. One thinks of such scenes as the rescue of Grete by Valtin during the Town Hall panic, the final dramatic quarrel between Grete and Trud, the return of Grete to her brother's house and her intense effort at self-abasement as she kneels at his feet, her dramatic appearance before the councillors, and finally, of course, the orgy of destruction and revenge upon the town. All incidentals in the story are cut to a minimum as the author strives for terseness and brevity. A great deal is left to the reader's own imagination, and events of great importance (e.g. the quarrel with Trud and the decision to leave home) are often only sparingly indicated. Again reminiscent of the ballad is the interruption of the action after chapter 14 for an interval of three years. The fact that the early part of the tale contains a half-hidden motif of predestined and inescapable disaster, the way in which coming events are hinted at in advance, and the striking manner in which the tragic figure of Grete dominates and unifies the action after Valtin's death, strengthen this impression of ' balladesque ' technique. On the other hand Fontane's genial nature finds it difficult to resist breaking through that sense of historical distance which ought here to be preserved. As the story develops, Valtin and Grete are sometimes allowed to analyse themselves and their problems, indeed to philosophise on life in general in a manner not strictly in accordance with formal requirements.

This *Novelle* indicates a conscious striving after stylistic perfection and an increased precision of description and portraiture. Compared with its diffuse predecessor, the full-length novel *Vor dem Sturm*, it also shows a new artistic self-discipline and conciseness. Although the atmosphere of small-town life in Brandenburg at the beginning of the seventeenth century is clearly conveyed, this remains strictly subordinate to the telling of the story. It is a tale of concentrated narrative interest; situations and incidents are depicted sparingly without any attempt to portray the entire milieu. In this connection we may notice a predilection for Romantic background scenes, for example the old castle of Tangermünde, the half-ruined convent at Arendsee, the stillness of the Lorenzwald or the delicate charm of the moonlit summer's night on which the lovers fled. Nature descriptions as such are brief but trenchant, setting as they often do the tone of an entire chapter. Fontane has captured with particular felicity the mood of the North German autumnal scene, especially in chapters 15 and 17 (at Arendsee and during the return to Tangermünde). Dialect and archaic forms are used discreetly to impart an old-world flavour to the tale.

As far as the subject-matter is concerned, we already have one of those unhappy love-relationships, complicated by social difficulties, which later form the central feature of so many of Fontane's novels about contemporary society. Even though requirements of the *Novelle* here prevented him from developing his gift for ' geistreiche Causerie ', so well illustrated in the Berlin novels which were to follow, one salient feature of his art does appear unmistakably—his ability to make his characters converse naturally and convincingly. ' Meine ganze Aufmerksamkeit ist darauf gerichtet, die Menschen so sprechen zu lassen, wie sie wirklich sprechen ', Fontane wrote,[8] and he added that in *Grete Minde* and *Ellernklipp* his ideal was to strive for ' eine absolute Simplizitätssprache ' as demanded by the material.

Despite its faults, *Grete Minde* still has much to recommend it as an introduction to the prose fiction of Fontane, especially for the younger student. Its strong narrative interest, sound characterisation and skilful evocation of historical atmosphere all contribute to the unsophisticated appeal of this simple tale.

The companion *Novelle*, *Ellernklipp*, shares many of the characteristics of *Grete Minde*, including the sombre undertones. The work was planned in outline late in the year 1879, then, after an interval of several months, was resumed in the early summer of 1880. The third and final draft was completed at Wernigerode, in the Harz Forest—the area of the story itself. The theme was taken from some notes in a local parish record and is set in the period immediately after the Seven Years War (1756-63) in the later years of the reign of Frederick the Great.

The central problem is that of a father's jealousy which leads to his becoming the murderer of his own son and finally taking his life in order to escape from an overpowering sense of guilt. The dominant figure in the work, however, is neither the father, Baltzer Bocholt, nor his son Martin, but the young adopted daughter, Hilde, who without conscious intent exercises a fatal influence on both father and son, thus becoming indirectly responsible for the tragic events which follow.

As in *Vor dem Sturm* and *Grete Minde* Fontane again makes use of chapter headings, and it is not by chance that the first eight of these all begin with the name ' Hilde ', e.g. ' Hilde kommt in des Heidereiters Haus ', ' Hilde spielt ', ' Hilde hat einen Willen ', etc. Hints are given early in the *Novelle* of Hilde's obscure origins, and it becomes increasingly clear that she is illegitimately related to the local aristocracy. During the first Christmas she spends at the Bocholt home we see from her eager and naïve questions that in her ten years of free-and-easy existence with her late mother, Muthe Rochussen, she has never received the least hint of Christian instruction. This, linked with her natural temperament, creates a dangerous situation from the start. As the percipient old minister, Pastor Soergel, says of her, even as a child : ' Ich fürchte, sie kennt nicht Gut und nicht Bös ', adding with unconscious irony in view of subsequent events, ' Darum hab ich sie zu dem Baltzer Bocholt gegeben. Der hat die Zucht und Strenge, die das Träumen und das Herumfahren austreibt '. But her life remains a mixture of dream and reality. By the time she has reached the years of young womanhood Hilde, like the female figures in the early *Novellen* of Storm, has an aura of other-worldliness about her.

Fontane describes his intentions when creating Hilde in the following words : ' Hauptfigur : ein angenommenes Kind, schön, liebenswürdig, poetisch-apathisch, an dem ich beflissen gewesen bin, die dämonisch-unwiderstehliche Macht des Illegitimen und Languissanten zu zeigen.'⁹ The apparent inevitability of her fatal influence on the other sex when she grows older is summed up by the ' conventicle ' preacher, Melcher Harms, who probably knows her better than anyone else : ' Ihr Blut ist ihr Los . . . Es geschieht was muß.'

The affinities between Hilde Rochussen-Bocholt and Grete Minde are not hard to find. Both yearn to escape from an unhappy situation into a romantic dream-life, both live in a half-world of imagination mingled with reality, both feel themselves as ' outsiders ' in the accepted pattern of society around them, in both there is a fundamental disharmony between elements acquired from parents of widely divergent background and temperament, both seem to have inherited a mystical streak which urges them to reject the strict Protestant dogma in which they have grown up, and both are self-willed and able to influence a weaker but devoted partner whom they lead to disaster.

Nor do the similarities between these two *Novellen* end with the principal female characters. We may think of the effective if slightly contrived use of the folk-song motif in both of them : in *Grete Minde* ' Es waren zwei Königskinder ', sung by the girls at their work, in *Ellernklipp* the ' Lied vom eifersüchtigen Knaben '. There are also obvious similarities between a number of the minor characters and the rôles they play, e.g. Pastor Gigas and Pastor Soergel, old Regine and Grissel.

Numerous points of technique are common to both tales. We observe the use of the supernatural element, the effective employment of a nature-mood in support of the main theme (for instance, the rainstorm in *Ellernklipp* and the creation of Lenau-like autumnal scenes in both stories). There are the sudden, compressed scenes of crisis (typical also of the later Fontane) and many items borrowed from the technique of the ballad. Here we remember the three-year interval, the fear of dark, inevitable forces ('Ewig und unwandelbar ist das Gesetz'), the threatening outline of the gaunt Ellernklipp, on which the tragedy takes place, the symbolism of the toy ships named 'Hilde' and 'Martin', the use of fire and destruction to indicate a break with the past, the hints and fragmentary information about a mysterious origin, the suggestions of future unhappiness ('Den Jungen reißt sie mit hincin'), and of course the major themes of jealousy, murder and atonement.

The affinity of these short tales with the ballad is twofold : it contributes not only to their charm but also to their stylistic and structural weaknesses. Fontane, the ballad-poet, has been successful to a certain extent in transferring the same technique into prose, but he found the task of sustaining a tone of detached objectivity throughout eighteen or twenty chapters too much for him. In both stories, therefore, he allowed more of his own personality and interests to creep in than was fitting, thus severely threatening the sense of distance in time required by the nature of the subject. This happened despite his own intense preoccupation with stylistic questions during the completion of the third and final version, which as usual took him as long as did the original composition. He laid particular stress on the importance of establishing the right tone from the very beginning in works such as these. Writing on 18 August, 1880, to his publisher Karpeles, he stated : ' Das erste Kapitel ist immer die Hauptsache und in dem ersten Kapitel die erste Seite, beinahe die erste Zeile ... Bei richtigem Aufbau muß in der ersten Seite der Keim des Ganzen stecken.' Certainly he was more successful in creating a crisp, effective opening chapter in *Ellernklipp* than in its sentimental counterpart, *Im Garten*, in *Grete Minde*.

We are, however, left with a number of nagging questions

at the conclusion of *Ellernklipp*—more, probably, than after completing *Grete Minde*. Certain aspects of the story only partially convince us of their probability. Would, for example, a man of Bocholt's reserved temperament really disclose so much of his inner self to his family, even when mellowed by wine at his birthday celebration ? Is his act of cruelty to his own son really convincing after what we have seen of him up to this point, and, still more, can we accept his total lack of remorse after the deed or his speedy assumption of the rôle of hardened criminal intent on hiding all traces of guilt ? Would a girl of Hilde's temperament really marry her foster-father after being in love with his son and, moreover, do so ' aus Furcht und Dankbarkeit ' ? Is her conversion at the very end of the tale to a life of contemplation and good works (reminiscent of Renate von Vitzewitz, a very different temperament) consistent with what we know about her already ? Or is this an artificial and contrived ending ? We notice, too, that there are still occasional intrusions by the author, even though these have become fewer, e.g. ' Ja, es waren unsere plauderhaften alten Freunde ' in Chapter 18. This is, of course, a more serious fault than in *Vor dem Sturm*, since it totally destroys the ballad-like distance between reader and subject.

Nevertheless, in spite of their weaknesses, these two *Novellen* show that considerable advances have been made since the completion of *Vor dem Sturm*. The stricter requirements of the *Novelle* have forced Fontane to abandon the diffuse and form-less succession of independent incidents and personalities found in the first long *Roman*. He had learnt to give his charac-ters a more distinct and coherent function in the story, and to develop and complete a narrative within a limited space without lengthy digressions.

The two ' balladesque ' *Novellen* cannot stand up to a de-tailed comparison with the later masterpieces, either in style or structure. But they deserve a place in the gallery of Fontane's prose fiction and offer a far more encouraging introduction to his prose works, because of their eminently readable quality, than their ponderous, eighty-two-chapter predecessor. Despite recent gallant attempts to upgrade *Vor dem Sturm* amongst the earlier works at the expense of the allegedly ' weak ' balladesque tales, its effect as an introduction to Fontane, especially on a younger reader, would almost certainly be to frighten him away from future contact with the novelist altogether. *Vor dem Sturm* is for the initiated, perhaps even for the connoisseur of Fontane, as is his last novel, *Der Stechlin*, whereas *Grete Minde* and *Ellernklipp* may safely be offered as a stimulating *hors d'œuvre*, designed to whet the reader's appetite for more.

Chapter 6

THE CRUCIAL YEARS

Schach von Wuthenow

IN order to maintain strict chronology one would need to consider the Novelle *Schach von Wuthenow* after *L'Adultera*, which appeared a few months earlier in the same year, 1882, but this would run counter to the inner pattern of Fontane's development as an author. In spirit and in technique *Schach* belongs to the last stages of the earlier phase, whereas *L'Adultera* signals the beginning of a new era. In terms of actual composition, moreover, *Schach von Wuthenow* precedes the other work in all but its final stages. It was simply put aside for a while as the result of a sudden inspiration for a new tale which the author wished to complete by means of one sustained effort.

For the material of *Schach von Wuthenow*, begun in 1878, Fontane goes back for the last time into the past, but he uses it in a fashion which clearly points forward to the so-called ' Berlin novels ' of the immediate future. Not only is the subject-matter closely related to the twin themes of love and marriage, which henceforth dominate his prose work, but there is an obvious maturity of style and technique which link this tale with those still to come. One hallmark of Fontane's prose, common to all phases, is meticulous research into the background—historical, geographical and social—of every new work of fiction. The training provided by the long years spent in writing the *Wanderungen* was never forgotten. The problem facing him in *Schach von Wuthenow* was the need to differentiate unobtrusively but effectively between the atmosphere of Prussia in the period 1804-6, the setting of this *Novelle*, and that of 1812-13 already presented in *Vor dem Sturm*. Only a few years separate these two pictures of Prussian life—but they are momentous years. In 1804-6 the country still echoed with the sounds of the old régime and reflected the spirit of Frederick the Great. After the shattering defeat at Jena in 1806 it would all be gone for ever.

The events which form the substance of this *Novelle* are also drawn from historical facts, although Fontane has taken mild liberties with both names and dates. The chief characters, von Schack and Fräulein von Crayn, become in his version von Schach and Fräulein von Carayon. The central theme remains unchanged, although it is linked more specifically with the social and political background of the era and becomes both a symbol and a symptom of the pre-Jena mentality in Prussia. Problems of love and marriage, the secret motives of society, the Prussian military concept of honour, are all investigated in depth for the first time. Only one bold step still remains to be taken—from the historical setting to the present day.

The course of events may be described in brief by one of the characters in the *Novelle* itself, von Bülow, who says in a letter at the end of the work :

"Wie lag es denn ? Ein Offizier verkehrt in einem adligen Hause ; die Mutter gefällt ihm, und an einem schönen Maitage gefällt ihm auch die Tochter ... und die Natur zieht ihre Konsequenzen. Was, unter so gegebenen Verhältnissen, wäre nun wohl einfacher und natürlicher gewesen, als Ausgleich durch einen Eheschluß, durch eine Verbindung, die weder gegen den äußeren Vorteil, noch gegen irgendein Vorurteil verstoßen hätte ? Was aber geschieht ? Er flieht nach Wuthenow, einfach weil das holde Geschöpf, um das sich's handelt, ein paar Grübchen mehr in der Wange hat, als gerade modisch oder herkömmlich ist ... Er flieht also, sag ich, löst sich feige von Pflicht und Wort, und als ihn schließlich, um ihn selber sprechen zu lassen, sein ' Allergnädigster König und Herr ' an Pflicht und Wort erinnert und strikten Gehorsam fordert, da gehorcht er, aber nur, um im Momente des Gehorchens den Gehorsam in einer allerbrüskesten Weise zu brechen ... Er greift zu dem alten Auskunftsmittel der Verzweifelten : un peu de poudre."

Von Bülow, who is also a profound critic of the values and philosophy of his own day and plays the part of ' raisonneur ' throughout the story, sums up the Schach tragedy with the words : " Da haben Sie das Wesen der falschen Ehre !" But Schach's suicide is more than just an indictment of the old Friderician code of honour. He is a highly complicated personality and the strands are not easily unravelled. There are many things we should like to know about his relationship with the von Carayon family. To what extent was he involved at an earlier date with the still-attractive widow, Josephine von Carayon ? What are we to make of her quotation to him in Chapter 19 of the saying : ' On revient toujours à ses premiers amours.' ? How can we explain his momentary affair with her disfigured daughter, Victoire, whom he had always addressed cordially but with a noticeable degree of reserve, as, for example, during the excursion to Tempelhof, when he accords her mother obvious preference ? Surely it is not very convincing to ascribe his lapse, as some critics have done, to the after-effect of a frivolous party conversation with Prinz Louis Ferdinand on the supposed attractions of the ' beauté du diable ' ? Schach is, after all, a man of keen aesthetic feeling, and, even when his fortunes are at their lowest ebb, he is still described by all who knew him well as a man of honour and chivalry. The Queen of Prussia tells him : " Ich habe Sie jederzeit als einen Kavalier und Mann von Ehre befunden." Even Frau von Carayon comforts her daughter with the remark : "Habe Vertrauen, Kind. Ich kenne ihn so lange Zeit. Er ist schwach und eitel nach Art aller schönen Männer aber von einem nicht gewöhnlichen Rechtsgefühl und einer untadligen Gesinnung." We have, on the other hand, Sander's cynical comment, made in a general context : " Unsere Prinzipien dauern gerade so lange, bis sie mit unsern Leidenschaften oder Eitelkeiten in Konflikt geraten, und ziehen dann jedesmal den kürzeren."

Much about this outwardly conventional, urbane man remains a mystery to the reader, as it does to his own circle of acquaintances in the story. Alvensleben, who is closer to Schach than are many of the others, recognises his complicated psychological pattern. He hazards a guess that aesthetic factors will lead him to reject marriage with a widow just as they would prevent a union with the scarred Victoire. He also points out Schach's abnormal sensitivity to public opinion, particularly within his own professional circle : " Er ist krankhaft abhängig, abhängig bis zur Schwäche, von dem Urteile der Menschen, speziell seiner Standesgenossen." His reaction to the series of malicious caricatures at his expense leaves us in no doubt about this. Linked with this sensitivity is a certain exaggerated formality which Victoire dubs " etwas konsistorialrätlich Feierliches ". An affront to his dignity, however slight, can affect him deeply. Again Victoire : " Ein spöttisches Lächeln verstimmt ihn auf eine Woche." This is echoed by Schach himself in chapter 13, when considering in despair his own situation : " Ich bin rettungslos dem Spott und Witz der Kameraden verfallen."

Much is revealed about the character of Schach when the reader sees him in the relaxed atmosphere of Schloß Wuthenow, the family seat, away from the conventions and pressures of Berlin and his fashionable regiment, ' Gensdarmes '. Here, in the setting of his childhood, Schach can rediscover his true self, and the reader can gain a fuller picture of the real man behind the mask of the professional soldier. Here, too, Schach can visualise the kind of rural existence which awaits him if he marries Victoire and settles in Wuthenow rather than become the butt of his comrades' wit in Berlin. " Jetzt bin ich zwölf Stunden hier, und mir ist als wären es zwölf Jahre." The picture of the future unfolds before his mind's eye . . . the Sunday sermon, the unchanging view of the park, the growing family, the traditional portraits of Victoire and himself for the gallery—he as a mere captain (retired) amongst the generals, she, with her physical imperfection, amongst the rows of beautiful women. He knows it can never be—and resorts to the traditional way out of an impossible dilemma. This choice reveals a certain intellectual limitation, for, having first placed himself in a vulnerable situation and attracted derision from members of his own circle, he now commits another absurdity. By going through the motions of obedience to the King's command and marrying Victoire, only to take his own life immediately afterwards in order to avoid the long-term consequences, he becomes a pathetic rather than a tragic figure.

The psychological conflict in Schach goes deeper than the problem involved, namely the prospect of a shot-gun wedding with a pock-marked former beauty whom he does not really love. Let us suppose that Victoire had not suffered the illness which led to her disfigurement and that there had been a greater depth and sureness in his feelings for her ; would the path of love have been straightforward ? It is very doubtful, for some of Schach's objections to what lay ahead of him— domesticity, family life, an undistinguished rural existence— would have applied in almost any matrimonial situation. Victoire herself is perceptive enough to realise this eventually, and she recognises the underlying conflict between Schach's ambitions as a fashionable officer and member of the court circle on the one hand and the counter-claims of conventional domestic life with an unfashionable wife on the other. She writes at the very end of the *Novelle* to her confidante, Lisette von Perbandt, on the subject of Schach's dilemma and says : " Er gehörte durchaus, und mehr als irgendwer, den ich kennengelernt habe, zu den Männern, die nicht für die Ehe geschaffen sind." Later, in the same letter, she adds : " Noch jetzt darf ich Dir versichern, und die Sehnsucht meines Herzens ändert nichts an dieser Erkenntnis, daß es mir schwer, ja fast unmöglich ist, ihn mir au sein de sa famille vorzustellen. Ein Kardinal . . . läßt sich eben nicht als Ehemann denken. Und Schach auch nicht."

When we look back at the end of the *Novelle*, we understand a great deal more about the motivation of Rittmeister von Schach and the inevitability of the outcome. We are helped, too, by the additional light cast on him by the letters of his friends and associates—a device much used by Fontane. But he still remains a partly obscure personality, and we must agree with Victoire's comment to Lisette von Perbandt on this subject : " Wie lösen sich die Rätsel ? Nie. Ein Rest von Dunklem und Unaufgeklärtem bleibt, und in die letzten und geheimsten Triebfedern andrer oder auch nur unsrer eignen Handlungsweise hineinzublicken, ist uns versagt."

The figure of Schach, of course, dominates this short prose work, but the strength of the characterisation does not depend exclusively upon him. Undoubtedly Victoire will intrigue the reader, for here also there are elements of contradiction. Her own sudden involvement with Schach is not easily explained, for she shows a remarkable degree of cool detachment, both before and after the crisis, in her assessment of him as a man, witnessed by her letter to Lisette as early as chapter 5. Against this, however, it must be added that she was clearly drawn to him emotionally, if irrationally, and still preserves a good deal of illusion about his feelings towards her when she writes after his death : " Ich hatte früh resigniert, und vermeinte kein Anrecht an jenes Schönste zu haben, was das Leben hat. Und nun hab ich es gehabt. Liebe." The reader's sympathy is with Victoire from the start, for her whole existence is conditioned by the misfortune which struck her in the early bloom of adolescence, when her beauty was already a subject of admiration. Nevertheless, her tragedy has not embittered her but rather brought out a certain saintly quality of passive heroism, expressed in the line : " In meiner Lage lernt man milde sein, sich trösten, verzeihen."

With a still young and attractive mother in the late thirties, Victoire might be forgiven for showing signs of jealousy where Schach is concerned, but she does not, and this enhances her strength of character and the reader's respect for her. Josephine von Carayon, the mother, combines an attractive vivacity with an impressive degree of emotional maturity and sound common sense. She is admirably characterised by Schach in chapter 4, where he calls her his feminine ideal and admits to what he calls her " stille Macht über mich ". We recognise her social tact in the soirée of chapter 2, when she skilfully and unobtrusively fends off an incipient quarrel between Schach and von Bülow on a political theme and quietly steers the conversation into safer channels by mentioning the topic of the theatre. Her fundamental kindliness, especially towards Schach, is matched only by her deep concern for the welfare of her daughter, Victoire, with whom she has a rare bond of mature understanding. It is this maternal protectiveness which provokes her wrath against the vacillating Schach and eventually leads also to her bold step of approaching the King with a plea for royal intervention—an episode in which she shows great dignity and strength of character.

Among the less prominent characters are several who deserve special attention, including the old General von Köckritz, a Fontane military portrait of distinction. The thumbnail sketches of the King and Queen are brief but highly effective, forming an interesting contrast with the lengthier presentation of the bon-vivant Prinz Louis. Other examples of considerable merit are to be found in the circle of visitors who frequent the von Carayon home, including the agreeable and sensitive von Alvensleben from Schach's regiment, the arrogant but intelligent retired officer, von Bülow, and the enigmatic figure from the publishing world, Sander. On the distaff side, the *Novelle* would have been poorer without the presence of Tante Marguerite, a delightful Fontane ' original ' who gets all her names and facts mixed up, lives for news and gossip from the Court, with which she has tenuous connections, and pronounces words like *Kirche* as *Kürche*. As always in Fontane's stories, the humbler social classes contribute their miniature masterpieces of human characterisation to the gallery, here in such village personalities as Krist, Mutter Krepschen and Ordonnanz Baarsch.

Many features in this *Novelle* are typical of Fontane's prose work in both early and later phases. One may note, for example, the effective use of conversation as a means of revealing character. The topics which come up for discussion are those which we associate with Fontane and his interests— the theatre, the political background, the social values of the period, the outlook of the military and aristocratic circles of Berlin. Typical, too, are many of the descriptive passages— the landscape, castles and villages around Berlin, the country people of Mark Brandenburg, visits to old churches, to cafés and restaurants in or near the capital. Often the reader is reminded most vividly of the style and content of the *Wanderungen*. Then there is the favourite motif of the effect on the principal characters of a ' Landpartie ', or country excursion, with its subtle change of mood. Victoire clearly recognises its influence upon people and events when she writes to her intimate friend, Lisette von Perbandt, about the walk near Tempelhof : " Solche stillen Abende, wo man über Feld schreitet, und nichts hört als das Anschlagen der Abendglocke, heben uns über kleine Rücksichten fort und machen uns freier."

The characteristic use of absolute discretion, when dealing with delicate situations, is seen to advantage in chapter 8 (*Schach und Victoire*). The full significance of this meeting is never spelt out for the reader. It is merely hinted at by subtle means, such as the unobtrusive change from ' Sie ' to ' du ' after the emotional episode—which is completely omitted, apart from the insertion of a space in the text and a single asterisk ! Similarly there is no description of the ' shotgun ' wedding between Schach and Victoire; the reader is transported directly from the preparations at the end of chapter 18 to the announcement at the start of the following chapter : " Die Trauung hatte stattgefunden ". Schach's farewell letter to

Victoire, which must have been a revealing document, is alluded to but not reproduced.

Typical of the earlier Fontane is the occasional use of such conventional devices as a personal intrusion into the story with phrases like " Armer Schach !" or by referring to him as " unser Schach ". He also still employs formal chapter-headings and is inclined to involve the reader in minor 'Wande-rungen ', as in the first part of chapter 16. We are introduced in some detail to the buildings and scenery of Wuthenow, Potsdam and Paretz as well as to the fashionable area of Berlin where the von Carayons have their home. The device of an exchange of letters continues to be employed (and very effect-ively) as a means of conveying viewpoints and information. An interesting feature is the use of symbols, e.g. the swans in chapter 7 and the ' Schlittenfahrt ' masquerade in chapter 11. Some of the symbolism applies to the tale as a whole, since Schach himself is to a certain extent a symbol of his age. He and the society in which he moves are both inwardly divided, and both are doomed, as von Bülow is quick to point out. Not without reason, therefore, has this Novelle been regarded as a ' kritischer Zeitroman ' in miniature.[1]

L'Adultera (1882)

This short *Roman*, which held up the completion of *Schach von Wuthenow* and appeared just before it, represents the beginning of a new stage in Fontane's creative writing. Now he takes a bold step and places his characters and their problems in the setting of contemporary Prussia in the 1880's, and it is that society as much as the characters of the novels which is henceforth the object of his analysis.

Again the subject-matter is taken from a real-life occurrence, and the problem involved so fascinated the author that he was able, while in the middle of another work of fiction, to complete the novel within about three months. As well as representing the transition from past to present, *L'Adultera* shows a remark-able advance in the author's mastery of style and characteris-ation. The subject is a variant of the love-and-marriage theme which is to remain Fontane's special field of interest, especially in its more problematical aspects. The original title he chose for this tale was *Melanie van der Straaten*, the name of the principal female character, but, reluctantly, Fontane allowed himself to be persuaded that *L'Adultera*, the subject of a Tintoretto painting which plays a symbolical part in the story, was a more satisfactory choice. Certainly it pleased his publishers and doubtless promoted sales of the book, but at the same time it led to widespread misunderstanding of the author's purpose.

Melanie de Caparoux, of French-Swiss origin, was married to Kommerzienrat van der Straaten when she was only 17 and he was 42. There is, then, an age-difference of no less than 25 years, a factor in broken marriages which Fontane later investigates in depth. Here, however, it is not the major cause. The marriage has already lasted for 10 years, the young girl has become a woman of 27 and mother of two children, Lydia and Heth, and by dint of good humour and self-control has achieved a remarkable degree of accommodation to the noticeably different temperament of her husband. Van der Straaten adores her, is indulgent towards her when their interests diverge, and allows her a wide measure of personal freedom—but he does not understand her, and this is to determine the outcome. He is a man of business, a financier, who typifies much of the parvenu spirit of Berlin during the ' Gründerzeit ' in the last decades of the 19th century. He is not without some very attractive qualities as well, and these are given full recognition in the latter half of the story, but neither his basic kindness nor his bluff good humour can out-weigh his moodiness and irritability, his consummate lack of tact and brash approach to life and people. Nevertheless the marriage has survived for a whole decade and might well have continued along the same superficial lines, neither particularly happy nor unhappy. But it is an example of what Fontane terms 'eine Scheinehe', and the arrival of Rubehn, a younger man with precisely those qualities of sensitivity and good taste lacked by van der Straaten, breaks the existing union into fragments. Melanie and Rubehn quickly discover mutual interests, especially in the realm of music, where both are devotees of Richard Wagner, and, for the first time, Melanie begins to feel deeply embarrassed by the social maladroitness of her husband, rather than just mildly irritated, since she now has other standards by which to judge him.

The drift towards disaster continues, a drifting which is

emphasised by some fairly obvious symbolism, as for example when their little boat is caught in the current of the river Spree and the question springs to Melanie's mind : ' Wohin treiben wir ?' With a deft touch of realism, which pleased Fontane's younger contemporaries in the Naturalist movement, he brings about the climax through the influence of an exotic environment. While wandering with Rubehn through a hot-house, rich with the scent of orchids and shaded by tropical palm-trees, Melanie feels her resistance crumbling into a feverish insecurity, and it is here that they admit their mutual love. With typical Fontane delicacy our participation is limited to the knowledge that " sie flüsterten Worte, so heiß und so süß, wie die Luft, die sie atmeten ".

An unexpected feature of this novel is the fact that Melanie and Rubehn find the inner strength to survive the social opprobrium, inseparable in the late nineteenth century from a divorce action, and to begin a new life together, still in Berlin. There is even a hint of partial reconciliation with society as a result of their courage in adversity and their steadfast love. This is the last occasion on which such a compromise with society is presented to us ; in later Berlin novels the victory of society is complete and the price of defeat is tragically high.

How much more convincing the background of Berlin appears to be in this novel, set in Fontane's own time, than that of 1806 in *Schach von Wuthenow*—and how greatly this helps to bring alive the characters who move against it ! Melanie dominates the scene, and deliberately so, for it is with her temperament and the revelation of its hidden depths that we are concerned. Rubehn, by way of contrast, remains an outline figure ; we are told enough about him to make the spiritual kinship convincing, but he is not analysed in the same depth as Melanie. Van der Straaten is presented to us in greater detail, and we are shown the abrasive side of his personality as well as its humorous and kindly elements. To do this effectively Fontane makes good use of his two favourite devices—the dinner party and the country outing, both occasions on which tongues wag freely, and we can thus learn about the main characters through the conversation of others.

The dinner-party described in chapter 5 is a masterpiece of

its kind, as is the subsequent analysis of events by the guests on
their way home. The occasion is a hostess's nightmare, poised
repeatedly on the brink of verbal disaster as van der Straaten's
love of *double-entendre* and provocative statements gets the
better of him, and the reader senses at once the social pre-
dicament in which Melanie finds herself. In addition to
providing this illumination of the marriage situation, however,
the conversation at the dinner-table reproduces the whole
social and political atmosphere of the era in which Fontane
was writing. The discussion moves among contemporary
personalities and topical events. Bismarck—usually referred
to indirectly as ' the Prince ' or ' His Highness ', though
occasionally named openly—is the subject of heated argument.
The possibility of renewed war with France is debated. We
hear the stilted, artificial conversational tone cultivated by
fashionable Berlin society during the heady period of the new
Second Reich. With seemingly effortless skill Fontane then
steers the table-talk from politics to art, and from art to music
and the current Wagner cult. A superb example is included
of van der Straaten's love of indelicate expressions, here
quickly masked by expert intervention and well-timed diversion. This in its turn provides us with an instance of the offender's
own sensitivity to rebuke on questions of taste and his liability
to fits of sudden anger, which nevertheless subside as quickly
as they arise, making way for humour and sentimentality
again.

Several secondary characters are introduced on this occasion,
prominent amongst them being the elegant, aristocratic Major
von Gryczinski, an officer on the General Staff and brother-in-
law of Melanie, Baron Duquede (Legationsrat a.D.), a cynic
who finds everybody and everything ' überschätzt ', so earning
himself the nickname of ' Herr Negationsrat ', and Polizeirat
Reiff with his fund of after-dinner stories of a kind much
appreciated by the host.

The ' Landpartie ' of chapters 8-10 takes us to the village
of Stralau and Löbbekes Kaffeehaus, where signs and portents
of coming disaster are by no means lacking, even for the less
discerning reader. The heading of chapter 10, ' Wohin
treiben wir ?' has already been cited, while other equally
obvious ones are to be found in chapter 8 (' Weil die Leute,

die mit dem Feuer spielen, immer zu sicher sind und immer die Gefahr vergessen ' ; or the incident when a ball aimed by Melanie at her husband is caught instead by Rubehn and there is much play on the word ' Glück '.) In the subsequent visit to the café we experience what is in fact a verbal anticipation by van der Straaten of the scene ' Unter Palmen ' (chapter 12) and an unconcious analysis of what is in reality his own marital situation. Even more blatant in its symbolism is the incident of the falling stars, heavily underlined by van der Straaten's observations : ' daß alles in der Welt eigentlich nur des Fallens wegen da sei : die Sterne, die Engel, und nur die Frauen nicht '. In later works the use of symbols continues, but they are handled more subtly. Events swiftly follow the many portents of this chapter ; an over-venturesome remark made by van der Straaten in the presence of Rubehn draws a sharp rebuke from Melanie, and the evening threatens to end on a disagreeable note. Chance then determines that Melanie and Rubehn shall share a small boat on the river, and, in her distress over her husband's lack of feeling and tact, she makes Rubehn her confidant, and he takes her hand. Distant singing of the ballad *Schön-Rottraut* provides a significant folk-song motif similar to that given in chapter 9 of *Grete Minde* by *Es waren zwei Königskinder*.

This ballad-like anticipation of events continues unremittingly. Even the climax in chapter 12 (*Unter Palmen*) is preceded by a lengthy peroration in dialect by the old gardener, Kagelmann, on the perils and instabilities of marriage. Some time before the final breakdown of the marriage, too, the reader is treated in the 14th chapter to some reflections by Rubehn on the trials and tribulations ahead (' Mut, Melanie, nur Mut. Es werden schwere Tage kommen . . . . ').

Dominating all this wealth of symbolism (an *embarras de richesses* indeed) is that of the Tintoretto painting *L'Adultera* which gives the story its title. How much is revealed, albeit in a rather over-deliberate, self-conscious fashion, by the conversation between husband and wife which arises from his purchase of this reproduction . . . Melanie's instinctive sympathy with the erring woman, van der Straaten's underlying pessimism on the subject of his own marriage, based on similar unhappy experiences in his family (' denn es ist erblich in unserm Haus' and 'Es kommt, was kommen soll.') In case the reader may somehow (though how, is difficult to imagine) have missed the significance of all this, the motif is reintroduced at the end of the tale by the arrival of a miniature of the same *L'Adultera* painting, contained in a locket.

Among the most impressive chapters of this work is that which deals with the final break between Melanie and her husband, chapter 16, with its significant title *Abschied*. The parting was intended to take place at night, without dramatic confrontations, but somehow van der Straaten discovers what is happening and makes a sudden appearance on the scene. But the expected angry reproaches and threats never materialise. Instead he is humble, conciliatory and understanding, showing an unexpected capacity for love and forgiveness. This, too, has just been foreshadowed by Christel, Melanie's maid, who pleads with her to stay and says of van der Straaten : ' Er ist eijentlich ein juter Mann, ein sehr juter, un bloß ein bißchen sonderbar '. Christel, like the coachman Ehm and the gardener Kagelmann, occupies a worthy place in the long series of Fontane servants, just as the shrewd, bird-like figure of Fräulein von Sawatzki (' Riekchen ') does in his portrait gallery of elderly spinsters with little physical charm but a heart of gold. She, too, senses the basic goodness in van der Straaten and offers Melanie a brief but trenchant analysis of him as early as chapter 7.

While there are numerous items in this work which look back to the past—chapter titles (used for the last time here and in *Schach von Wuthenow*), ballad-like motifs and over-use of symbols, for instance, there is much also that looks to the future and will later be taken up again and developed to perfection. One example is Melanie's reunion—if such it may be called—with her children, only to find the elder one, Lydia, (not a very convincing portrait of a small girl, it must be admitted, with her old-young outlook and adult suspicions of Rubehn from their very first encounter) completely alienated from her. She drags her younger sister with her from the room, shouting : ' Wir haben keine Mutter mehr !' This theme of child-alienation is taken up once again in *Effi Briest*, where it receives a more subtle if less dramatic treatment. Similarly the speed with which events move after the parting of husband

and wife is also found in later works such as *Effi Briest*, but this too acquires a new subtlety and is not so apparent, rather as though the author were seeking to reach a conclusion as soon as he could do so with decency.

Graf Petöfy

Having just seen Fontane established in his new rôle as an author of controversial social novels set in the Berlin and Prussia of his own day, it comes as something of a surprise to discover that *Graf Petöfy* (1884), though contemporary, plays against an Austro-Hungarian background. Stylistically speaking, this is an elegant and impressive work. As an attempt to bring alive the scenes, atmosphere and personalities of the old Habsburg empire, its achievement is much more limited. The reason for this soon becomes apparent. Fontane was a man of the North, a Prussian (despite his French ancestry) and above all a Berliner. Let him deal with people and places known to him intimately—in the capital city, the Harz, or his other favourite holiday resort, Silesia, and both the characters and their surroundings vibrate with life. Take him away from his own roots, as here and again in the second part of *Quitt* (1891), and he is lost, despite all his conscientious researches. Book-learning can never replace for him the intimacy of personal experience. One only has to compare the reminiscences of the North German sea-coast in chapters 9 and 22 of *Graf Petöfy* with the rest of the book to realise this.

Fontane once again takes his material from real-life sources, a marriage between a Berlin actress and a Hungarian count of advancing years. He transfers the scene to, first of all, Vienna and later to Schloß Arpa in Hungary. It is a tragedy of youth married to age, without any compensating inner spiritual link. The situation is made more complicated by Franziska's misinterpretation of her own temperament and by the untimely arrival on the scene of a young and attractive man when she is suffering from a sense of loneliness at the somewhat mournful Schloß Arpa with its alien setting. But the age factor is the most important one. ' Er ist alt, und du bist jung ', Hannah warns her mistress, Franziska Franz, before the marriage. Unlike van der Straaten, Graf Adam is not really in love with his young wife. He is 70, she is 26; he loves the theatre, she is a successful actress. They both enjoy lively, cultured discussions together and with others. That is about all there is to the relationship. The count wanted to secure for himself her amusing conversation, the ornament of her beauty and the companionship of her interest in matters connected with the theatre. She, on the other hand, appreciated the kind of life and background he could offer her, with security and the dignity of a title. It is thus a ' Scheinehe ' from both points of view. The tell-tale episode of the ring worn by his young nephew, Egon, warns the elderly count of the real trend of events. He realises his mistake, which it is now too late to correct, foresees the coming scandal, and somewhat quixotically ends his own life in order to clear the way ahead for the young lovers. Ironically, despite this self-sacrifice, Franziska and Egon do not find happiness together, for the shadow of their guilt falls over the relationship.

As in *L'Adultera*, there is much ' Vordeutung ' of coming events. In chapter 2 Graf Adam, when speaking of his sister, remarks : ' Sie sieht in mir einen ewigen Jüngling und beweist mir, daß mein Leben eine Kette von Jugendtorheiten sei, ja, sie hat sich, glaub ich, in den Kopf gesetzt, eine Jugendtorheit werde auch mein Leben beschließen.' This early warning to the reader is reinforced by a discussion of suicide and its ethics in the following chapter. He is aware of difficulties in the way of this unusual marriage, but concentrates rather on those of secondary importance in the discussion (chapter 10) with his sister Judith, namely ' Geburt und Stand und Konfession '. Judith sees these as negotiable ; in a family of humbler origin they could perhaps prove a stumbling-block, ' . . . aber das Haus Petöfy darf sich freier bewegen, und in dem Augenblick, wo das Ja gesprochen ist, ist auch ausgeglichen, was Geburt und Stand vermissen liessen.' Confessional differences, too, can be adjusted. But the vast gap in ages cannot, and the elderly Judith is woman enough to see that this is the real sticking-point. Graf Adam puts his case in plain terms : ' Ich weiß genau, was siebenzig Jahre bedeuten, und daß sie der Zypresse näher stehen als der Rosenlaube. Der Sprosser im Fliederbusch hat für mich ausgeschlagen. Ich weiß das.' He explains to his sister that he is not embarking on any kind of amorous adventure, but is tired of an old bachelor's solitude and its artificial solutions. He seeks diversion, a soothing influence, and stimulating conversation, bringing, he hopes, the kind of inner peace which has always eluded him. Judith warns him, just as Hannah had warned Franziska : ' Junges Blut will junges Blut '. At this, Graf Adam shows that he is capable, like van der Straaten, of making unusual and indeed remarkable concessions : ' Weiß ich doch, daß sie jung ist. Und sie *soll* jung sein und Freude haben und jede Stunde genießen.' He merely asks for the maintenance of outward appearances and the dignity due to his station in life : ' Diskretion also, Dekorum, Dehors.'

A parallel discussion takes place between Franziska and Hannah, who is more a confidante than a maid. Hannah's chief objection is also on the score of the age-gap, as we have seen. In addition she points out the contrast between Graf Adam's background of Vienna and Hungary and Franziska's Prussian-Pomeranian origins, their religious differences (very important to the strongly Protestant Hannah), and the disparity of rank between a count and an actress. Here Franziska is able to put an opposing viewpoint ; as a trained actress of some repute she will be able to transfer her histrionic abilities from the stage to real life and play the rôle of countess with some skill. As far as the age-difference is concerned, she believes that the days of the ' große Passion ' are behind her— if ever they existed—and is more concerned with the possibility of losing her freedom of action in small, everyday matters as a result of marriage. Her total lack of awareness of the hidden depths within her own personality is a major factor in bringing about the tragedy.

Signs and portents abound in the chapter after the marriage ceremony. There is the ominous cracking of the old bell at Schloß Arpa, when it is rung to greet her arrival. There is the ' Lied von Barcsai ', which attracts Franziska with its haunting folk-song melody and proves to be on the theme of the unfaithful wife of a Hungarian count. The scene on the lake, which brings about the emotional crisis, is worthy of the Romantic movement—there is the dramatic change to icy cold, an uncanny whistling sound, the stars all disappear from view behind an inky cloak of darkness. As their boat gets caught in the whirlpool and death seems imminent, Franziska

suddenly addresses Egon as ' du ' and there is no more pretence
between them. It all strikes the reader as somewhat contrived
after *L'Adultera*. The major climax occurs in chapter 32, when
an improbable chance reveals to Graf Adam the fact that Egon
is wearing a small ring of Franziska's, hidden under a large
one of his own. This fresh opportunity for symbolism and
double-entendre is fully utilised in such barbed phrases by the
Count as : ' Und solch Ringelchen ! Man sollte nicht glauben,
daß es so tief verletzen könne.'

After her husband's death Franziska, rather surprisingly,
returns to Arpa and renounces all intention of marrying Egon.
Instead, she proposes what is a kind of penance, a life of contemplation and good works—with strong implications of an
imminent conversion to the Catholic faith. As she reaches the
castle it hardly surprises the reader, inured by now to this
profusion of symbolism, that her arrival coincides exactly with
the return of the bell which was broken at the time of her
unfortunate marriage to the former *Schloßherr*.

One senses the lingering influence of *Schach von Wuthenow* on
this work, with the underlying problem dominating the
characters at times. It is discussed at great length by everybody most intimately concerned and analysed in detail. This
naturally tends to give the characters a cipher-like quality,
illustrating an abstract problem but somewhat remote as
people. Nor do the social occasions sparkle quite in the same
way as those with a Prussian setting, for the author was not
acquainted with Austro-Hungarian society or its distinctive
atmosphere and tone. While there is much in this work to
interest the Fontane-lover who is familiar with the whole range
of this author's novels, it is perhaps best regarded as a preliminary study for the treatment of this same problem in a surer
fashion and on familiar ground in a work which lies only just
ahead chronologically, namely *Cécile* (1887).

Unterm Birnbaum

Meantime, however, Fontane presents us with another
surprise, for in 1885 be brought out a completely different
kind of prose tale, one within the field of the ' Kriminalge-
schichte '—an experiment not repeated by him after *Unterm
Birnbaum*.

A Polish representative of a firm, to which Abel Hradschek owes a good deal of money, disappears early one stormy morning soon after (presumably) leaving Hradschek's village inn. His carriage is found in the flooded river, but not the body. The reader is left in little doubt about the fact that Szulski has been murdered by Hradschek with the complicity of his wife who later impersonates the traveller as ' he ' steps, muffled up, into his carriage and drives off. There are suspicions in the village and tongues wag freely. Despite legal investigations, however, and Hradschek's arrest for questioning, nothing can be proved against him, and he is released. There is indeed a body found in the innkeeper's garden, ' unterm Birnbaum ', but it is of a long-dead French soldier from an earlier war. The case becomes almost forgotten—but not quite, as the occasional double-edged remarks of Hradschek's neighbour, Mutter Jeschke, clearly indicate. In a moment of panic Hradschek decides to move the victim's remains, which are buried beneath the cellar floor, only to be caught himself by a thousand-to-one chance. He unthinkingly removes a wooden chock, and a huge barrel rolls across the trap-door of the cellar, incarcerating him with the evidence of his guilt. In his terror, he suffers—or so we must presume—a heart-attack and dies, leaving his partly disinterred victim pointing the hand of mute accusation at him.

Here we have a detective story of an unusual kind. We know almost for certain who committed the crime and why. Towards the end of the tale we also gain a fairly accurate impression of where the evidence is likely to be found. Interest is centred mainly on the question : will Hradschek be found out and, if so, how ? Many ballad-like touches lead us to expect discovery. There is as a result a comparatively low degree of tension, which is hardly typical of the ' Kriminal-geschichte '. There is no titillating of the imagination by means of any description of the deed itself, nor is there a dramatic confrontation with the authorities or the laying of a capital charge against the innkeeper. Gruesome and sensational elements are almost entirely absent.

Unterm Birnbaum is as much a piece of genre-painting as a murder story, an extension into the realm of fiction of the *Oderland* section of Fontane's *Wanderungen durch die Mark*

Brandenburg. Our interest is not focussed constantly on the mystery, which is hardly a mystery at all, but strays appreciatively over the whole scene of village life and its wide range of local characters. It is these local people—and one in particular—who eventually solve the case which has baffled both police and magistrates, for it is as a reaction to their gossip that Hradschek makes his fatal blunder of attempting to move the evidence of his crime. Several questions, however, remain to worry us ; chief among these is our difficulty in believing that the jovial, somewhat nervous Hradschek is capable of murder at all, still less his pious wife. And what would have happened to the plan to fake an accident in the storm if the weather had not obligingly remained in angry mood till the following day ?

Cécile

Cécile (1887) brings us back on to the main track of Fontane's prose fiction. Although a large part of the *Novelle* is set in the Harz, it may nevertheless be counted as one of the ' Berlin ' series, not only because the main action (which occurs towards the end) takes place there, but also because all the principal personalities are from Berlin and take with them on holiday their Berlin attitudes and social values. As a prose work it looks forward to the peaks just ahead in time but also back to what has gone before. Wandrey, in his 1919 monograph, *Theodor Fontane*, suggests that it shows similarities with the tone of *Schach von Wuthenow* and that the author's interest in his characters here is a cool and detached one, adding: " Cécile . . . liegt unter Fontanes reifen Werken seinem Lebenszentrum am fernsten."[2] H. H. Reuter, on the other hand, in his 1968 study, *Fontane*, takes a different view.[3] He sees this work as Fontane's reaction to Schopenhauer and the latter's views on the rôle of woman in society and on the subject of marriage. He also feels that *Cécile* belongs with the following two tales, *Irrungen, Wirrungen* and *Stine*, forming with them a kind of loose trilogy. Both of these viewpoints can be defended, but perhaps the most satisfying solution is to regard *Cécile* as a bridge, linking together two adjacent stages of the author's rapid development in the field of prose fiction.

On one point, however, there is little doubt. *Cécile* shows clear evidence of further striking progress in matters of style and technique, not only as compared with *Schach von Wuthenow* but also with *L'Adultera*, its spiritual next-of-kin in the immediate past. Once again Fontane is dealing with a marriage problem, and again there is a considerable age-difference between the partners—over twenty years, in fact—but this is not the crucial factor. Temperamental differences play a major part in the situation, as do social elements which only become apparent towards the end of the story.

Pierre St. Arnaud, a retired army officer of energetic and ruthless temperament, has little understanding for his hyper-sensitive and ailing young wife, Cécile, with her need for constant reassurance and attention. In such circumstances it is not surprising that she should accept gratefully from an admirer, von Gordon, the kind of considerate devotion that she fails to receive from her husband. Nor is there initially much danger of this relationship getting out of hand, thanks to Cécile's cool and determined attitude (despite an obvious liking for him). Unfortunately, however, Gordon's feelings are less firmly under control, and the aura of mystery surrounding Cécile's past life adds curiosity to his ardour. The revelation of her early history as a ' Fürstengeliebte ' leads him to break the barriers of conventional respect for her as St. Arnaud's wife. In a frenzy of jealous rage over an incident that was really without significance, he insults Cécile in front of another person, who promptly informs St. Arnaud. The result is a duel, in which St. Arnaud kills Gordon, just as he had earlier on killed the officer in his own regiment who had objected to the marriage with Cécile on the grounds of her past. Cécile, realising that she has again been the unwitting cause of a man's death at the hands of her unloving but possessive husband and unable to face the emptiness of the years ahead, ends her own life in despair.

Virtually all of the action takes place in the final seven chapters out of a total of twenty-nine. The first sixteen are set in the Harz and are devoted largely to a leisurely delineation of the principal characters against their holiday background. Indeed this background frequently becomes the foreground, as Fontane lovingly weaves into the story his own happy memories of the district in which he so often spent his summer holidays and where the draft version of this tale was completed.

It is one of the interesting peculiarities about Fontane's so-called ' Berlin novels ' that most of them were written miles away from the capital. So the ghost of Fontane, the 'Wanderer', creeps in and out of the first half of *Cécile*. We follow excursions he had himself just made, and we visit with him once again old churches and castles. But these are not mere 'Einlagen' or irrelevant digressions, as they tended to be in the earliest works. In each case the incident is turned to good account as a means of illuminating the characters. There is, however, a strong sense of actuality about this Harz background ; the Hotel Zehnpfund in Thale, where St. Arnaud and Cécile stayed and where they first met Gordon, existed in reality and was several times the holiday home of the author. Fontane did the ramble from there to Altenbrak, described in chapters 13-15 ; indeed, it was during this very walk that he worked out the plan for the *Novelle*, summarising it in skeleton chapters of one page each the next day at the hotel in Thale, where his own table d'hôte companions supplied certain aspects of the characterisation. The ' Präzeptor von Altenbrak ', too, was a real person with whom Fontane had conversed. There is a happy, relaxed atmosphere about this vacation in the Harz, and one cannot really accuse it of holding up the action—since the action has not yet begun. It does so with an almost frightening suddenness, however, once the scene moves to Berlin, and the leisurely day-by-day account of the characters and their activities gives way to an intense, almost ballad-like episodic approach. Just before this change of setting there is a masterly example of Fontane's ability to present a psychological crisis with the utmost brevity and in a completely casual manner. On the way back to Thale from Altenbrak, Cécile, in a sudden mood of fatigue and irritation, reveals to Gordon her unhappiness in marriage with St. Arnaud. Gordon, we are told : ' nahm ihre lässig herabhängende Hand und hielt sie und küßte sie, was sie geschehen ließ.' The incident is not emphasised in any way—almost the reverse—and the conversation occupies only about ten lines. None the less it represents the ' Wendepunkt ' of the *Novelle*.

As in *L'Adultera* the central female character dominates the scene throughout, and we tend to see all situations from her point of view. Again the husband and the aspiring lover play

largely supporting rôles in strong contrast with each other.
Here there is one major difference, however. For a long time we
cannot understand *why* Cécile reacts so often in the way she
does. We realise that she suffers from nervous debility without
knowing the reason for this. We note her sudden swings from
apathy to lively participation and back again to apathy. We
sense the underlying melancholia, but not its cause, likewise
the constant need for flattery and attention to sustain her
morale. Like Gordon, we, too, are intrigued by the baffling
contrasts in Cécile's personality—the apparent absence of
formal education or any intellectual interests combined with
an undoubted graciousness of bearing and manner suggestive
of a distinguished background. Constant hints are given but
the revelation is deferred. Even in the first chapter there is the
odd behaviour of General von Saldern, who salutes the couple
most courteously on Potsdam station but then avoids them.
There is the curious fact that St. Arnaud, a first-rate professional
soldier, should have retired at 50 from the command of a
Guards regiment. There is Cécile's inexplicable embarrassment on hearing the story of Jagdschloß Totenrode and (the
broadest hint of all) on learning the history of Gräfin Aurora,
the former ' Fürstenfavoritin ', while visiting the castle gallery
at Quedlinburg. Only in chapter 21, when the long-delayed
letter from Gordon's sister Klothilde has reached him, do we
learn the truth about Cécile—and then expressed in the most
delicate terms imaginable . . . she had been ' Vorleserin ' at a
small princely court, had been asked ' not to leave the court '
when the Prince's nephew succeeded him, had been for some
time ' under the protection' of a chamberlain, and so forth.
But Fontane sums up the reality rather more bluntly in the
thoughts expressed by the disillusioned Gordon : " Fürstengeliebte, Favoritin *in duplo*, Erbschaftsstück von Onkel auf
Neffe ! Und dazwischen der Kammerherr . . . ." He cannot
help regarding her in a new light, and his changed attitude is
reflected in the freer tone he adopts. Cécile is sensitive enough
to feel this change and to suspect the reason behind it. Her
whole desire after marrying St. Arnaud—for protection rather
than love—has been to free herself from her past and earn the
respect of society ; but now she begins to realise the truth
which Fontane expressed in a letter (of 2.6.87 to Paul Schlen-

ther) about the theme of this work : ' Wer mal drin sitzt, gleichviel mit oder ohne Schuld, kommt nicht wieder heraus.'

Gordon and St. Arnaud, though clearly sketched, are not shown in such detail as Cécile, just as was the case with the central male figures in *L'Adultera*. St. Arnaud emerges distinctly at an early stage, though his past, too, is veiled in mystery until Klothilde's letter reveals it. Again we are given hints by Fontane before this . . . his distinguished military record in the Franco-Prussian War of 1870-71 and his narrow escape from death in action, his premature retirement, his bitterness and empty way of life since then, much of it whiled away at his club—not, be it noted, a military club but one frequented by financiers and gamblers. We hear through the painter, Rosa Hexel, that he is capable of momentary acts of courtesy towards Cécile but is also a person of extreme moods, egoistic by nature, and capable of forgetting his wife altogether for days on end. She is a beautiful woman and one of his valued possessions, to be brought out or put aside at will. It is quite obvious that his anger with Gordon over the scene he made in front of Geheimrat Hedemeyer is not connected with the embarrassment caused to Cécile, but rather with his own sense of property and rights : ' Er geriert sich, als ob er legitimste Rechte geltendzumachen hätte,'' he says angrily. Fontane explains his anger thus : ' denn er war an seiner empfindlichsten, wenn nicht an seiner einzig empfindlichen Stelle getroffen, in seinem Stolz.' The picture of the real St. Arnaud, ' der Mann der Determiniertheiten ', is then presented clearly in the words : ' Gefürchtet zu sein, einzuschüchtern, die Superiorität, die der Mut gibt, in jedem Augenblicke fühlbar zu machen, das war recht eigentlich seine Passion '. Typically, he includes in his letter to Cécile, after the duel, the observation : ' Aber nimm das Ganze nicht tragischer, als nötig : die Welt ist kein Treibhaus für überzarte Gefühle.'

Of Gordon the reader knows far less. We follow his every movement and see Cécile through his eyes, but much of his own temperament remains obscure. We are taken by surprise in chapters 25 and 26 when the impetuous, self-willed streak in him suddenly reveals itself in impulsive, ill-considered action. In retrospect, however, the words of Hofprediger Dr. Dörffel to Cécile, giving his first impressions of Gordon, take on new import : " Er hat, so lebhaft und sanguinisch er ist, einen eigensinnigen Zug um den Mund und ist mutmaßlich fixer Ideen fähig. Ich fürchte, wenn er sich etwas in den Kopf gesetzt hat, so will er auch mit dem Kopf durch die Wand. Das Schottische spukt noch in ihm nach. Alle Schotten sind hartköpfig."

Of the minor characters in *Cécile* comparatively few make sufficient impact to merit individual attention, and one of them—the Privatgelehrte Eginhard Aus dem Grunde—does so only in a negative sense. When the work first appeared, Eginhard came in for a good deal of criticism, and understandably so, for he holds up its progress with his tedious lectures without contributing anything of value. In a sense this was deliberate, since Fontane intended him to be a caricature of similar persons from whose loquacity and self-importance he had suffered at meetings of historical societies in Berlin. But the figure of Herr Eginhard remains too much an abstraction and the boredom he exudes is sometimes intolerably real. Fontane later admitted the superfluity of this character.

In the case of the two Berlin tourists at Thale, however, he has been outstandingly successful. Jovial, loud and self-assured, they typified the Berlin male of the 1880's on holiday —as seen by the non-Berliner. Fontane's mastery of every nuance of Berlin dialect was here turned to good effect and delighted his contemporaries. The part they play in the main theme is slight, but their contribution to the atmosphere of the holiday idyll represented by chapters 1-16 is appreciable.

Rosa Hexel, the woman painter specialising in animal studies, must surely have appealed to the Naturalist writers with their emphasis on the new rôle of woman in society, namely as an independent personality with her own contribution to make. Not that Rosa is presented to us as a militant suffragette-figure ; far from it, for she has much personal charm. She forms an excellent contrast with the aggressive, masculine Baronin von Snatterlöw on the occasion of the St. Arnaud dinner-party in chapter 20, as well as serving a useful function in supplying Gordon with information about Cécile and her husband. The other members of the St. Arnaud circle make little more appeal to the reader than the Baroness (' eine hochbusige Dame . . . mit Ringellöckchen und Adlernase ',

Fontane calls her). All, like St. Arnaud, have a sizeable chip on their shoulder and tend to express themselves in sarcasm and aggression; all move, or have moved, in similar circles, military or governmental, and all have met with disappointment of some kind.

The dinner-party, at which these people come together, is itself another masterly example of Fontane's art of self-characterisation through conversation, an art already far advanced by the time he wrote *L'Adultera*, where it was similarly used to great advantage. Once again the table-talk ranges over the current political scene of Bismarckian Germany, and once again the vociferous speakers tell us at least as much about themselves indirectly as about the topics under discussion. How skilfully, too, Fontane knows how to deflate pomposity, as in the case of the ebullient Geheimrat Hedemeyer, trapped in full oratorical flood by the sorry mischance of entangling his spectacles, while removing them, in his curly hair—which we know to be a toupet !

Other familiar stylistic features are present in this tale, all handled with increasing skill and discretion. Symbols and portents still play their familiar (but no longer obtrusive) part. There is the idyllic country house of chapter 5, concealing a story of unhappiness and death ; Cécile is compared with the tragic and guilty figure of Mary, Queen of Scots; she sees Gordon bathed in the fiery sunset glow, filtering through the leaves of a copper beech, and regards this as a warning ; there is the funeral procession which confronts Gordon early in chapter 19 and reminds him of life's transience ; most clearly of all, there is the twice-uttered, prophetic remark by Rosa : ' Gebe Gott, daß es ein gutes Ende nimmt '. Letters are again used as an occasional means of conveying information about the characters (notably in the Gordon-Klothilde correspondence), and one remembers that Fontane himself was an enthusiastic and fluent correspondent. Considerable use is also made of the ' Selbstgespräch ', e.g., by Gordon in chapters 16, 17 and 22, as a means of indicating the state of mind of a principal character. A few old tricks of style reappear, including the familiar linking of author and reader with the characters by means of such phrases as : ' Unsere Reisenden ', ' unsere Reiter ', ' unsere Freunde '. The choice of unusual and in some cases foreign-sounding names is one feature which remains with the author at all stages : here we have Robert von Gordon-Leslie (von Gordon), Pierre and Cécile St. Arnaud, (all good Germans none the less !) and the improbable Eginhard Aus dem Grunde. The characteristic feature of ' toning down ' crises has already been mentioned in connection with the first avowal of affection between Gordon and Cécile ; a further instance is the way in which her suicide is reported. We are not told directly that she took her own life, merely that she died, and we draw our conclusions from the note left behind and recall the emphasis placed on the permitted maximum dosage of the digitalis prescribed for Cécile in chapter 23 (" Aber zählen Sie richtig und bedenken Sie, welch ein kostbares Leben auf dem Spiele steht.")

One feature of this *Novelle* differentiates it sharply from *L'Adultera*, and that is the tragic ending. No longer is it possible to reach some sort of compromise with society. Cécile's marriage was an attempt at such a compromise, at social rehabilitation, but it failed. After the scandal caused by the second duel her position would be even more hopeless. Here Fontane diverges markedly from his sources. For, in the real-life story of a dispute between Gardeleutnant Graf Eulenburg and his commanding officer, Oberstleutnant von Alten, over a proposed marriage by the young lieutenant, tragedy was averted and the affair gradually forgotten. Fontane takes this incident as the basis of his tale but gives it a new and terrible intensity.

Chapter 7

THE GOLDEN AGE, I

Irrungen, Wirrungen

IT comes as a shock to the modern reader to discover that *Irrungen, Wirrungen* (1888), a masterpiece of Fontane's art and presented with typical delicacy of feeling, was once referred to as 'die gräßliche Hurengeschichte'.[1] At the time of its publication it was regarded by many readers as an outrageous novel. So strong were the initial reactions against it, when it appeared as a serial in the *Vossische Zeitung*, that Fontane had some difficulty in obtaining a publisher for the book. Practically all the objections were based on a complete misunderstanding of the author's purpose, and it remained for the passage of time to confirm the favourable opinion of a discerning minority. It was almost as though the now elderly author were writing for an era later than his own. What he unmasked in *Irrungen, Wirrungen* was not the moral code in the genuine sense but hypocrisy and convention. The love between Lt. Botho von Rienäcker, a young nobleman, and Magdalene Nimptsch, a seamstress, can by no stretch of the imagination be ranged alongside the casual affairs of his brother-officers with women of low repute. This point is clearly made in the Hankels Ablage chapters, where the two kinds of relationship are brought into vivid contrast.

What we are confronted with in this novel is a situation involving sincere love and spiritual affinity between two young people of different classes in an age of acute class-consciousness. At first the theme appears to be a simple one. Botho and Lene meet by chance on a river excursion, develop the acquaintance and fall deeply in love. Under family pressure Botho has to marry within his own social class and renounce Lene, who later follows his example. Both remain inwardly bound to the memory of their idyllic relationship, but both come to terms with the society in which they live and so avoid tragic consequences. To understand and feel the inevitability of this parting today requires an ability to transport oneself in imagination back to a world of rigid social barriers which crumbled away after the 1914-18 war. To this extent the work may be said to have become ' dated '. But the theme of frustrated love, doomed by factors quite outside the control of the lovers, is an eternal one, and the present-day reader living in a far less rigid social order should not find it difficult to interpret the underlying problem in terms of his own era and its barriers, be they national, religious, sectarian or political.

Structurally the story may be divided into two parts : the love affair between Botho and Lene occupies the first fifteen chapters, while chapters 16-26 are concerned with the outwardly separate destinies of the lovers in their respective social spheres. In the longer first part, the last three chapters (13-15) represent the transition—during and just after the Hankels Ablage visit—from idyllic happiness to an abrupt and final separation. Part of the idyll rests on the unforced bridging of the social gap, not only between the lovers themselves but also between Botho and those who form Lene's immediate background, namely old Frau Nimptsch (her foster-mother) and the Dörr family. Significantly, Lene does not meet Botho's circle until the unfortunate rencontre at Hankels Ablage, which presages the end. There is never any suggestion of patronage on the part of Botho either towards the sensitive, intelligent Lene or her less gifted but worthy relatives and associates. Nor is it a mere phrase when he claims to feel as much at home by the fireside of the elderly washerwoman, Frau Nimptsch, as in the heart of fashionable society. Whether strolling in the countryside with Lene or sitting in her simple homestead by the Tiergarten, Botho finds those elements of simplicity and sincerity for which his honest nature craves. It is against this kind of background that we first come to know him—in the tumbledown ' Schloß ' with its absurdly pretentious, broken-down clock tower, surrounded by the Dörrs' market garden, and guarded by its watchdog Sultan. Here Botho can relax and shed the artificialities of both military and aristocratic social life. We learn of the lovers' first meeting through a casual conversation between Lene and Frau Dörr, leading to the older woman's friendly warning not to forget the reality of the situation. Lene's reply is characteristic of her open and sincere nature : ' Ich bilde mir gar nichts ein. Wenn ich einen liebe, dann lieb ich ihn. Und das ist mir genug.'

We have already formed an impression of Lene after hearing

the conversation between Frau Nimptsch and Frau Dörr early in the first chapter, while the two lovers are out walking. Lene's foster-mother likewise fears that the girl may have illusions about the future, and this leads Frau Dörr to voice her gloomy philosophy : ' O du meine Güte, denn is es schlimm. Immer wenn das Einbilden anfängt, fängt auch das Schlimme an.' She too has had a ' Liebschaft ' with a member of the aristocracy in her youth, but one of a very different kind, and recollections of her ' Graf mit seine fuffzig auf'm Buckel ' form a useful foil against which we can study the Lene-Botho relationship. Frau Dörr pays tribute to Lene's character : ' Jott, ein Engel is sie woll grade auch nich, aber propper und fleißig un kann alles und is für Ordnung und fürs Reelle.' We learn also from the same source that there is some kind of mystery connected with Lene's origin. We have already been told that she is a ' Pflegetochter ' ; Frau Dörr also hints that she may be of noble birth—' Vielleicht is es eine Prinzessin oder so was.' This secret, however, is left unrevealed.

From Lene's own conversations we quickly learn the salient features of her character, above all her frankness and honesty : ' Sich zieren und zimperlich tun, das hab ich nie gekonnt ' she says in recollecting her first meeting with Botho. The same forthright realism is reflected in her statement to her lover about the future : ' Glaube mir, daß ich dich habe, diese Stunde habe, das ist mein Glück. Was daraus wird, das kümmert mich nicht.' She foresees the social inevitability of their eventual parting and accepts this as a fact of life : ' Aber wegfliegen wirst du, das seh ich klar und gewiß. Du wirst es müssen. Es heißt immer, die Liebe mache blind, aber sie macht auch hell und fernsichtig.' She realises too, with the sure feeling of a strong character, that there is a weak strain in Botho, which will lead him to conform : ' Du liebst mich und bist schwach. Daran ist nichts zu ändern. Alle schönen Männer sind schwach . . . . '

Botho is not only analysed for us in Lene's conversations with him and by random remarks between Frau Nimptsch und Frau Dörr. Chapter 8 provides a kind of parallel with the earlier scenes at Lene's home, introducing Botho's comrades in the officers' club and allowing the reader to hear their views of him. Here, amidst the flip of cards and the clipped tones of the officers' mess, we see Botho through the eyes of his regimental companions, who clearly recognise the subtle differences between him and themselves. His attachment to Lene is known and not taken too seriously, whereas the news of his impending engagement (albeit under family pressure) to Käthe von Sellenthin, a distant cousin, arouses great interest. It is considered ' eine glänzende Partie ' both from the personal viewpoint and as a means of reviving the family fortune—a factor which is considered to be decisive. Only Wedell has some doubts, reminding the others : ' Rienäcker . . . war immer fürs Natürliche ' and reiterating the point made earlier by Lene, namely that he is ' schwach und bestimmbar und von einer seltenen Weichheit und Herzensgüte '. But the others recognise that circumstances will eventually triumph over sentiment : ' Aber die Verhältnisse werden ihn zwingen, und er wird sich lösen und frei machen, schlimmstenfalls wie der Fuchs aus dem Eisen.'

Between the several chapters showing the Botho-Lene relationship against her family background and this cool, detached assessment of the situation by his fellow-officers, there is the important lunch-party episode of chapter 7. We see Botho for the first time in company other than that of Lene and her circle ; although the changes in Botho's manner are only minimal, consisting of a lightly-worn mask of aristocratic convention in speech and jargon, we realise at once that Lene's presence at such a gathering would be impossible. We also learn at first hand some of the pressures being brought to bear upon him. The chapter is an outstanding one, and its appeal goes far beyond its function in the story. Fontane's growing skill in the presentation of dinner-table scenes and conversations has already been commented upon ; in this case his technique is excellent. Several elements, each important in its own right, are blended effortlessly into one artistic whole. There is, for a start, the superb portrait of the choleric Baron von Osten, Botho's uncle and prototype of the Prussian landowner. He is deeply emotional, although attempting to conceal it behind stock phrases of his class and former military profession, intensely loyal to his concept of honour and fatherland (in which the heart clearly plays a larger rôle than the mind), contemptuous of Bismarck and all his works, and slightly out of his depth in this brash, up-to-date ' Weltstadt ' which has replaced the Berlin of his youth. Through him the reader learns a good deal about the controversy which raged around the figure of Bismarck in Fontane's day as well as about the characteristic values and attributes of the Prussian country aristocracy.

As so often in this author's works, the brilliant table-talk leads its participants to the brink of social disaster. An incautious remark by Botho brings the fiery old gentleman on to the dreaded topic of Bismarck (still Chancellor, when the story opened), while a well-meant attempt from the same source to steer the conversation on to other subjects simply gives his uncle an opportunity to introduce the matter of Käthe von Sellenthin and Botho's duty to marry. Despite his nephew's obvious embarrassment he pursues this theme (one of the incidental purposes of his visit to Berlin) and virtually talks Botho into enforced agreement. The reader also gains a good deal of information concerning the background of this strongly favoured match ; he learns of the financial insecurity of the Rienäcker estates with their sandy, unproductive soil, of the improvidence of Botho's parents in money matters and his obligations towards other members of the family, of the understanding between the Rienäckers and the Sellenthins which has existed for years on the question of a marriage between Botho and Käthe . . . ' die bloß darauf wartet, daß du kommst und in einem regelrechten Antrag das besiegelst und wahrmachst, was die Eltern schon verabredet haben, als ihr noch Kinder wart '. Plainly Uncle Kurt Anton fears two possibilities, which he expresses thus to Wedell : ' Er vertut sonst sein bißchen Vermögen oder verplempert sich wohl gar mit einer kleinen Bourgeoise '—and in the latter assumption he is far nearer the truth than he realises. Without waiting for Botho's formal assent to the proposal that he should return triumphantly with the news of his nephew's agreement to the marriage, he calls for champagne in which to celebrate his diplomatic victory. So Botho, weaker of will than his uncle and conscious of family duty, is caught in a trap and henceforth his relationship with Lene survives only on borrowed time.

For a while the sword of Damocles is forgotten and the

interest of the tale shifts back again to Botho and Lene, seen in the old familiar setting. Then follows the fateful excursion to Hankels Ablage. The choice of the little resort on the Spree is significant. Other places are considered, then dismissed : ' alle waren noch zu besucht '. This factor has influenced all their movements—the need to avoid prying eyes and society gossip. Even early in the first chapter we were told by Frau Nimptsch that the young couple had gone for a walk towards Wilmersdorf—' den Fußweg 'lang, da kommt keiner '. Chapter 9 provides another example, when Lene suggests taking the footpath across the meadows, adding without pathos : ' Hier bleiben wir. Das ist der hübscheste Weg und der einsamste. Da kommt niemand.' For similar reasons Hankels Ablage is chosen, although fate frustrates their purpose.

This key episode begins on a note of idyllic happiness. The two lovers are alone for almost the first time and they have not included Frau Dörr in the excursion, as originally proposed. As Botho says : ' Frau Dörr, wenn sie neben deiner Mutter sitzt oder den alten Dörr erzieht, ist unbezahlbar, aber nicht unter Menschen. Unter Menschen ist sie bloß komische Figur und eine Verlegenheit '. Nevertheless ' Verlegenheit ' is not entirely lacking, even on the first happy evening, for the innkeeper's wife causes Lene embarrassment by misconstruing her tiredness and offering much unwanted advice of a highly personal nature to the young woman. Yet it is happiness which predominates on that first evening at Hankels Ablage, albeit of a somewhat feverish quality which indicates the awareness of Lene in particular that it will be short-lived. This is underlined by the pessimism in her remark concerning the choice of rowing-boat :

' Welches nehmen wir,' sagte Botho, ' die " Forelle " oder die " Hoffnung " ?'

'Natürlich die "Forelle". Was sollen wir mit der "Hoffnung"?'

We feel also the sadness which makes her reluctant to acquiesce in Botho's sentimental request for a hair with which to bind a bouquet of wild flowers : ' Du hast es gewollt. Hier, nimm es. Nun bist du gebunden.' Each becomes silently aware of the fragile nature of their happiness, and the chapter closes on the uneasy note : ' Jeder aber hing seinem Glück und der Frage nach, wie lange das Glück noch dauern werde.'

One is reminded at times in these three chapters of the skilful blending in Beethoven's *Pastoral* Symphony of happiness with undertones of disquiet and rising tension before the dramatic onset of the storm. In chapters 11 and 12 the note of happiness remains the dominant one. Chapter 13 also opens in all serenity but contains an early warning of the short duration of their happiness reflected in Lene's thought : ' Und wenn diese Stunde die letzte war, nun, so war sie die letzte . . . ' Ironically, they are both already within a minute of escape from impending disaster as they prepare their sailing boat for a half-day's excursion. But, before they can leave, they are surrounded by three of Botho's fellow-officers, together with their ' Damen '. The idyll is shattered as the two worlds meet.

Hitherto Lene has only known the smart, superficial world of Botho's circle through his own ironical imitations (as in chapter 4) or by distant observation from the outside. Her introduction at Hankels Ablage is not to its nobler aspects. She is at once ranged alongside the women of the *demi-monde* who have accompanied Pitt, Serge and Balafré and assumed to be one of them. Shamefully, Botho compromises in this situation of *force majeure* and shows the reader all too clearly the truth of Lene's intuitive realisation that he is basically a weak, conforming nature, despite his many virtues and the marked individuality of his tastes. Instead of insisting, after a brief exchange of courtesies, on carrying out his original plans with Lene, he allows the others to take charge and organise a combined excursion which cannot but be painful to both of them. So Lene, too, receives an ironical nickname, like the other ' Damen ' and Botho drops into the casual, superficial jargon of the mess. Fontane does not linger unduly over the remainder of this ruined day, which had begun in such promising fashion. Enough is however shown to emphasise the basic difference between Lene and her temporary female companions. Characteristically she makes no reproaches to Botho, but senses with intuitive feeling that it is a symbol of the end : ' Ach, mein einziger Botho, du willst es mir verbergen, aber es geht zu End '. Und rasch, ich weiß es.' As they part, she is even more specific : ' Gestern, als wir über diese Wiese gingen und plauderten und ich dir den Strauß pflückte, das war unser letztes Glück und unsere letzte schöne Stunde.'

It is hardly a surprise when the following morning brings the decisive letter from Botho's mother, outlining the sudden crisis in the family's finances, warning of the growing impatience on the part of the Sellenthin family and making the marriage with Käthe a matter of some urgency. The inevitability of parting has to be faced, and Botho does so while out riding alone. In a prolonged self-examination he concedes : 'Es liegt nicht in mir, die Welt herauszufordern' and claims that all he sought with Lene was 'ein verschwiegenes Glück' for which he hoped to gain the tolerant understanding of his circle. Why was this intimacy with Lene so important to him ? Because she alone possessed those qualities which he valued above all others—'Einfachheit, Wahrheit, Natürlichkeit'. Hence the powerful hold she had on his emotions. The prospect of giving her up in exchange for the artificialities of a socially acceptable match without inner harmony appears intolerable. Nevertheless his conclusion is that one's social origins and sense of order ultimately triumph over all else. 'Denn Ordnung ist viel und mitunter alles. Und nun frag ich mich : War mein Leben in der "Ordnung" ? Nein. Ordnung ist Ehe.'

The very brief chapter 15, which deals with the lovers' final parting, is probably the culmination of all Fontane ever achieved in both style and content. Botho and Lene take leave of each other without scenes or tears, preserving a classic dignity which in no way belies or conceals the depth of underlying feeling. 'Ich hab es so kommen sehen, von Anfang an,' says Lene, 'und es geschieht nur, was muß.' It is clear none the less that the parting is merely an outward act and that more than just memories will remain. Lene's prescient remark at Hankels Ablage—'Nun bist du gebunden'—was more than a mere phrase.

When writing in defence of *Irrungen, Wirrungen* and drawing a careful distinction between adultery and 'eine Schneidermamsell mit einem freien Liebesverhältnis', Fontane points out that there may nevertheless be disagreeable consequences, 'die mitunter sehr hart sind'.[2] These 'natürliche Konsequenzen' have, however, nothing to do with morality in his view, only the structure of society. In the second part of the novel, which begins unobtrusively and without formal division with chapter 16, we are concerned with these consequences. In undertaking a lengthy study of them, Fontane exposed his story to the risk of an anti-climax. That he has avoided the pitfall is obvious, though the reasons for his success are perhaps less so. He has achieved a kind of aesthetic balance between past and present, which remain firmly united despite the break between Botho and Lene. Käthe is judged in the light of Botho's experience of Lene ; Gideon Franke, whom Lene eventually marries, lives in the shadow of Botho's influence on Lene. That the old feelings are still alive may be seen in the effect on Lene of a chance sight of her former lover with his wife. She does not begrudge him happiness within his own social sphere but cannot bear to be a witness of it. "Ja, mein einziger Botho, du sollst glücklich sein, so glücklich wie du's verdienst. Aber ich kann es nicht sehen . . . ' She is, however, partly mistaken in her conclusions after having seen Botho and Käthe laughing and chatting together. This is essentially the level of their contact with each other, the fullest extent of Botho's happiness. As Wandrey puts it: ' Er . . . lebt in keiner unglücklicken Ehe, aber ohne rechte Freude '.[3] But he cannot help contrasting Käthe's superficial nature with Lene's ' Einfachheit, Wahrheit und Unredensartlichkeit '. A case has been made on Käthe's behalf, based largely on her calm reaction after the discovery of the burnt love-letters, to the effect that her frivolity and apparent lack of spiritual depth are merely a well-bred façade, hiding deeper wisdom and prefounder emotions. The question remains open, but one is inclined to agree with Pitt, an admirer of Käthe, however, when he says of her : ' She is rather a little silly. Oder, wenn du's deutsch hören willst : sie dalbert ein bißchen.' We cannot help noticing, too, that while Lene is able to mention her past affair to Gideon Franke, Botho cannot discuss it with Käthe, even when a natural opportunity has presented itself. In chapter 17 she even goes so far as to admit her jealousy of old love-affairs : ' Auf alte, ganz alte Geschichten bin ich eifersüchtig, viel, viel eifersüchtiger als auf neue.' His description of the three years since he parted from Lene to marry Käthe von Sellenthin seems to summarise the situation : ' Viel Freude, gewiß. Aber es war doch keine rechte Freude gewesen. Ein Bonbon, nicht viel mehr. Und wer kann von Süßigkeiten leben !' Despite the symbolic burning of the wild flowers and Lene's letters he remains inwardly bound to her .... ' Alles Asche. Und doch gebunden.'

What of the other marriage, that between Lene and Gideon Franke, the pious, hardworking artisan ? It is three years before Lene can contemplate marriage with another, and it is clear that Gideon with all his virtues is no replacement for Botho in Lene's heart. She respects him, none the less, and he is a sufficient judge of character to know the value of the woman who becomes his wife. On this point his estimate agrees precisely with that made by Botho during their strange but dignified interview. For Lene, typically forthright, has confessed to her previous liaison with Botho— indeed, to the reader's surprise, she also mentions an earlier attachment as well, about which we knew nothing. Botho is then able once again to summarise for us, as well as for Gideon Franke, the qualities in Lene which had won his admiration—her honesty, directness and simplicity, her underlying seriousness : ' Denn so heiter und mitunter beinahe ausgelassen sie sein kann, von Natur ist sie nachdenklich, ernst und einfach.' His conclusion is a worthy tribute to his memory of her : ' Denn sie hat das Herz auf dem rechten Fleck und ein starkes Gefühl für Pflicht und Recht und Ordnung.' All this is echoed by Franke himself who, in spite of his phrase-mongering and formal piety, has a realistic and discerning eye for human qualities. It is no mere play on words when Botho replies to Käthe, who sees the marriage announcement in the paper but only as a source of fun in the names ' Nimptsch ' and ' Gideon ' : ' Was hast du nur gegen Gideon, Käthe ? Gideon ist besser als Botho.'

Stylistically this tale shows clearly the seemingly effortless perfection Fontane has now attained. Previous works have reached similar heights in places, but the distinctive feature of *Irrungen, Wirrungen* is its consistently high level. There are occasional survivals from the earlier novels, e.g., a reference to ' unsere Frau Nimptsch ' in chapter 1 and a slight touch of the ' Wanderungen ' tone in the discussion with the landlord of Hankels Ablage about the nature and history of his establishment. Symbols continue to be used, but discreetly and sparingly ; there is the appearance of the persistent bluebottle just before the arrival of the fateful letter from Botho's mother :

' Diese Brummer sind allemal Unglücksboten und so hämisch zudringlich, als freuten sie sich über den Ärger, dessen Herold und Verkündiger sie sind.' The sudden discovery of the ' Hinckeldey-Kreuz ' by Botho while out on a solitary ride in search of a solution to his problem leads fairly obviously to the discovery of certain parallels with his own dilemma and the conclusion that ' das Herkommen unser Tun bestimmt '. It seems also more than mere chance that causes the singers on the road to the Neue Jakobikirchhof to strike up with ' Denkst du daran ', last sung with Lene on their walk near Wilmersdorf. The re-introduction of an early theme when Botho dances with Käthe to the music wafted across from the Zoologischer Garten is an effective touch, linking past and present in symbolic form. To a lesser extent this same purpose is served by the view seen from the balcony of the newly-wed couple in the Landgrafenstraße, which looks towards open country and the village of Wilmersdorf—the associations of which cause Botho to lose countenance when asked by Käthe : " ' Und das Dorf daneben. Wie heißt es ?' ' Ich glaube Wilmersdorf ', stotterte Botho." These symbolic traits, though obvious enough in isolation, are in fact so skilfully woven into the fabric of the tale that they no longer obtrude in pointed fashion as was the case in some of the earlier works already discussed.

A close examination of the text reveals many other stylistic advances. Notice, for example, the technique Fontane has developed for breaking up a lengthy letter or solitary rumination by means of a brief interruption—not long enough to destroy the train of thought, but sufficient to avoid monotony. This is used when Botho von Rienäcker receives the long and important letter from his mother (chapter 14) urging his marriage ; he stops reading, gets up and paces the room in agitation. Again, when he rides across the Jungfernheide in solitary contemplation of the crisis, his exposition is divided into sections of palatable size by means of similar momentary diversions. There is first the impact of the gunfire which suddenly resounds from the Tegel ranges and upsets his horse. Further on there is another short break as the horse scares up a hare from the grass.

Most impressive in this tale is the complete fusion of characters and background. Fontane is depicting the Berlin in which he lived and which he knew so intimately. He does not select some rare instance or a limited social circle, as sometimes was the case in earlier works. Within the compass of about 135 pages he introduces characters from almost the whole range of humanity to be found in the German capital in the 1880's, from the military aristocracy to the washerwoman. Only the factory worker and the new industrial proletariat of the 'Gründerzeit' remain slightly outside his picture, though receiving a brief mention in chapter 14. Through the love attachment between Botho and Lene, high and low estate are brought into close contact. The middle class, a segment of which is represented by Gideon Franke, has to wait for the publication of *Frau Jenny Treibel* five years later before occupying the centre of the stage.

It is clear that the author himself regarded this work with particular affection, calling it on one occasion ' diese von mir besonders geliebte Arbeit ',[4] though he does not appear to be unduly troubled as to whether it was considered a novel or a *Novelle* (he sometimes calls it by the latter term in his correspondence). Today it is generally regarded as a short *Roman*. Part of the secret of its success lies in the intense evocation of atmosphere ; this applies not only to the chapters set in Berlin, but also to those outside the city. To achieve this, Fontane made special trips to places such as Hankels Ablage, the Neue Jakobikirchhof and Jungfernheide. Indeed, as H. H. Reuter has pointed out,[5] he completed eight chapters while staying at Hankels Ablage himself.

Stine

Closely related to the above work in both theme and form is *Stine* of 1890. The date of publication is misleading, for it antedates *Irrungen, Wirrungen* in composition and may be regarded as a preliminary study for it or perhaps as a tragic alternative version. Once again we are faced with the problem of love between members of two differing social classes in an era which frowned on marriages outside one's own clearly defined circle. At the same time society tacitly accepted illicit liaisons, usually of a purely expedient character and not involving any depth of affection, so long as they remained discreetly hidden. Graf Waldemar von Haldern and Stine (Ernestine) Rehbein, the seamstress, are therefore faced with exactly the same problem as were Botho and Lene. However, Waldemar does not possess Botho's ability to accept the hard realities of the world in which they live. He has been severely wounded in the Franco-Prussian War and was obliged to leave the service, and this had increased within him a tendency towards brooding introspection and unhappiness. It is Stine who eventually faces the facts and breaks off the relationship. As so often in Fontane's novels, it is the woman who possesses the strong and decisive traits. Deprived of his one hope of understanding and consolation, Waldemar finds himself unable to face the future alone and takes his life. As a kind of ironical contrast-motif, we see that his uncle, the old roué Graf von Haldern, is able to maintain a casual relationship of a very different kind with Stine's more worldly sister, the widowed Pauline Pittelkow, without dire consequences of any kind.

The interest should be concentrated primarily on the two central figures of Stine and Waldemar, but in fact a good deal of the limelight is stolen by Stine's sister, Witwe Pauline Pittelkow. Waldemar is, in Frau Pittelkow's brutal words, ' ein armes, krankes Huhn ', a shadow of a man left over from the war. However, his war-injuries only intensified the tragic discord in Waldemar's soul and did not create it. He tells in chapter 14 of his unhappy home life as a child and young man, of the hours of boring lessons with his house tutor, the ill-concealed hostility of an arrogant stepmother, and the failure of his weak-willed father to protect him from her. He was, he admits, a stranger in his own home. In Stine, the virtuous and hard-working sister of his uncle's mistress, he finds understanding and spiritual comfort. So vital does she become that he is prepared to abandon all ties of class and family, marry her, and emigrate. It is clear, however, that Waldemar lacks the physical and mental stamina for such a radical break. Moreover his unpractical nature is shown by the way in which he approaches this crisis. He reveals his plans to Baron ' Papageno ', then to his uncle—without taking the simple precaution of first discussing them with his intended bride and obtaining her consent ! After witnessing his failure to win his uncle's support, one already doubts Waldemar's ability to carry out his intentions. Stine's implacable refusal to marry him and her despairing outburst : ' Unser Glück ist hin ' remove the last strands of hope, and he is finished. Whereas Botho, in *Irrungen, Wirrungen*, can steel himself to part from Lene, the less robust Waldemar cannot even accept that state of limited happiness, termed by Botho ' ein verschwiegenes Glück '. Without being forced by Botho's need to marry someone else for family reasons, he pursues a course of ' everything or nothing ' and loses all. His is the stubbornness of the sick man, as his uncle recognises when he says of him : ' Waldemar ist eigensinnig (alle Kranken sind es)'. His sickness expresses itself in many subtle forms, such as his preference for the dying willow-trees by the river-bank (' halb abgestorben und immer noch grün '), his comparison of the Invalidenpark with a graveyard, and his morbid interest in memorials.

If Waldemar is a sick, unhappy man, Stine appears at first sight to be a robust, independent and decisive personality by contrast—but only by contrast. We are told in the second chapter of the points of resemblance between Stine and her sister, Pauline, except that ' die Ränder der überaus freundlichen Augen zeigten sich leicht gerötet, was, aller sonst blühenden Erscheinung . . . unerachtet, doch auf eine zartere Gesundheit hinzudeuten schien '. Fontane describes her as ' Typus einer germanischen, wenn auch freilich etwas angekränkelten Blondine '. Stine has the virtues of industry, thrift, honesty and moral integrity. When her sister attempts to justify her own liaison with Graf Haldern by posing the question : ' Wovon soll man denn am Ende leben ?' she replies bluntly : ' Von Arbeit.' Once again, as in the companion work, the virtues of ' Arbeit ' and ' Ordnung ' are extolled, and not only in the person of Stine. She says of her sister : ' Meine Schwester ist arbeitsam und ordentlich . . . . ' and explains to Waldemar that even in her basically deplorable liaison with his uncle, Pauline at least shows a certain loyalty. Stine, though practical and down-to-earth like her sister in some respects, has in addition a romantic, imaginative streak, and it is this which attracts Waldemar from the start. There is an instinctive recognition of basic affinities between them on the evening of the party at Witwe Pittelkow's flat, when ' nur der junge Graf und Stine schwiegen und wechselten Blicke '. Nowhere does this romantic streak come out more clearly than in the last unhappy meeting between the couple, when she refers to the fairy-tale drama seen in her childhood. Like the happy pair in that play, she and Waldemar would lose their magic bliss if certain words were spoken—and Waldemar had uttered them, thus breaking the spell. At the same time Stine had no illusions about the situation, knew it must some day end, and entertained no false ambitions of becoming Gräfin Haldern. Her only fault was that of a *carpe diem* attitude of mind, which allowed the situation to develop as it did, so that the less realistic Waldemar could build castles in the air and tell others of their dream-world. ' Und nun ist alles falsch gewesen, und unser Glück ist hin, viel, viel schneller als nötig, bloß weil du wolltest, daß es dauern solle '. Only now, as she renounces her happiness, does Stine admit the full intensity of her love for Waldemar : ' Sieh, es war mein Stolz, ein so gutes Herz wie das deine lieben zu dürfen ; und daß es mich wieder liebte, das war meines Lebens höchstes Glück '. Fontane does not give a detailed account of Stine's life after the harrowing experience of her lover's death, but there are strong indications that the shock has been too great for her delicate constitution.

It is Stine's more down-to-earth sister, Pauline Pittelkow, who leaves the clearest impression on the reader's memory. Fontane himself admitted that she had grown beyond the stature he had originally planned for her, but, like the elder Graf Haldern, he had fallen for the charms of his ' lieben schwarzen Deibel '. We have noted from Stine's remarks to Waldemar that Witwe Pittelkow was not really attracted to her rôle of mistress to an older member of the aristocracy, but, once having accepted the position and the material advantages that it brought, she adhered to it conscientiously and did not complain about the inevitable gossip. Her view of her lover is an unflattering one ; she refers to him casually as ' Der Olle ' or, in certain moods, as ' Alter Ekel '. The incidental benefits of their arrangement are to be seen in a number of luxurious items of furniture which contrast oddly with the rest, in the arrival of food-hampers and crates of wine before the Graf's parties, and the knowledge : ' daß er für alles

sorgt ', including the first-floor apartment itself. Despite her
financial dependence, however, Pauline Pittelkow remains
outspoken and honest, refusing to allow her benefactor to
treat her in a patronising or degrading fashion. His toast,
for instance, ' Es lebe meine Mohrenkönigin, meine Königin
der Nacht !' is badly received. We note the quickness of her
temper when the talk is not to her liking—and so does the
Count, who has learned to respect it. All in all, she is a remarkable combination of qualities, ranging from the aggressively
vulgar to almost queenly dignity, and she never alienates the
reader's basic respect for her. Through her earthy acceptance
of life and society as she finds them, Pauline Pittelkow, ironically enough, offends far less against the current concept of
' Ordnung ' than does Waldemar with his marriage plans or
even Stine with her attempted compromises. In drastic terms
she sums up the whole situation at the end of chapter 10 ;
despite her indifference towards rank and noble birth, she
cannot alter the realities of society—nor can the nobleman,
and, if he dares to try, he will be prevented by the others of
his class. Then one day he will just cease to call—' er sitzt
erster Klasse mit Plüsch . . . und sie hat 'nen blauen Schleier
an 'n Hut, und so geht es heidi ! nach Italien. Un das is denn,
was sie Hochzeitsreise nennen.' For Waldemar the journey
was of a more tragic nature ; in the case of Botho von Rienäcker the description would have been all too accurate.

Compared with the dynamically vital personality of Pauline
Pittelkow, her aristocratic lover, Graf Haldern, is a somewhat
stock figure—an ageing roué who takes a mistress as casually
as he might rent a hunting lodge for the season. Despite the
check of Pauline's lively temper on his natural arrogance, it
still breaks through on occasions, as for example with his
brusque tone in chapter 4, when he introduces his nephew to
the ladies, asks if the wine has been delivered, and indicates
his command of the situation in an unceremonious ' Nun,
dann bitte ich also . . . '. Nor does he hesitate to remove the
lilies (which he dislikes) from the floral arrangement and hurl
them out of the window in annoyance. In his own aristocratic
circle he affects a liberal outlook, ridiculing the prejudices of
his class, but, as soon as his family is threatened by a
mésalliance, he reveals a very different attitude. Nevertheless

he possesses a number of likable traits, including his affection
for his ailing young nephew—though this does not extend to
his acting as an intermediary on his behalf with the rest of the
family when the marriage question arises.

Baron ' Papageno ' is a more shadowy figure, one of his
main functions being in chapter 11, where he advises the
young man to consult his uncle, Graf Haldern, on whose
personality he sheds a good deal of new light. Frau Pittelkow
dismisses him in the contemptuous phrase ' Ein Dummbart '.
More interesting among the lesser characters are Wanda
Grützmacher (the suburban actress), Frau Pittelkow's il-
legitimate daughter Olga, and the upstairs family, the Polzins,
whose tenant Stine is.   As a theatre critic of many years'
standing, Fontane was familiar with the world of actors and
actresses, and his portrait of Wanda is a worthy example of
the various theatrical characters presented by him.   Contrasting with her world of make-believe greatness on the stage are
her humble lodgings in the Tieckstraße, where she had to
learn her lines against the din of constant hammering from the
landlord's workshop in the yard behind.   She is consoled by
the knowledge that she enjoys the favour of the audiences who
patronise the Nordend-Theater, as well as, apparently, that
of its Director. At Frau Pittelkow's parties she is regarded as an
essential guest : ' Wenn Wanda nicht da is, is es immer bloß
halb . . . alle von's Theater haben so was un kriegen einen
Schick un können reden '.   Her entrances, even at Pauline
Pittelkow's gatherings in the Invalidenstraße, are not without
their proper effect, and her acting abilities are welcome in a
new, if minor, rôle. After the evening's entertainment, when
Pauline and her sister are sitting over ' eine braune Kanne
voll ' (more to their taste than the Count's choicest wines), the
guests are discussed—Wanda in particular.   Stine, typically,
takes a kindly view of her as ' eine nette Person, und jedenfalls
eine sehr gutmütige '.   Her sister, on the other hand, expresses
herself in her usual drastic fashion on the subject, accusing
Wanda of being ' wichtig und zierig ', an accusation already
made in her presence when Wanda demurred at the words of
a song on the questionable grounds of ' es ist noch zu früh '.

Olga presents us with a slight mystery. She is not, it appears,
the child of the late Herr Pittelkow, but the result of an earlier

misadventure. In his brief sketch of her Fontane has given us a
shrewd analysis of the child's mentality. Particularly engaging
is the scene of mingled gluttony and ingratitude at the end of
the third chapter, when Olga bites greedily into the generous
helping of cake presented to her by ' Tante Wanda '. ' Aber
schnöder Undank keimte bereits in ihrer Seele, und während
es ihr vorzüglich schmeckte, sagte sie schon vor sich hin:
' Eigentlich is es gar kein richtiger . . . Ohne Rosinen . . .
Einen mit Rosinen ess' ich lieber '.

Although they play only a peripheral part in the events of
the tale, Stine's landlord and his wife, the Polzins, represent
one of those Berlin thumbnail sketches by Fontane which the
reader would be loth to miss. Polzin is an intriguing mixture
of industry and greed, boundlessly admired by his wife in
typical late nineteenth century Berlin fashion, and lives partly
by manufacturing his ' Polzinsche Teppiche ', partly by
evening work as a waiter. In addition, he and his wife let every
available room in the upstairs flat they rent above Frau
Pittelkow. Frau Polzin thereby enjoys the extra bonus of a
little gossip, for she is a great listener at walls and keyholes.
Like Lady Macbeth she draws attention to her guilt by protesting too much, her catch-phrase being ' Wir sehen nichts
und hören nichts '.

As well as dealing with the themes of the socially unsuitable
marriage and the superficial affair in late nineteenth century
Prussia, this work provides a good deal of incidental social
comment. On the positive side, we hear from Stine about the
kindness of her employer and his enlightened, responsible
attitude towards his workers. Not all firms, it would seem,
treated their employees in the manner illustrated by Fontane's
younger contemporaries of the Naturalist circle. There is also
the timely reminder placed by Fontane in the mouth of
Pauline Pittelkow that the victories of the 1870-71 war were
not all won by the great families of Prussia : ' Alle Wetter ',
she exclaims, ' ich bin auch fürs Vaterland und für Wilhelm '
and points out bluntly to Graf Haldern that poor men from
unknown families were also there and many of them likewise
sacrificed their lives.

Perhaps the most telling commentary on the social relationship between the classes is that provided by the evening party

at Witwe Pittelkow's home in the Invalidenstraße. Present are three members of the nobility, (Waldemar Haldern, Waldemar's uncle and the elderly Baron) also the two working-class, or marginally lower-middle class, sisters Pauline and Stine. Because of the illicit but intimate relationship between Graf Haldern and Pauline Pittelkow the normal class barriers are suspended—but not altogether. We have already noted the brusqueness of Graf Haldern's introductory remarks and his high-handed behaviour with the table-decoration. At no time does he forget that he is paying for everything, not only in connection with that evening but generally. This attitude shows itself in a variety of patronising remarks and he is only held in check by fear of his mistress's vitriolic tongue. The evening's humorous exchanges are often forced, having as they frequently do a double significance, which is fully under-stood only by the better-educated noblemen. Pauline Pittelkow can only partly follow the banter from the two men, but is defensively suspicious, while Stine is embarrassed. As a result the conversation contains a false note, lending the whole evening a brittle, artificial tone. This artificiality is reinforced by the device of using nicknames (as in *Irrungen, Wirrungen*) to conceal the identity of the aristocratic guests, in this case names drawn from Mozart's *Magic Flute*—Sarastro and Papageno.

Technically we find more devices in *Stine* which look back to the earlier Fontane than were noticeable in *Irrungen, Wir-rungen*, once again reminding us of the real order of composition of these two works. It is rather a surprise to discover, after the introduction of Stine's landlord and his wife in chapter 2, the lame summary : ' So waren die Polzins '. Again, after the description of the actress, Wanda, and her background, we have : ' So Wanda Grützmacher, Tieckstraße 27a '. In chapter 15, paragraph 2, Fontane resorts once more to his earlier mannerism of calling a central character ' unser Freund'; shortly afterwards it recurs as ' unser Kranker '. The symbolism is sometimes rather heavily stressed, as for example the motif of the setting sun, which so fascinates Waldemar when he sees it from Stine's room and which also suggests a parallel with his own sad life and declining health. Just in case we have missed the point of this, Fontane includes in Waldemar's valedictory letter a reference to the ' Sonnenuntergangsstunden ' of their brief happiness. Equally obvious is the stress laid on Waldemar's symbolical long, lingering look back at his usual seat in the riverside café, reinforced by the observation ' . . . als ob er ein bestimmtes Gefühl habe, daß er's nicht wiedersehen werde'. On the other hand we find elsewhere instances of the unobtrusive skill noted in *Irrungen, Wirrungen*, as for example the way in which the sunset motif is used in chapter 8 to break up what might otherwise have become an over-lengthy explanation by Waldemar. The dialogue between Waldemar and Stine is neatly concluded by reference to the same scene a page or two later. The technique of word or phrase-repetition is employed here in the same effective fashion as in the companion tale ; see for instance Pauline Pittelkow's drumming insistence on the term ' Liebschaft ' in chapter 10. We can also note the manner (similar to that of *Irrungen, Wirrungen*) in which the reader is thoroughly immersed in the Invalidenstraße environment, seeing the aristocratic characters only in their limited contacts with this humble background, before suddenly switching in chapter 11 to the home of Baron ' Papageno '. This visit not only emphasises the social gulf between Invalidenstraße and Zietenplatz but also affords the author a natural opportunity to give an intimate character-sketch of Waldemar's uncle as seen through the eyes of his friend ' Papageno '. The new environment is subsequently emphasised by a visit to Graf Haldern in the Behrenstraße.

Read in conjunction with *Irrungen, Wirrungen, Stine* leaves a slighter impression as well as a sense of inner dissatisfaction that the central character, Waldemar, should have handled the situation with such ineptitude. The long discussions of chapters 10-14, analysing the problem from differing viewpoints, also tend to obtrude. The focus of the reader's attention is here kept more firmly on the point of issue, whereas in *Irrungen, Wirrungen* the eye is allowed to stray over a wide range of visual pleasures in and around Berlin. Despite these and other criticisms which have been levelled at *Stine*, it nevertheless offers a fascinating portrait of Berlin life in the latter years of the nineteenth century through the many incidental vignettes which accompany the main theme. If its two ostensibly principal characters, Stine and Waldemar, suffer in comparison with the fuller, livelier portraits of Lene and Botho, there is on the other hand the bonus of that vigorous and original personality, Witwe Pittelkow.

Quitt

Between the peaks represented by *Irrungen, Wirrungen* on the one hand and *Frau Jenny Treibel* and *Effi Briest* on the other, two prose works of a lesser calibre must be considered. One of these, the ' Tendenzroman ' *Quitt* (1891), cannot claim to be anything other than a minor work, despite its length. There are two clearly defined parts, although no formal indication is given of this, except that chapter 17 starts with the words : ' Sechs Jahre waren hin '. The first sixteen chapters are set in Silesia, near Krummhübel in the Riesengebirge, an area which Fontane knew intimately from repeated holidays. The following twenty-one take place in the United States, a country not visited by the author. The result is that, while chapters 1 to 16 sparkle with life, all the zest goes out of the story thereafter and it drags its slow, colourless way through another 117 pages without retaining the reader's emotional participation.

Lehnert Menz, wheelwright in the village of Wolfshau (and occasional poacher in the local landowner's forest) maintains a constant feud with Förster Opitz, the district gamekeeper—a feud which goes back to their military service, when Opitz was a bullying NCO who prevented his subordinate, Menz, from obtaining a decoration for gallantry. Despite the efforts of the minister, their mutual hatred deepens and ends with a dramatic confrontation on the mountain slopes and the death of Opitz, who lay alone for hours with his wounds before a merciful oblivion descended. Suspicion, later backed by evidence, points to Lehnert, who flees the country. His subsequent life in the United States occupies the larger part of the novel, but the background, although painstakingly constructed after extensive reading, fails to convince   We learn of Lehnert's gold-digging exploits in California, his accumulation of wealth and its subsequent loss in San Francisco. He has since come east, and has joined a Mennonite community near the lonely railway settlement of Darlington on the line from Galveston to St. Louis, where it ran through Indian

territory. The life of this community is described in considerable detail, including much about the European background
and family connections of its inhabitants, but the tale now
seems to have lost all direction and purpose. The only point
at which it briefly recovers a little life is when Lehnert and his
friends are caught in a blizzard on the mountainside. These
three pages recapture something of the atmosphere evoked
earlier on by descriptions of the Silesian forests, but they are
only a momentary flicker. When Lehnert Menz meets his
death on the mountain-top while hunting for a missing friend,
and the parallels with the long-drawn-out agony of Förster
Opitz are stressed, the contrived element of this symbolic
expiation of guilt is manifest.

From the technical aspect there are a number of factors,
even in the more successful first part, which seem to suggest
a retrogressive step. A minor example is the occasional use
of the old form ' unser Förster Opitz '. Chapter 3 is largely
expository and reads accordingly. There are also some
rather too obvious attempts to foreshadow the future, e.g.
' . . . und meinen Dienst tu ich und wenn es mir ans Leben
geht ' in chapter 4, or ' . . . vor seiner Seele stand es, wie's
kommen würde ', the closing words of chapter 8. Even more
dramatic is Lehnert's outburst in chapter 11 : ' Einer muß das
Feld räumen, gewiß . . . ' Symbolism is used fairly extensively
in both parts ; on his way up to the mountain-top in Silesia
before the fatal deed, Lehnert meets a party of schoolgirls
singing the song ' Schlesierland ! Schlesierland !', so often
recalled by exiles because of its undertones of ' Heimweh ',
which he too feels at this moment, as though he were about to
leave his homeland for ever. His entry into the game preserves
is accompanied by repeated hints of evil to come (' Er war nun
drin in dem Waldgehege. Was war geschehen oder doch
vielleicht geschehen, wenn er wieder heraustrat ?') Reinforc-
ing such thoughts is the brilliantly evoked atmosphere of the
darkening forest and its sinister stillness. Contrasting with
this tense, highly successful description, there is the irritating
irrelevance of chapter 16, with its tedious intrusion of the
Espes and Dr. Unverdorben, who are to make an equally
unwelcome reappearance in the final chapter (37).

One may perhaps conclude this short survey of *Quitt* with the perceptive words of Wandrey : 'Fontane war ein großer Beobachter, kein Phantasiemensch, ein Realist und Finder, kein Erfinder.'[6]

Unwiederbringlich

The second of these two lesser works, *Unwiederbringlich* (1891), is of a more consistent character, attaining neither the dramatic heights of the first part of its predecessor nor sinking to the colourless unreality of the second. During its first appearance as a serial it aroused the instant admiration of another outstanding prose stylist, Conrad Ferdinand Meyer, because of its masterly interpretation of human psychology, its firm contours and convincing characterisation. Subsequent disappointment on the part of both readers and critics has been attributed mainly to the conclusion, which has been condemned as inconsistent and arbitrary. Ironically, both story and conclusion were taken by Fontane, as so often, from a real-life source and merely disguised by transposition of the setting from Strelitz to Schleswig and Copenhagen. In so doing Fontane did not run the risk involved in *Graf Petöfy* and the second part of *Quitt*, for the area chosen was sufficiently close to his native Prussia and familiar enough to him personally to be infused with life in his descriptions. In his treatment of the story itself, however, he remained astonishingly true to the real-life model.

In *Unwiederbringlich* the reader is introduced to another variation of the marriage-theme which dominates the author's prose work. In this case it is a marriage which breaks down as a result of an incompatibility in temperament. Between Christine and Helmuth Holk there is no appreciable difference of age or social standing but a considerable one of outlook and emotion. Only a part of Graf Holk can be satisfied by the quiet, domesticated existence offered at Schloß Holkenäs on the coast of Schleswig ; another side of this somewhat immature man is excited by the very different way of life represented by the court and capital city of Copenhagen, where he periodically serves as gentleman-in-waiting under the system of 'personal union' which linked the duchy of Schleswig to the Danish crown until 1864. The unstable element in Holk is further provoked by the excessive piety of his intelligent, sensitive but melancholy wife. She is a woman with fine

principles and a stern sense of duty, but, despite a fundament-
ally kind heart, she leaves a dark, chilly impression, and her
doleful nature serves only to aggravate the existing conflict
in her husband's mind. The provocative and intriguing
personality of Ebba von Rosenberg at the Danish court merely
completes the inner process of alienation between Holk and
his wife. That a man should, on the basis of a brief flirtation
(for such it is as far as Ebba is concerned) make the kind of
assumptions made by Holk and formally announce his separation from wife and family, indicates the degree of emotional
immaturity which lurks within this married man of more than
seventeen years standing. His subsequent dilemma, after a
summary and scornful rejection by Ebba, is pathetic rather
than tragic. Neither the contrived outward reconciliation
with his wife and family, after a period of aimless exile, nor
Christine's suicide are really convincing, despite their faithful
adherence to the real-life model. Why should this be ? Probably
because the character of Christine, as presented by Fontane,
seems to preclude either of these possibilities, whatever may
have been credible in the case of the actual persons, unknown
to Fontane, at Strelitz.

Fontane's portrait of Christine becomes clear before that of
Helmuth Holk. As early as chapter 2 we note her morbid
preoccupation with the family burial vault, a matter which is
of little importance to her husband—although he later accedes
to her wishes for its restoration out of kind-hearted concern for
his wife's feelings. Her antipathy towards the worldliness of
court life in Copenhagen is expressed in chapter 4, in which
also takes place the incident of the song, *Der Kirchhof*, on
hearing which Christine is so moved that she has to leave the
company. Her brother Arne well knows the melancholia
which underlies his sister's piety and expresses his fears in a
frank talk with Pastor Schwarzkoppen : ' Immer Erziehungs-
fragen, immer Missionsberichte von Grönland oder Ceylon
her, immer Harmonium, immer Kirchenleuchter, immer
Altardecke mit Kreuz. Es ist nicht auszuhalten '. By contrast,
she has no real interest in mundane matters or any need for
social enjoyment. When Holk receives the letter summoning
him to Copenhagen on duty, Christine's repudiation of everything connected with the way of life there is too strong to be

influenced by her husband's remarks about the cultural and
religious life of the city. For her it remains a centre of godless
frivolity : ' Tanzsaal, Musik, Feuerwerk. Es ist eine Stadt für
Schiffskapitäne, die sechs Monate lang umhergeschwommen
und nun beflissen sind, alles Ersparte zu vertun und alles
Versäumte nachzuholen. Alles in Kopenhagen ist Taverne,
Vergnügungslokal '. She can manifest frankness bordering
on contempt when upbraiding her husband for his easy-going
attitude to life : ' Alle Körner fallen aus deinem Gedächtnis
heraus, und nur die Spreu bleibt zurück '. At the same time
she is not entirely unaware of her own shortcomings and that
it is the combination of two such temperaments which causes
the strain : ' Du bist leichtlebig und schwankend und wandel-
bar, und ich habe den melancholischen Zug und nehme das
Leben schwer. Auch da, wo Leichtnehmen das Bessere wäre.
Du hast es nicht gut mit mir getroffen, und ich wünschte dir
wohl eine Frau, die mehr zu lachen verstände... Ernst bin
ich gewiß und vielleicht auch sentimental '. Christine's brother,
Arne, identifies part of the source of the conflict when he
differentiates between a strict outlook on life and a lack of
moderation in representing that outlook, protesting in terms
reminiscent of Hebbel that an excess of virtue can become a
danger. Even kindly old Pastor Petersen is castigated for his
harmless interest in geology, which provokes Christine into
critical comments on the subject of giving stones instead of
bread to his flock.

When, however, the question of a reconciliation between
man and wife has arisen, we see that Christine's reasons for
opposing it for so long are not founded on religious or moral
conviction. Her pride as a woman is injured by the thought
that Holk wants her back *faute de mieux*, after failing to attain
his object. The reader may even feel a sense of relief at this
discovery of normal human pride, for her Christian sense of
duty must have at least suggested the opposite course. When
she does finally succumb to the pleas of friends and relatives,
her depressive personality disintegrates beneath the strain and,
Christian piety or not, she seeks a way out of the dilemma in
suicide.

If Christine seems to dominate the scenes at Holkenäs,
Helmuth Holk's personality appears to open like a flower in

the social warmth of his Copenhagen environment. None the
less he is in some respects a feeble plant. Though expressed
with unnecessary tactlessness, Christine's analysis was not far
from the truth. We also learn a good deal more about him
from the conversation in chapter 5 between Schwarzkoppen
and Arne—that he is, for example, ' ein Augenblicksmensch ',
that he had been attracted to his wife in earlier years partly
by the very piety which he now finds so oppressive, as well as
by her intelligence and, possibly most of all, by her beauty.
His recognition of her intelligence persists, as we see in chapter
6 ; ' Nun, Christine,' he says, ' du bist nicht bloß viel charak-
tervoller als ich, du bist auch viel klüger.' Though intellectually inferior to his wife and more vacillating by temperament,
Helmuth Holk nevertheless possesses character traits which
command the reader's respect. His good-humoured indulgence
of Christine's foibles, his jovial bonhomie and patent honesty
and lack of guile all help to offset his erratic, slightly naïve
qualities. Even Fräulein Dobschütz, attached though she is
to Christine Holk by ties of close friendship, provides a glowing
testimonial to his nobler attributes, when she tells her : ' Aber
gleich nach dir kommt dein Mann. Er ist in dem, um das
sich's hier handelt, ein Muster . . . Holk ist aufrichtig und
zuverlässig . . . ,' but her calculations leave out the possibility
of an Ebba von Rosenberg. It is precisely Ebba, with her
analytical approach and dislike of German ways, who sees
through so much of the man she simultaneously ensnares. Her
first impressions are of his stiff awkwardness as a courtier.
Later, in her conversation with the Princess, she enlarges on
the theme of his personality ; ' Ich glaube, er hat ein gutes
schwaches Herz ' is her initial summary. To the Princess's
reply that character is more important than matters of the
heart, she retorts : ' Dann ist Holk verloren, denn ich glaube,
sein Charakter ist das recht eigentlich Schwache an ihm.'
From this Ebba proceeds to a detailed analysis, from which the
infatuated Holk emerges but poorly. Not only is he a weak
person, according to Ebba, but he has no inkling of this ; he is
a good-looking man but one of modest talents only, which he
has failed to develop in a suitable direction. Above all, she
finds him ' unklar und halb, und die Halbheit wird ihn noch
in Ungelegenheiten bringen '. As one of the worst examples

of this, she cites what she suspects to be his duality in moral questions : ' Er ist moralisch, ja beinah tugendhaft und schielt doch begehrlich nach der Lebemannschaft hinüber '.

Holk, however, is not so strongly attracted to the rôle of man-of-the-world as driven on by his deeper need for companionship, tenderness and inner harmony. When looking back over his seventeen years of married life, he realises the gulf which has opened up between Christine and himself, also the lack of just those very qualities in his wife which Ebba seems to offer. ' Ich sehne mich nach einem anderen Leben, nach Tagen, die nicht mit Traktätchen anfangen und ebenso aufhören, ich will kein Harmonium im Hause, sondern Harmonie, heitere Übereinstimmung der Seelen, Luft, Licht, Freiheit.' So he makes the same fantastic assumptions as did Waldemar in *Stine*, nearly blurts out his intentions to the Princess herself, informs his wife to her face of their coming separation, and dreams his romantic dreams of blissful days in Sorrento with Ebba—all before he has ascertained the lady's own views on the subject.

The interview between Holk and Ebba, which shatters his dreams, is a masterpiece of compression—a quality for which this work is not especially notable—and the illusory nature of their previous relationship is made manifest. They part like strangers which, deep down, they had always been.

What sort of woman is this Ebba von Rosenberg for whose sake a forty-five-year-old husband and father of noble background and good repute has sacrificed his family connections and honour ? In the first place, she is a born courtier, which— as she instantly perceives—Holk is not. Despite her non-Danish origins (she was born in Sweden), she knows exactly how to adapt herself to Danish court life, which Holk, the German from the Duchy of Schleswig, does not. She flatters the Princess with the same adroitness as she does Holk or any other reasonably attractive male. She readily admits her own moral limitations, as in her conversation with the Princess in chapter 18, but denies any responsibility for men too weak to defend themselves against her charms, using the age-old formula from the Book of Genesis : ' Soll ich meines Bruders Hüter sein ? '

Holk himself, in his more reflective moments, recognises

the evanescent quality of Ebba's attraction : ' Ebba war eine Rakete, die man, solange sie stieg, mit einem staunenden "ah" begleitete, dann aber war's wieder vorbei, schließlich doch alles nur Feuerwerk.' In harmony with such a character is her love of dangerous situations, whether skating on thin ice literally as in chapter 25 or in a metaphorical sense. As the Princess expresses it : ' Ebba liebt mit der Gefahr zu spielen, und sie darf es auch, weil sie ein Talent hat, ihren Kopf klug aus der Schlinge zu ziehen.' By contrast, Holk has no such instinct for survival as the Princess foresees.

In the final interview with Holk, Ebba shows this instinct to a marked degree. She knows how to accept what the moment offers, without seeking to make it into an eternity, just as she knows when the illusion has to stop. For her, love and its language are a game with which to beguile the tedious hours of court life, and she expects others to accept the same convention. Intelligent, attractive and worldly-wise, she lacks depth and warmth of personality.

Stylistically *Unwiederbringlich* is open to serious criticisms as well as praise, but opinions vary as to the just proportions of each. There is much in this work which could be ruthlessly pruned away without real loss to the story but with distinct advantage to the reader's patience. Some of the local gossip and Copenhagen social trivialities could well have been dispensed with (e.g. in chapter 10), while the relevance of Brigitte Hansen's Siamese adventure in chapter 11 is hard to find. Descriptive passages of buildings and interiors tend to become over-long at times and suggestive of Fontane's *Wanderungen* style, as for instance in chapter 20. Similarly, the liberal use of correspondence as a means of conveying information palls on the reader after a while. By contrast, the description of the fire at Frederiksborg is given with admirable terseness, and this whole incident stands out from the discursive preceding chapters like a mountain at the far end of a featureless if agreeable plain. It is the only dramatic moment involving concentrated action in a tale devoted almost entirely to the depiction of environment and the workings of human psychology.

Features familiar from a study of the earlier tales are again to be found here. Coming events are hinted at, even in the opening chapter, when Uhland's poem is quoted as a kind of double omen for the new Schloß Holkenäs by the sea. The outcome is foreshadowed by Christine's dream in chapter 9, with its motif of the combined marriage and mourning procession. The dim awareness in Holk's own mind that he is treading on dangerous ground during his stay at Copenhagen is made the excuse at the end of the fifteenth chapter for a ballad-like final line, warning of evil things to come. His nightmare of a shipwreck, involving a hostile Ebba-figure (chapter 21), renews the *Leitmotiv* of danger and ultimate disaster. The symbolism of the escapade on the ice of the Arresee again warns us explicitly, though not obtrusively, of dangers ahead and risks taken, ending in Holk's dramatic, double-edged question to Ebba : ' Hier ist die Grenze, Ebba. Wollen wir darüber hinaus ?' Even the outbreak of fire at the castle of Frederiksborg is anticipated in the previous chapter (26) by a pointed discussion between Schleppegrell and Bie on the subject of the primitive heating arrangements and the potential danger they represent. As late in the story as the end of chapter 32 this technique is again used, for we are told about the mood of sadness at the reunion festivities, suggesting that the new-found happiness at Holkenäs might well be of a temporary nature. The impression is reinforced by Holk's despair about his wife's attitude of melancholy resignation (chapter 33), and his pessimistic conclusion : ' Wir treiben einer Katastrophe zu.' The final disaster is preceded by a melancholy folk-song by Waiblinger, evocative of bygone days and ending with the ominous lines : ' Doch die mir die liebsten gewesen sind, Ich wünsche sie *nicht* zurück ', a theme taken up and repeated by Christine.

One of Fontane's stylistic idiosyncrasies is the use of drastic generalisations through the mouths of his characters, and *Unwiederbringlich* provides some notable examples, e.g. ' Alle Portugiesen sind eigentlich Juden ' (Pentzin in chapter 10) or Holk's remark to Witwe Hansen in chapter 11 : ' Alle Kapitäne sind hübsch '. A technique less frequently employed by him elsewhere is illustrated by the manner in which he has emphasised the character of the mother by the creation of a precocious daughter, Asta, who echoes Christine Holk's melancholy sentiments in such phrases as ' Ich mag nichts Lustiges ' or her somewhat elderly analysis in chapter 7 of the respective philosophies of her parents.

Looking back over the thirty-four chapters of this *Roman*, one is left with a feeling of regret that Fontane appears to have slipped back into something of the rambling, discursive frame of mind which characterised the earliest novel, *Vor dem Sturm*. The reader's impatience with long passages of Copenhagen gossip, architectural description, or irrelevant personal reminiscence by the characters themselves is only sharpened by the contrast presented in such succinct passages as the tactfully hinted at love scene between Holk and Ebba at the conclusion of chapter 26 or the great fire in the castle which follows immediately afterwards. Any such irritation with the prolix nature of parts of this work should not, however, blind us to the fact that it contains a brilliant study of human psychology. One may not admire the divided character of Holk or feel drawn to the pallid, depressive personality represented by his wife, but as a literary investigation of a tragic human situation in a marriage between incompatibles, it can be regarded as the most significant of Fontane's lesser *Romane*.

Mathilde Möhring

It is to this period of the author's creative writing that the short prose tale *Mathilde Möhring* properly belongs, although it was laid aside in favour of larger undertakings such as *Frau Jenny Treibel* and *Effi Briest* and eventually appeared posthumously in 1907. While it is convenient to list a writer's works according to the dates of publication, these may not necessarily correspond with the actual time of composition. One must remember too that several new works may be in the process of creation at the same time. Such considerations are relevant in any study of Fontane, especially at the point of his life now under review. A full account of the dates and stages of composition relating to Fontane's novels may be found in the detailed study by Hans-Heinrich Reuter listed in the bibliography.

The first draft of *Mathilde Möhring* was written during August and September 1891, but the final stages of revision had not been carried out by the time of the author's death in 1898. The brevity of this tale (it is approximately 86 pp.) makes it difficult to classify as either a *Novelle* or an unusually short

Roman. Stylistically it has characteristics of both. It cannot be called a long fragment, either, despite the somewhat abrupt conclusion, which leaves the reader expecting more. Another striking feature is the complete absence of formal chapters. Fontane had abandoned the use of chapter headings some time before, but the chapter division was of considerable importance to him as representing a phase of the work's inner development ; it was often a psychological rather than a time-division. In *Mathilde Möhring* the only indication of a break is a space marked by an asterisk.

Hans-Heinrich Reuter characterises the tale as ' ein Frauen-roman ',[7] and this is justified inasmuch as interest is centred on the personality of Mathilde herself, and the second fully-developed character is probably Mathilde's mother rather than the male partner, Hugo.

The action is comparatively simple. Hugo Großmann, a law student already in his middle twenties, takes rooms at the home of the widow, Frau Möhring, and her daughter Mathilde; he is looked after by them during an illness and then becomes engaged to Mathilde. She is able to exert the pressure which he needs in order to concentrate on and complete his studies, and it is she who urges him to apply for the post of *Bürger-meister* in the little town of Woldenstein in West Prussia. Once there, she continues the process of building up her easy-going husband into a local figure of importance, and he appears to be heading for a brilliant career which he would never have attained single-handed. However, Hugo is not as robust as he appears to be and succumbs to a severe chest infection in the bitter West Prussian winter. After his death, Mathilde, with remarkable adaptability, returns to Berlin and the little *pension* in the Georgenstraße, trains to become a teacher (thus realising an earlier thwarted ambition) and accepts life with her complaining, self-pitying old mother just as she had endured it for so many years previously.

We are concerned throughout with the character of Mathilde and its effect on the malleable Hugo. The theme of a strong woman dominating a weak man is not confined to this one tale by Fontane ; it is the *absolute* quality of her dominion over Hugo's passive nature which is unique. She is determined, intelligent, reliable, highly observant (as witnessed by her shrewd assessment of Hugo from his books, clothes and other possessions) and socially adaptable, as well as being ambitious both for her husband's sake and on her own account. Even in her earlier rôle of landlady's daughter she has a sense of pride and is embarrassed at being seen wielding mop and bucket. Fontane is believed to have included some aspects of his mother's character in this portrait. It is this concentration on the personality of one single figure which is particularly suggestive of the *Novelle*-technique. At times the decisive, calculating quality in Mathilde's personality tends to alienate the reader and obscure her gentler characteristics which come to the fore so clearly during Hugo's two illnesses and in her patient relationship with her wearisome mother.

So completely does Mathilde dominate the story that it is difficult to find enough detailed evidence of Hugo Großmann's personality to construct an adequate portrait of him. He appears to be gentle, indecisive, lazy but not without modest ability when driven ahead by others. ' Er ist bloß faul und hat kein Feuer im Leib ', is Mathilde's summary of him. He has no real sense of mission about his studies or a legal career, preferring secretly to read literature or dally with the idea of turning actor, like his friend Rybinski. His frail health gives him a reasonable excuse for spending fine afternoons, like Fontane, his creator, on long walks instead of at his desk. In Mathilde he finds his counterpart, and their union is a credible, indeed highly successful one, despite its deviation from the conventional norm. We tend to see Hugo through the eyes of Mathilde from an early stage, and it is ironical to note the strong counter-influence he exerts on her posthumously, when she realises the full extent of his good nature.

Much attention is devoted to the personality of old Witwe Möhring, who is one of the not inconsiderable series of portraits of the ' Mutter aus dem Volk '. But she belongs rather to the type represented by Lehnert's mother in *Quitt* than to the more agreeable category which includes old Frau Nimptsch (*Irrungen, Wirrungen*). Perpetually complaining of her lot, fearful of destitution and the poor-house, distrustful of life and unsure of herself, she vacillates between transparent self-seeking and abject self-abasement. One redeeming feature is a recognition on her part of her daughter's abilities, and a strange bond of mutual affection unites them, which survives in spite of everything. As a contrast-figure to Mathilde, she is perhaps more unattractive than she need have been in order to achieve the necessary balance.

The atmosphere of the capital city is skilfully conveyed in the first part of this tale, though on a much smaller scale than in most of the longer *Romane*. The range of supporting characters is limited, but the presence of such 'originals' as old Frau Runtschen, the cleaner, and the spiteful gossip, Frau Schmädicke, gives the story an authentic flavour of Theodor Fontane's Berlin. Obviously there could be no room in a story of this restricted length for a broader canvas allowing the kind of detailed delineation of background found in most of the other Berlin novels. Only a small segment of society is involved in any case; there is no tragic class-conflict, for both Hugo and Mathilde are of bourgeois origin. Such social problems as do present themselves are those arising from sub-divisions within one class and hinge largely on the difficult personality of old Frau Möhring, since Mathilde possesses all the necessary social graces for her new rôle in the professional upper-middle class. On the one occasion when Hugo, while still just a lodger in the Möhring household, decides against accompanying the two women to the theatre, it is clearly because of the tenant-landlady relationship and its implications rather than through any feeling that Mathilde would let him down in public. Indeed her performance as Frau Bürgermeister Großmann in Woldenstein is superb and wins the admiration of all. Nor is it meant to excite the reader's laughter or ridicule, as in the pompous case of Frau Kommerzienrat Jenny Treibel, for it represents something of the new, independent woman as she was beginning to emerge in the society of the closing years of the nineteenth century. Reuter goes further and maintains that Fontane was already anticipating the greater degree of emancipation which lay just ahead: ' In *Mathilde Möhring* . . . suchte er einen Menschen des 20. Jahrhunderts zu schaffen.'[8]

Again, coming events cast their shadows before them. Hugo's actor friend, Hans Rybinski, has an early presentiment of the future engagement to Mathilde, while the Polish Count foresees Hugo's death. The familiar sweeping generalisations, such as ' Alle Logiker verstehen gewöhnlich gar nichts ', also recur in this work.

The ending remains a point of dispute. Should Fontane have drawn the story to a close almost immediately after Hugo's death, merely hinting in a few phrases at the widow's future life, or should he have expanded the remaining eight pages in order to provide a balancing counterweight to the earlier events, rather as he did in *Irrungen, Wirrungen* ? Certainly there is material enough in this short tale to provide for a considerable expansion, though it is doubtful whether Fontane had any such intentions. Possibly, had this version undergone the novelist's usual detailed revision, some compression might have taken place. As it is, the reader is left near the start of what appears to be a new and expanding section of the book which then suddenly comes to a disconcerting end.

Die Poggenpuhls

Like the preceding short work, this one also belongs to the productive period just before the author's illness of 1892. It was laid aside after the first draft, but, unlike *Mathilde Möhring*, was completed in the author's lifetime and published in 1896. It is a ' kleiner Roman ' of fifteen chapters, occupying eighty-six pages in the Nymphenburg edition. To the reader wishing to know at once what happens in the novel, one must frankly answer ' almost nothing at all '—but, despite this, the story has much to recommend it. Its appeal lies in the depiction of *milieu* and character, and it also has an incidental documentary value as a record of the changing social structure of Prussia during the closing years of the nineteenth century. Events mentioned in the text allow us to fix the date precisely at 1888.

The unfortunately-named Poggenpuhls (which in North German dialect signifies ' Frog-pond ') are members of a fairly distinguished Pomeranian *Junker* family which has served its king and country well through several generations but has now fallen on hard times. The Berlin branch of the Poggenpuhls consists of the widowed mother, Albertine, and three daughters—Therese, Sophie and Manon. In the background are two sons, Wendelin and Leo, both serving in the army, and an uncle, the retired General Eberhard von Poggen-puhl. We meet all these representatives except Wendelin, mainly against a Berlin background but also, in the later chapters, at Adamsdorf in the Riesengebirge.

The main theme is the family's struggle to maintain some kind of dignity worthy of its long history in spite of very straitened circumstances in the alien setting of a modern, industrialised capital city. A highly significant aspect of this struggle is the varying attitude of each member of the younger generation towards it and towards the tradition they are supposed to represent. The eldest daughter, Therese, adheres fanatically to the aristocratic conception of honour, the second shows a certain readiness to adapt her artistic talents to the changing society around her, while the youngest, Manon, turns frankly away from the past and seeks the company of newly-rich commercial and banking families. The old General, born and raised in an earlier tradition of the settled, rural aristocracy, believes implicitly in the rôle of his own caste, despite the humiliation of his dependence upon a rich wife, but shows more tolerance and insight when dealing with other social classes and different ways of life than does his eldest niece, Therese. This we see very clearly in the restaurant, when they are joined by Herr von Klessentin, an aristocratic ex-officer turned professional actor ; Thesese is embarrassed, regarding him as *déclassé*, but her uncle is fascinated and delighted by the encounter. Notwithstanding his age and family pride, the general senses that the old order of society is nearing its end, as did the elderly Fontane, and this insecurity is hinted at in a variety of ways, including the symbolism of the family portrait which keeps falling from its place on the wall. Of the two sons, we meet only the younger, Leo, a fashionable lieutenant of twenty-two, who retains certain of the old aristocratic weaknesses, notably in his penchant for duelling, gambling, dalliance and the acquisition of enormous debts. His elder brother, Wendelin, is by contrast a figure of immense respectability, carving out a career for himself in the army and clearly destined for the general staff—though he lacks the personal popularity of his charming but irresponsible brother Leo, even in the family circle. Their mother—like the Generalin—is of middle-class origins and feels herself to be something of an outsider when questions of Poggenpuhl honour are debated. Together they form a valuable foil to the other members of the family circle.

One must not forget the minor but important rôle played by two secondary characters, neither of them of bourgeois origin, let alone of noble birth. The faithful old servant, Friederike, provides a good deal of additional information about the family she serves, both by means of her candid conversations with various members (for, like most of Fontane's old retainers, she enjoys a status approaching intimacy) and through her own reflections and ruminations on their situation. The other humble personage of note is the hall porter, Nebelung, who symbolises the urban worker without the old loyalties and traditions of the countryman and who already questions the whole value of the aristocracy. Indeed, the inner stresses and strains of Wilhelmian society are strongly in evidence throughout this tale. While the position of the nobleman on his family estates in the country still seems secure enough, the aristocracy of the city is showing signs of uncertainty and decay. The former concepts of ' honourable ' professions for the nobleman—usually the army or civil service—are becoming blurred. Not many young aristocrats would go the length of Herr von Klessentin, the actor, but the dividing line between the sphere of the urban nobleman and that of the new, wealthy bourgeoisie has become very uncertain.

Complicating the situation still further is the new rôle of what is politely referred to as ' the third confession ', namely the Jewish bourgeoisie. During the years following national unification in 1871 the German-Jewish financial and business families were playing an increasingly important part in the public life of the newly industrialised country, acquiring both wealth and social standing in the process. As a part of their rising status, these Jewish commercial families sought connections with the German aristocracy, and this led to numerous cases of inter-marriage between the two classes. The Jews had wealth and growing power in the new industrial, urbanised Germany, while the old noble families had their prestige and titles, but were often woefully lacking in funds. Thus, in many instances, they complemented each other. Reflections of this situation are seen in the connection between Manon von Poggenpuhl and the banking family of Bartenstein, with which she would like to forge a link by means of a marriage between her brother Leo and their daughter Flora. There is an approximately parallel situation in Leo's own involvement with the Jewish family of Blumenthal, though (like many of Leo's plans) it leads nowhere.

Some of Fontane's own concern for the future expresses itself in this novel, especially his fear that the aristocracy of Prussia, despite all its aesthetic appeal for him, was failing to adapt itself to a changing world and would become an antiquated relic of the past instead of providing Germany's leaders in a new age. The aristocrats in *Die Poggenpuhls* seem to lack a sense of purpose ; as H. H. Reuter remarks : ' Der Zukunftslosigkeit der Helden entspricht die Handlungslosigkeit der Fabel.'[9] Indeed, the only major occurrence in the whole story is the death of Uncle Eberhard, the elderly general, which results indirectly in a slight amelioration of the family's financial position, but they still do not appear to have much future as a social group.

Much of the charm in this tale is found in the elements of characterisation and conversation, both of which are closely linked. The conversation is of a casual, domestic kind between members of the same family, their intimate friends and an elderly servant who is almost one of the family. They all reveal a great deal about themselves in their discussions as well as casting fresh light on each other. The atmosphere of Berlin pervades the novel, apart from the Riesengebirge section, but the actual glimpses we have of the city and its inhabitants are few and far between, as befits a work of this restricted size.

From a formal point of view *Die Poggenpuhls* has received a good deal of criticism, especially because of its lack of action and the somewhat prolonged use in chapters 10 and 11 of correspondence between Adamsdorf and Berlin, though this is skilfully employed as a means of characterisation. Conrad Wandrey, the doyen of Fontane critics, senses a marked slackening of the author's creative gifts,[10] but this overlooks the fact that the tale was completed in rough draft by 1892, before such masterpieces as *Frau Jenny Treibel* and *Effi Briest*. Fontane has admitted some structural and formal weaknesses, referring to its ' Bummelstil ' in a letter written to Paul Schlenther in 1896,[11] but he implies that the casual approach was deliberate rather than accidental. The present-day reader will undoubtedly discover shortcomings ; he may expect to find

Leo's part in the story developing into a central motif, whereas in fact it fades entirely into the background. The Bartensteins, too, look as though they are destined to play a larger rôle, possibly through a romance between Flora and Leo, but here also the reader's expectations are thwarted. This would have opened the way for a vivid contrast between two social classes. As in the case of *Mathilde Möhring*, there is material enough in this book for a full-length *Roman*, but it remains unexploited. Perhaps most disturbing is the way in which Adamsdorf and the affairs of Uncle Eberhard suddenly occupy the foreground, threatening to displace Berlin altogether and start an entirely new phase of this family chronicle.

With all its flaws, *Die Poggenpuhls* has, however, much to commend it as an ancillary work to the longer studies of Berlin life in the 1880's and 1890's. It is atypical, inasmuch as it appears to be purely a work of fiction, without any recognisable real-life source as is the case with so many other novels by Fontane. It emphasises, too, the importance which the elderly novelist placed on 'das Kleine'—the small things of life, around which so much of this story is woven. Stylistically, it looks forward in time both to the last and most discursive of the novels, *Der Stechlin*, and to the satirical study of the bourgeoisie represented by *Frau Jenny Treibel*, which occupied the author's attention immediately after the first draft of this story and which was eventually published before it.

Chapter 8

THE GOLDEN AGE, II

Frau Jenny Treibel

THAT Theodor Fontane was aware of major differences between the solid social virtues of the traditional 'Bürgertum' and the pretensions of the newly-rich 'Bourgeoisie' during the years of prosperity and industrial expansion after 1871 is evident in several of the works already discussed. In none of them, however, is the essential difference between these two middle-class groups so manifest as in *Frau Jenny Treibel* (1892). In this novel he has taken one outstanding example of the *nouveau-riche* class and analysed the workings of her mind so profoundly that she has lived on as the symbol of an entire era and its social structure. Nor is she a mere caricature, despite elements which border on this, but maintains credibility for the reader as a life-like figure.

Jenny Treibel, née Bürstenbinder, entered the world humbly as the daughter of a Berlin grocer. Seeking escape at first through sentimental fantasy, she later achieves it in reality through marriage with a prosperous manufacturer, Kommerzienrat Treibel. She endeavours in middle age to transfigure the memory of her own social origin, but remains very conscious of it. She has learned to respect one thing above all others—money, with its power to bring material security and social standing. Had she acknowledged these values openly, she would at least have been an honest representative of the era. Unfortunately she insists on concealing the reality behind a screen of pseudo-culture and an affectation of contempt for worldly wealth. At her glittering dinner-parties the entertainment normally includes her own rendering of a sentimental ballad in praise of 'Glück ohne Gold' and concluding with the noble phrase : 'Ach, nur das, nur das ist Leben, wo sich Herz zum Herzen find't'. Unfortunately, however, 'heart *does* find its way to heart' in her own family circle between young Leopold Treibel and Corinna Schmidt, the penniless daughter of her schoolmaster friend from earlier days—and, ironically, the author of the sentimental poem. Jenny is transformed instantly, and it is clear that she will tolerate no idyll of ' Glück ohne Gold ' in the Treibel family. Her mask of tender feeling is dropped and replaced by cold anger and ruthless determination. Corinna, on whom she had only recently lavished much affection, suddenly becomes ' diese gefährliche Person ' filled with ' Professorentochter-dünkel ', and at Schmidt's home, near her own point of origin in the Adlerstraße, she vents her indignation in a brief but tense scene.

At the end of the novel, when her will has finally prevailed, she makes an unexpected appearance at Corinna's wedding to Cousin Marcell, a ' Gymnasial-Oberlehrer '. She is her former gracious, sentimental self once again, having come to the con-clusion that the whole Corinna-Leopold incident could most appropriately be dismissed as a childish aberration.

Naturally, a figure of such dimensions tends to dominate the novel and its other characters, most of whom are like putty in her hands. Only the young Corinna Schmidt puts up any serious degree of resistance to her will, and so the tale becomes essentially a conflict between these two women. The menfolk of the Treibel family represent no serious obstacle to her plans. Her husband, the jovial Kommerzienrat, is far more anxious to preserve a peaceful domestic life than to oppose Jenny's determination with his own more tolerant philosophy. Jenny's domination in their relationship comes out very clearly in chapter 8, though she is not entirely invulnerable to his re-proaches. This may be seen in chapter 12, where she is criti-cised for being ' blind und vergeßlich ' in her social snobbery, and has the good grace to turn pale and tremble.

There is much down-to-earth common sense in Treibel, apart from his aberration in the field of make-believe politics, but unfortunately he usually submits his will to that of his wife. Notice, for example, his strictures on the subject of class distinction near the conclusion of chapter 12. His hint to Jenny to remember her own humble background is brief, and he links it with an equally deprecating reference to his own side of the family. ' Wir sind auch nicht die Bismarcks oder die Arnims oder sonst was Märkisches von Adel, wir sind die Treibels, Blutlaugensalz und Eisenvitriol, und du bist eine geborene Bürstenbinder aus der Adlerstraße.' But Jenny's snobbish attitude nevertheless finds an echo even in his tolerant nature, for ' der gute Treibel, er war doch auch seinerseits das Produkt dreier, im Fabrikbetrieb immer reicher gewordenen Generationen, und aller guten Geistes- und Herzensanlagen unerachtet ... der Bourgeois steckte ihm wie seiner senti- mentalen Frau tief im Geblüt.'

Corinna Schmidt belongs to the younger generation of Berlin womanhood during the last two decades of the nine- teenth century, already on the threshold of social emancipa- tion. Determination and pride are as much a part of her temperament as they are of the Frau Kommerzienrat, but in place of Jenny's money-conscious materialism she possesses qualities of imagination and judgement in human affairs which differentiate her sharply from the older woman. Her frankness, when admitting her motives and ambitions to Frau Jenny in chapter 13, is also impressive. She is not unaffected by the prevailing respect for wealth and rank. Having spent her early life in an atmosphere of economy, she is at first attracted by the comfort and luxury seen in the Treibel home, and so she decides to marry Leopold purely for the sake of the social advantages offered by such a match. Somewhat spoilt by an indulgent father and lacking the advice of a mother, she is in danger of losing touch with the sound qualities of her ' bürgerlich ' way of life. Fortunately, her essentially healthy nature—that which her father has immodestly called ' das Schmidtsche '—finally triumphs, and she recognises the intrinsic worth of her patient, ever-faithful cousin Marcell, whom she marries. With him she is typically frank in her sum- ming-up of the situation. She had intended to marry Leopold and might well have been tolerably happy, in spite of his weakness and the family's materialism. ' Ich habe von früh an den Sinn für Äußerlichkeiten gehabt ', she admits. But the combination of materialism and false sentimentality proved too much for her. In creating the figure of Corinna Schmidt, Fontane is believed to have borrowed a number of character- istics from his daughter, Mete.

Professor Wilibald Schmidt, who has known Jenny from her earliest years, has a profound insight into her character and motivation, but nevertheless maintains a friendly relationship, tinged though it may be with irony. He is in many respects the most likable of the main characters and has certain traits

in common with Fontane, such as his mild scepticism and love
of anecdotes, though not enough to justify the term 'self-
portrait' which has sometimes been applied. He is a kindly,
tolerant individual with scholarly rather than material interests in an era which respected the latter. Part of his attractive-
ness lies in his sense of humour which frequently hovers on the
brink of irony. Although not without a certain schoolmasterly
pomposity and self-preoccupation, he is a perspicacious judge
of human character. He knows his old friend Jenny thoroughly,
perceiving ' daß sie, völlig unverändert, die, trotz Lyrik und
Hochgefühle, ganz ausschließlich auf Äußerlichkeiten gestellte
Jenny Bürstenbinder von ehedem war '. He also has an unusual sense of detachment which enables him to analyse for
the benefit of Marcell the strong and weak points in his own
daughter. He is happiest when indulging his interest in Greek
antiquities, but at the same time he is not without a shrewd
insight into the ways of the world around him, as for example
in his terse analysis of the difference between the aristocratic
and bourgeois outlook, when he observes to Marcell : ' In
eine Herzogsfamilie kann man allenfalls hineinkommen, in
eine Bourgeoisfamilie nicht.'

Of the minor characters in this work one figure stands out
clearly, namely Professor Schmidt's housekeeper, Frau
Schmolke. Enjoying, like so many of Fontane's servants, a
privileged relationship with the family, she looms larger in the
story than one might have anticipated. In the late-night
conversation between Corinna and Frau Schmolke, following
the fateful excursion to Halensee, it is the servant who plays the
major rôle and leaves the stronger impression on the reader.
She too sees through the Kommerzienrätin and her motives :
' Es ist eine geldstolze Frau, die den Apfelsinenladen vergessen
hat un immer bloß ötepotöte tut.' Her reminiscences during
the course of the novel show us glimpses of her former married
life with the late Schutzmann Schmolke, whose influence
lingers on most powerfully in her mind and expresses itself in
the recurrent phrase : ' Schmolke sagte immer . . . ', or ' Das
war ein Hauptsatz von Schmolke '. In her recollections of the
good man's unshakable belief, despite his experiences with the
Berlin police, in ' Proppertät und Strammheit und Gesundheit',
we have another example of the emphasis so often placed on

the virtues of ' Ordnung und Gesetz ' by the humbler figures in
Fontane's world.   Because of her intimacy with Corinna, it
seems entirely natural that she should be the first person to
hear in confidence of the secret engagement to Leopold.   In
this connection it is interesting to note that her frank observation : ' Glaube mir, Marcell wäre besser gewesen, denn ihr
paßt zusammen ', is entirely correct.   It costs Corinna herself
much anguish and humiliation to discover this simple fact
which Frau Schmolke has understood intuitively, and it is not
mere chance that she is the first to hear of Corinna's change of
heart.   The two households of Schmidt and Treibel provide
an effective contrast between the modest scale of lower-middle
class living conditions on the one hand and the lavish display
of the newly-rich bourgeoisie on the other.   At the Schmidts'
the reader witnesses a ' Lehrerkränzchen ', at which a number
of schoolmasters gather informally to smoke, chat and discuss
archaeology over supper.   The keynote is one of extreme
simplicity.   At Frau Treibel's suburban villa, on the other hand,
an elaborate dinner is staged to impress an English business
associate of her elder son, and this is presided over by Jenny
with great virtuosity, despite her humble social origins.   The
description of this dinner-party is one of the finest of its kind
in Fontane's novels, which abound in such scenes.   The conversation moves effortlessly from one group to another and from
one topic to the next, with the Frau Kommerzienrat controlling
the movement with the skill of an orchestral conductor.   But
the tone of the occasion is marred by insincerity, especially
when compared with that of the ' Oberlehrerkränzchen '.
One senses that Frau Jenny's wealthy guests are just ' making
conversation ', that they are really bored with the whole
affair, with each other, and with the kind of society in which
they move.   It is true that Wilibald Schmidt's schoolmaster
friends only come together when they have nothing more
exciting to do, but, once assembled, they do have interests in
common and their talk flows naturally without any contrived
direction.   At the Treibels' dinner it is more sparkling and
polished but is basically unnatural, being developed as a
social accomplishment.   Since the *nouveaux-riches* lack both the
culture of the aristocracy and the professional interests of the
older ' Bürgertum ', their conversation has neither depth nor

significance.

Josef Ettlinger has neatly described this novel as follows :
' In seiner ungetrübten Lustspielstimmung sticht dieser Roman
wie ein Intermezzo aus der langen Reihe der übrigen, fast
durchgehends tragisch ausklingenden Werke ab.'[1] For all the
underlying element of social satire, ironical humour remains
the dominant note in *Frau Jenny Treibel*. The whole relationship between Jenny and Wilibald Schmidt is tinged with
delicate irony, for, despite a certain genuine liking for his
one-time sweetheart, Schmidt has no illusions left about her.
After their strained meeting at the time of Corinna's attempt
to capture Leopold, Wilibald sees off his old friend Jenny with
the parting phrase : ' Freilich, wie Sie schon sehr richtig
bemerkt haben, die Zeit . . . alles will über sich hinaus und
strebt höheren Staffeln zu, die die Vorsehung sichtbarlich
nicht wollte.' Unmindful of any personal application of this
stricture, Jenny nods in solemn agreement : ' Gott bessre es.'
The circumstances of her own marriage with Kommerzienrat
Treibel are conveniently forgotten ! Then, after previously
setting her face against the acceptance of a second member of
the haughty and patrician Munk family from Hamburg as a
daughter-in-law, Jenny performs a remarkable *volte-face,* treats
the hitherto distrusted Helene, wife of her elder son, as a
natural ally and throws her entire earlier policy into reverse.
Honeyed words are written to Hildegard Munk in Hamburg,
entreating her to visit Berlin as soon as possible. This letter,
perhaps more than any other single factor, exposes for the
reader the hollow sham of the Treibel family relationship.
As her facile phrases flow on from page to page, she compounds
her insincerity by implicating her husband and son as well
without their knowledge. ' Treibel vereinigt seine Wünsche
mit den meinigen, und Leopold schließt sich an.' In fact the
guileless Herr Treibel only learns of the invitation when he
receives Hildegard's telegram of acceptance. In a significant
postscript she indicates quite openly the direction of her hopes
with regard to Leopold. To complete the irony of this situation,
Jenny's real attitude towards the Munks and their superior
Hamburg airs is, as the reader knows, no secret to the recipient
of this gushing missive. Hildegard has merely become the
lesser of two evils in Jenny's view. In pushing on this match

with the socially acceptable Hildegard Munk, Frau Treibel incidentally performs a signal service for the self-willed Corinna Schmidt, who is saved from making—largely through caprice —what would certainly have proved a disastrous marriage with the spineless Leopold. Having been used as a pawn in Jenny's family plans, the unfortunate Hildegard is allowed to fade quietly into the background, and the reader is left to assume her marriage to Leopold.

Stylistically this novel offers much that is of interest to the student of the mature Fontane. He will note the way in which the reader is offered an immediate explanation in chapter 1 of Jenny Treibel's childhood background, which is the key to her outlook as a woman in the late fifties, when he meets her. Her superficial sentimentality and ' Herz für das Poetische ' are indicated immediately afterwards in the conversation with Corinna, which also gives further details of her past life. Corinna's seemingly light-hearted response : ' Ja . . . die Jugend ist gut. Aber " Kommerzienrätin " ist auch gut und eigentlich noch besser. Ich bin für einen Landauer und einen Garten um die Villa herum ', offers us at the same time an indication of the materialistic streak which will shortly lead her along false paths and provoke the battle of wills between the two women. She is sceptical about Frau Jenny's praise of ' kleine Verhältnisse ', objecting that : ' Das sagen alle die, die drüber stehen und die kleinen Verhältnisse nicht kennen.' Hints are also given at this early stage of the tensions which exist between the essentially Berlin Treibels and the Hamburg in-laws with their patrician airs and international connections.

One of Fontane's favourite techniques is to allow his characters to comment on a social event immediately after it has happened, so giving the reader their candid, first-hand impressions. This he employs to good effect at the end of chapter 1, where Schmidt reviews in private the scene with Jenny that has just ended. He comments ironically on her use of the modish expression ' unentwegt ' and reflects on how little she has changed basically in forty years. Out of the dolled-up greengrocer's daughter has sprung what he frankly calls ' das Musterstück von einer Bourgeoise '.

The ' rumination ' technique is used again at the beginning of chapter two, just before the start of the dinner scene at the

Treibels, when husband and wife give vent to their private
thoughts while dressing, Jenny's preoccupations are of a social
and practical kind, fully in accordance with her class-conscious
nature, and run smoothly and naturally. Kommerzienrat
Treibel is concerned principally with his political ambitions,
and the result is less convincing, leaving a somewhat forced and
unnatural impression. The same rather stilted tone prevails
in his after-dinner conversations with Vogelsang and Gold-
ammer. This dinner-party also provides an example of
Fontane's whimsical choice of names, inasmuch as the two
Court ladies, Fräulein von Ziegenhals and Fräulein Bomst,
each appear to have got the name most suited for the other,
while the 'Gesellschaftsdame', Fräulein Honig, has little
that is suggestive of sweetness in her nature.

Attention has already been drawn to the skill with which
Fontane (and consequently Jenny) has handled the flow of
conversation at the formal dinner given by the Treibels. By
way of contrast, he then goes on to adapt his conversational
technique to fit the small-scale, more intimate discussion
between Corinna and her cousin Marcell as they later make
their way home. This he employs skilfully as a means of
revealing Corinna's inner thoughts and plans, at the same time
bringing out the sterling qualities of Marcell and indicating
his deep attachment to Corinna.

Much of our knowledge about the character—such as it is—
of Leopold Treibel is acquired indirectly, particularly through
the comments of his mother, Frau Jenny. In chapter 8, during
some candid exchanges with her husband, Jenny deplores the
feebleness of both her sons, especially Leopold whom she
admits to be 'eine Suse'. Yet, at the same time, she hinders
any possibility of growing independence by interfering at
every turn. 'Da hat mir die Frau Mama gesagt : "Hören
Sie, Mützell . . . eine Tasse ; nie mehr" ', says the waiter when
the unfortunate Leopold orders a second cup of coffee. To her
old friend Wilibald she says bluntly : 'Leopold ist ein Kind
und darf sich überhaupt nicht nach eigenem Willen ver-
heiraten . . .' When the fateful engagement does occur between Leopold and Corinna after the Halensee excursion,
Jenny summarises the situation with brutal frankness to her
son : ' *Sie* hat sich verlobt,' she says, ' und du bist bloß verlobt

worden.' There will be no acknowledgement of the event in Villa Treibel. ' In meinem Haus existiert keine Verlobung und keine Corinna.'

Kommerzienrat Treibel complements Jenny's views of their son in his rueful comments at Halensee, where Leopold cuts such a poor figure, and Leopold himself later confirms the impressions already received from his parents. ' Pluck, dear Leopold ', his friend Mr. Nelson had counselled him privately, but this, he admits, he has not got. ' Da liegt es ; nirgend anders. Mir fehlt es an Energie und Mut, und das Aufbäumen hab ich nun schon gewiß nicht gelernt.' To prevent this self-analysis from becoming tedious, Fontane inserts an unobtrusive pause ; Leopold feeds the sparrows before resuming his meditations. He concludes : ' Ich weiß, ich bin kein Held, und das Heldische läßt sich nicht lernen.' Despite his wild fantasies about eloping to Gretna Green with Corinna, the reader senses his spiritual impotence when faced with disagreeable facts.

Another use of the internal monologue is to illuminate the mind of Jenny's husband, Kommerzienrat Treibel, especially the fantasy-world of his political interests. These contrast sharply with his practical sense in the world of business, and their absurdity is heightened by the ludicrous impression made by Lt. Vogelsang, his political agent in the election campaign. The reports on the supposed progress of this in chapter 9 can have little relevant purpose in the story apart from underlining the futility of Treibel's candidature and provoking some reflections by him which are useful pointers to the understanding of the man and his motives. The reader's picture of him is given additional detail by means of a variation of this technique ; he makes a speech during the trip to Halensee which, in its pomposity and prolixity, pleases the reader as little as it pleased some of his fellow-excursionists.

The Halensee episode is by no means as incidental as it may appear on first reading. It is an outstanding example of Fontane's use of the ' Landpartie ' in order to take the main characters out of their customary habitat, place them slightly off their guard, and so provoke a decisive step which leads to a crisis. In this particular instance the way ahead is clearly signposted for the alert reader, for at the beginning of chapter

10 it is stated with reference to Corinna : 'Denn in ihrer Seele dämmerte eine unklare Vorstellung davon, daß die Landpartie nicht gewöhnlich verlaufen, sondern etwas Großes bringen werde.' This ' etwas Großes ' is, of course, the engagement of Leopold and Corinna. Even in the relaxed atmosphere of a country walk, however, Leopold finds it impossible to talk freely to Corinna until he has overtaken his mother and no longer sees her looming in front of him like a warning !

Corinna's supreme skill in leading the pliant and impressionable Leopold to his ' decision ' is indicated by a verbatim account of their conversation, interspersed with brief glimpses of the mood and internal reflections of the participants. Fontane's discreet irony blends well with the assumed pathos of Corinna's emotional speech near the end of the tenth chapter, when she declares : 'Hier unter diesem Waldesdom, drin es geheimnisvoll rauscht und dämmert, hier, Leopold, mußt du mir schwören, ausharren zu wollen in deiner Liebe.' In the background they have the favourite Fontane motifs of the crescent moon (' die Mondsichel ') and a distant snatch of sentimental song.

Not only the two young people find themselves affected by the mood of woodlands, lakes and moonlight ; sentimental memories of former days fill the ample bosom of the Kommerzienrätin as she walks with her old love, Professor Schmidt, and gives full expression to her ' poetic ' self. Only an incautious mention by Schmidt of a rumour that a second Hamburg daughter-in-law from the house of Munk is about to be welcomed into the Treibel fold momentarily disturbs this mood : ' " Wer sagt das ?" fuhr jetzt Jenny heraus, plötzlich aus dem sentimental Schwärmerischen in den Ton ausgesprochendster Wirklichkeit verfallend. " Wer sagt das ?" ' But a few minutes later she has returned into her world of pseudo-sentiment, laying her hand over her heart as she declares : ' Glück, Glück ! Ach Wilibald, daß ich es in solcher Stunde gerade vor Ihnen bekennen muß, das Glück, es ruht *hier* allein.'

Lovers of Fontane's drastic generalisations will find them plentifully strewn amongst the pages of this work. ' Landpartieen also sind immer fröhlich ', declares Treibel in chapter

10, and shortly afterwards : 'Erinnerungen sind immer das Beste.' 'Alle Gesellschaften sind Unsinn', scoffs Wilibald Schmidt. 'Denn was ein Professor sagt, is immer wahr', asserts Frau Schmolke somewhat unconvincingly in the early part of the sixteenth. There are also, for good measure, a few examples in English from the mouth of Mr. Nelson, whose frequent comments in that language remind us that, despite the passage of the years since Fontane's sojourn in Britain, his mastery of English has not deserted him, even though some of the colloquialisms may have become dated.

The canvas of *Frau Jenny Treibel* is a broad one, as befits the study of a whole *milieu*, and there are no heroes and heroines, no great deeds and no catastrophes. Yet the way of life and inner values of a class and an era are preserved for the future in forms and personalities which arouse our interest in their own right and make this novel one of Fontane's most successful works. Conrad Wandrey has neatly summarised the author's purpose : 'Fontane will die lügnerische Phrasenhaftigkeit, den leeren Hochmut, das Hartherzige der Bourgeoiswelt zeichnen, die Herrschaft des Geldsacks und der Geldsacksgesinnung, die ständig den Anspruch auf das "Höhere" erhebt, vom Schönen, Guten, Wahren redet und im entscheidenden Augenblick, die Maske werfend, das goldne Kalb umtanzt.'[2]

Effi Briest

Whether *Effi Briest* (1895) or *Irrungen, Wirrungen* (1888) may claim the honour of representing Fontane's highest achievement in prose fiction is likely to remain a subject for debate. Certain it is that, with the appearance of *Effi Briest*, Fontane began to transcend the boundaries of the German-speaking world and invite comparison with the author of *Madame Bovary*. As Wandrey succinctly remarks : 'Mit *Effi Briest* ragt Fontane in die Weltliteratur.'[3] Its composition was, on the novelist's own admission, an effortless, instinctive process—though this did not spare him the later detailed stylistic revision, which often took longer than the actual writing. 'Es ist so wie von selbst gekommen, ohne rechte Überlegung und ohne alle Kritik', he wrote of the original draft.[4] The starting point was again a real-life story and was based on the unsuccessful marriage of an aristocratic cavalry

officer and a young girl of good family from Parez, near
Magdeburg. The figure of Effi was derived from a young
English girl seen by the author while on holiday at Thale in
the Harz. Although the actual events took place in the Rhine-
land, Fontane wisely transferred them to the more familiar
areas of Pomerania and Berlin. Nor was he content with a
mere reproduction of existing facts ; in the figure of Effi and
in the depiction of her tragic marriage, he has created a work
of prose fiction which completely transcends the original
stimulus, based on events known to him principally through
gossip.

The background pattern of this novel forms a circle, starting
at Effi's childhood home of Hohen-Cremmen, moving from
there to Kessin on the Baltic coast, then to Berlin (with a brief
interlude at Bad Ems), and finally back to Hohen-Cremmen.
Each setting has its own particular mood and significance for
the development of the theme, and there are also sub-divisions
within this background frame, for example the two phases of
Effi's life at Kessin and again at Berlin.

The reader is introduced to Effi as an unsophisticated
seventeen-year-old, scarcely more than a child in emotional
development and experience of life. This is amply illustrated
in her conversation with three close friends, as they talk about
family affairs, marriage and the expected visit from Baron
von Innstetten, a former admirer of Effi's mother. It is further
emphasised by the sudden transition from light-hearted chatter
to high-spirited, boisterous games, in which Effi plays the
leading part, showing the impulsive element in her temperament. From this scene of adolescence, Effi is called away to
meet the important visitor who has arrived, unbeknown to
her, to ask her parents for her hand in marriage. He is nearly
forty, a former army officer turned civil servant, and at present
occupying the position of *Landrat* at the little coastal resort of
Kessin. ' Ältlich ist er auch, er könnte ja beinah mein Vater
sein ', says Effi of him before she goes in. As they meet, and a
new world is about to open for Effi, her childhood friends,
impatiently waiting to resume their games, appear at the
window and call out : ' Effi, komm !' The engagement is
announced, and Effi's immaturity is again stressed through her
comments to her friends Hertha, Bertha and Hulda. When

asked : ' Ist es denn auch der Richtige ?' she replies : ' Gewiß ist es der Richtige. Das verstehst du nicht, Hertha. Jeder ist der Richtige. Natürlich muß er von Adel sein und eine Stellung haben und gut aussehen.' It is hardly an exaggeration when Erich Schmidt says of the engagement : ' Das Kind wird von der Schaukel weg in die Ehe geschickt.'[5]

During the preparations for the wedding, practically everything is discussed and arranged by Effi's mother and Geert von Innstetten, while the bride herself shows more interest in the excitement of a Berlin visit than in the purchase of her trousseau, except for one or two personal items which take her fancy and, typically, are all of the very highest quality. Typical also of her naïve fantasy-world is her longing for an exotic Japanese bedcover and a lamp with a warm red glow—both of which suggestions meet with marked disfavour on the part of her practical mother. Lost in the wonder of her newly acquired importance, Effi tends to forget about the man who caused this transformation, even to the extent of putting his letters absent-mindedly into her pocket, unread.

After the marriage ceremony at Hohen-Cremmen, the couple travel extensively through South Germany, Austria and Italy, and the reader is given numerous glimpses of the underlying differences of temperament through the remarks made by Effi on the stream of postcards sent to her parents. The honeymoon is virtually a cultural tour through half the galleries and museums of southern Europe, along the endless corridors of which the dutiful Effi is led by her enthusiastic husband. Her attempts to echo his sentiments are less convincing than her complaints of tired feet and her happy anticipation of feeding the pigeons in St. Mark's Square. Even more revealing are the signs of her longing for Hohen-Cremmen.

Kessin comes as an anti-climax after the hustle and bustle of the previous weeks of travel. Obviously based on Fontane's childhood memories of Swinemünde, it incorporates many of the less attractive aspects of small-town life at the end of the nineteenth century. Its society is rigidly stratified, its diversions during the long winter are extremely limited, while the interests and conversational topics favoured by her own small circle are hardly those likely to appeal to a lively, seventeen-year-old girl from an unsophisticated country background. Added to all this is the gloomy atmosphere of her new home, with its reputation of being haunted by the ghost of a Chinese serving-man who once lived there. Innstetten's cold, pedagogic attitude towards his young wife and his frequent absences on duty do not help the situation. In his own way he obviously cares deeply for Effi but cannot express his affection spontaneously. During the first few lonely months at Kessin Effi relies increasingly on the society of a sensitive and high-minded cripple, Alonzo Gieshübler, whose own inner suffering has given him uncanny insight into the unhappiness of others.

The arrival of Major Crampas, the new commanding officer of the district *Landwehr*, provides an alternative and far more dangerous distraction. A "ladies' man" in his forties, saddled with an ailing, unsociable wife, he regards the guileless Effi as fair game, despite his long-standing association with Innstetten during their army days. Slowly and skilfully he exploits her loneliness and inexperience until she finally succumbs in despair rather than through any real affection, betrayed by a side of her own nature of which she was hitherto unaware.

Sudden promotion for Innstetten, involving a transfer to Berlin, rescues Effi from this dangerous and basically unsatisfying situation only a matter of weeks after its commencement. With a thankful heart she looks ahead to brighter days and a fresh start. Indeed her hopes seem to be realised, for over six years pass, during which time the maturing Effi appears to be achieving a better understanding with her husband and fulfilling happily her rôle as wife and mother. At this point, however, the past reasserts itself and Effi's only half-conquered fear of discovery proves to have been all too justified. With typical insouciance, she has left in her sewing-box a little pile of notes and letters from Crampas, unheeded and of no further importance to her at all. During a frantic hunt for bandages, while she is away at Bad Ems, these are unearthed by the maid, left lying around, and later discovered and read by Innstetten.

From this point onwards the story progresses rapidly and with seeming inevitability towards its tragic outcome. After a historic discussion between Innstetten and his close friend Wüllersdorf, in which the whole ethic of the duel as a social convention is analysed, Innstetten concludes that so long as society remains as it is, men must obey its laws, unwritten as well as written ones. He returns to Kessin, with its bitter-sweet memories, meets Crampas at a lonely spot amongst the dunes, where formerly the three of them had walked, ridden and laughed together, and in the ensuing duel shoots Crampas dead. The convention has been satisfied, but nothing is solved, as quickly becomes evident. Having taken this first step, Innstetten is forced to take others as well, including the repudiation of his young wife for whom he still cares and with whom he has achieved a more stable relationship in the years following her one lapse.

The way in which Effi receives the news from her parents at Hohen-Cremmen is not only stylistically admirable but also reveals a new side of her character, the inborn aristocratic dignity which underlay her earlier immature frivolity. At no point does she betray herself in public or gratify the burning curiosity of the odious Geheimrätin Zwicker. Socially, however, her life has ended. She cannot return to Hohen-Cremmen, for her parents would then be ostracised. She cannot go back to her married home in Berlin or see her daughter, the custody of whom has been given to her husband as the blameless party. Her former circle of acquaintances in the capital is now closed to her. Supported by a modest allowance made secretly by her parents, Effi lives in virtual isolation in a small Berlin flat, an isolation only made tolerable by the return to her of Roswitha, her devoted maidservant. All attempts to reconstruct a meaningful existence by taking up social work as a form of employment are doomed to failure because of her aristocratic birth and the convention which makes it unacceptable in humble, day-to-day activities. Her always fragile health and nerves begin to suffer, and the fatal blow is struck by her own daughter, Annie, who is finally allowed—albeit grudgingly— to visit her. This visit—a scene of high emotion and unusual for Fontane—is a disaster, for the child has been trained carefully by Innstetten to regard her mother as an outsider. In this respect there is an important difference from the parallel scene in *L'Adultera* where one of the children feels spontaneous resentment. In reply to all Effi's gaily uttered suggestions for future meetings and joint excursions, the girl replies coldly : ' O gewiß, wenn ich darf.'

Only medical evidence from the old family physician, Geheimrat Dr. Rummschüttel, enables her parents to take back the inwardly broken Effi to her childhood home—and even then they are shunned by most of their aristocratic friends. There, amidst the scenes of her happy girlhood and in tranquil communion with the beauty of nature, Effi is allowed to enjoy a brief Indian summer of contentment and reflection on the meaning of her ruined life. These final chapters are written in a lyrical tone rarely found in Fontane's prose, and it is clear that the reader is being prepared for the inevitable end. Before her death—while still a young woman in her twenties—Effi has obtained a far deeper understanding of the nature of humanity and human society. She dies reconciled to her fate and to the inevitability of Innstetten's actions, indeed thankful to have been allowed to spend these last placid months at her native Hohen-Cremmen, home in its deepest sense for her and the only soil upon which she could ever truly flourish.

What is the reader of today to make of this tragic story, and to what extent is his understanding hampered by the subsequent changes in social structure and social convention?

It is known that, even at the time of its composition, some accepted usages and attitudes were being closely scrutinised by the more critical elements of society as it existed in Germany at the end of the nineteenth century. This is reflected in various ways in Fontane's novel, but nowhere more clearly than in the two long conversations between Innstetten and Wüllersdorf, the first in chapter 27 and the second in chapter 35. Obviously a period of social transition lay just ahead, but it had not yet arrived and could not be anticipated without incurring the kind of inevitable disaster which Hebbel had also portrayed in dramatic form earlier in the century. The duel between Innstetten and Crampas is not decided upon lightly. Wüllersdorf advances his ' Verjährungstheorie ' in view of the lapse of six-and-a-half years since the offence. He then warns Innstetten plainly that if he kills the wrongdoer he may be adding fresh grief to that which he must already bear : ' Innstetten, Ihre Lage ist furchtbar, und Ihr Lebensglück ist hin. Aber wenn Sie den Liebhaber totschießen, ist Ihr Lebensglück sozusagen doppelt hin, und zu dem Schmerz über empfangenes Leid kommt noch der Schmerz über getanes Leid.'

In answer to the direct question, ' Fühlen Sie sich so verletzt, beleidigt, empört, daß einer weg muß, er oder Sie ?' Innstetten cannot with honesty say that this is so. He is unhappy, insulted, deceived—but not filled with burning hatred or a desire for drastic revenge after such a lapse of time. He would prefer to forgive his wife, but his ' Paragraphenseele ' cannot tolerate this deviation from the accepted norm.

' Man ist nicht bloß ein einzelner Mensch, man gehört einem Ganzen an, und auf das Ganze haben wir beständig Rücksicht zu nehmen, wir sind durchaus abhängig von ihm.'

So, to placate what he calls ' jenes . . . uns tyrannisierende Gesellschafts-Etwas '—and because he has already admitted the truth to Wüllersdorf—there can be no concessions on the grounds of time since the event occurred or the love he still has for his wife. ' Ich habe keine Wahl. Ich muß.' Wüllersdorf is also convinced, despite himself : ' Unser Ehrenkultus ist ein Götzendienst, aber wir müssen uns ihm unterwerfen, solange der Götze gilt.'

An effective contrast is provided by the second meeting in chapter 35. Innstetten has just received news of his elevation to the rank of ' Ministerialdirektor ', but is more grateful for the kind words accompanying the promotion than for the supposed honour of the distinction itself. Since the fatal day at Kessin he has learned to measure life with new values and to appreciate its small pleasures more than the outward signs of success. But, as he admits to himself, his days have passed in an increasingly joyless fashion, deprived of love and weighed down with unhappy memories. ' Ich habe mich zu freuen verlernt ', he says to Wüllersdorf. The more he receives outward marks of official distinction, the more does he become convinced of their intrinsic worthlessness. He would rather get away from the whole empty farce and start a new life in some far-off place. Wüllersdorf dismisses the idea as ridiculous on the part of a middle-aged man of fixed habits and stresses the only real solution : ' Einfach hier bleiben und Resignation üben . . . In der Bresche stehen und aushalten, bis man fällt, das ist das beste.' He bids him enjoy the little things of everyday life—the kind of minor pleasures so loved by Fontane himself— and recommends to him the saying of a friend, an architect, whose life had gone to pieces : ' Es geht überhaupt nicht ohne

" Hilfskonstruktionen ".' The reader is left with the impression that Innstetten has paid for his ' Götzendienst ' to the social code nearly as heavily as Effi and Crampas. There is no going back and no real prospect ahead. The only gain has been in the form of spiritual insight—but at what a price !

When reading *Effi Briest* it must be borne in mind that Innstetten suffers a personal tragedy as well as Effi, even though he may be partly responsible for it. There is much that is worthy of respect in the character of Geert von Innstetten, despite his obvious shortcomings, as there was in Botho von Rienäcker. He is a just and high-principled man, 'ein Mann von Charakter, ein Mann von Prinzipien—auch ein Mann von Grundsätzen ',[6] possessing a punctilious sense of duty and of order which fit him admirably for his civil service career, and he is capable of genuine kindness. No doubt to his colleagues in the Ministry he is an exemplary figure, an impression implicit in the cordial letter accompanying the news of his promotion as well as in the tone of the conversations with his civil service friend Wüllersdorf. On the other hand, his insistence on rigid principles and reasoned conduct leads him into cold, even ruthless attitudes in his private life. ' Ihr Herr Gemahl . . . ist ein Mann, der nicht nach Stimmungen und Laune, sondern nach Grundsätzen handelt ', says the Minister's wife to Effi. Worst of all is the inner weakness which makes much of his conformity mere outward show ; ' Du bist ja der Mann der Formen ', Effi tells him. This moral cowardice does not diminish his undoubted physical courage, however, which manifests itself in his readiness to fight a well-matched duel. In his attitude towards his emotional, sensitive young wife a pedagogic streak comes out repeatedly, and he does not shrink from the deliberate inculcation of fear in order to serve his own ends. Too late does he achieve insight and refer sadly to ' mein Schulmeistertum, was ja wohl mein Eigentlichstes ist '. So, despite a genuine affection for Effi, he manages to infuse the marriage with a cheerless, impersonal flavour. Later he even succeeds in training his little daughter, Annie, to be a reflection of this chilly aspect of his character, so that she treats her own mother as a stranger. Yet his emotional capacity is clearly larger than appears on the surface, and the reader comes to understand that he has suppressed a good deal of his feeling. ' Denn so nüchtern er schien, eigentlich war er nervös.'⁷ His unexpected enthusiasm for Wagner reveals more than just his taste in music.

Clearly this marriage ran grave risks from the start, quite apart from the dangers normally inherent in a union between seventeen and forty. There had to be warmth of feeling, protectiveness and understanding if all were to go well. Given a situation of loneliness and fear, boredom and alienation, Effi was bound to fall victim to the first presentable man who appeared and offered those essentials lacking in her life with Innstetten. She, too, is a weak character in ways different from those detected in her husband, and has a certain ' Hang nach dem Aparten ' which can easily lead her into dangerous situations. This is recognised by Innstetten as well as by her mother ; noting her extravagant reaction to the romantic life-story of the singer Marietta Trippelli (born simple Marie Trippel, the local pastor's daughter), Geert von Innstetten takes her to task for constantly hankering after ' was Apartes '. ' Aber hüte dich vor dem Aparten oder was man so das Aparte nennt ', he says ; ' Was dir so verlockend erscheint, . . . das bezahlt man in der Regel mit seinem Glück.' Associated with this trait of Effi's character is her taste for the unusual and even morbid in literature and folk-lore ; whereas her young friends Hulda and the twins have forgotten the tale about the grim fate meted out to unfaithful wives by the Turks, Effi has not : ' Ich nicht. Ich behalte so was.' An element, later identified by Innstetten as ' was Verführerisches ', is already present, though dormant, in the teenage tomboy of chapter 1, who plays hide-and-seek like a child, races round the garden, and outshines her friends in daring antics on the swing— always, significantly, with a mingled thrill of pleasurable fear at the thought of the risks involved.

Effi seems at times to have a fairly clear idea of the contra-dictions in her disposition, even before marriage. During the confidential discussion with her mother in chapter 4, she replies to the question : ' Wofür bist du denn eigentlich ?' as follows : ' Ich bin . . . nun, ich bin für gleich und gleich und natürlich auch für Zärtlichkeit und Liebe.' But, in default of such qualities in marriage, she is prepared to settle for ' Reichtum und ein vornehmes Haus, ein *ganz* vornehmes . . . ' More specifically she adds : ' Liebe kommt zuerst, aber gleich hinterher kommt Glanz und Ehre, und dann kommt Zerstreuung . . . Was ich nicht aushalten kann, ist Langeweile.' Undertones of this may be found in her dull reaction to Geert's letter with its moderation, its endeavours to achieve what Effi's mother calls ' das rechte Maß '. Here is something which Effi Briest can never hope to emulate, for she is by nature mercurial and subject to sudden changes of mood.

Does she really love Geert, asks her mother, and the reply is so indicative of her immaturity that the reader is astonished at her mother's failure to react to it adequately. ' Warum soll ich ihn nicht lieben ? ', responds Effi . . . ' ich liebe alle, die's gut mit mir meinen und gütig gegen mich sind und mich verwöhnen.' The sudden transition to her new status at Kessin brings about a maturing process, at first uneven and sometimes unconvincing (as for example in the early conversations with Gieshübler), but later accelerated by the impact of her affair with Crampas. Despite these changes, however, her longing for her past life in Hohen-Cremmen remains undiminished, and the sight of an express train roaring past on its way to her old home can still bring tears to her eyes. Her long letters from Kessin to her parents continue to be filled with yearning for the past and betray a sense of guilt at their admissions of dissatisfaction, and the reiterated plea of ' don't tell Innstetten '. It is not that she fails to respect, even admire him for his basic kindness and upright character ; what she lacks is ' Huldigungen, Anregungen, kleine Aufmerksamkeiten'. In short, ' Innstetten war lieb und gut, aber ein Liebhaber war er nicht.' In addition there is the isolation and lack of entertainment to cope with, ' Aber immer das Alleinsein und so gar nichts erleben, das hat doch auch sein Schweres . . . ', she complains, and her husband's enthusiasm for an erudite recapitulation of their cultural discoveries in Italy does little to fill the void. Note by way of contrast her enthusiastic response to Crampas' plans for amateur theatricals : ' Effi war wie elektrisiert ; was wollten Padua, Vicenza daneben bedeuten ! Effi war nicht für Aufgewärmtheiten ; Frisches war es, wonach sie sich sehnte, Wechsel der Dinge.'

What she cannot experience in reality she achieves in daydreams of travel and excitement to which she is greatly prone, even when faced with the imminent prospect of motherhood. Sometimes during her holidays at Hohen-Cremmen all that has happened since her marriage seems unreal and she forgets both husband and child in the joys of rediscovered adolescence. When, however, imaginary cravings for diversion and the forbidden are changed into reality she feels oppressed and trapped in a situation from which she cannot escape : ' sie fühlte, daß sie wie eine Gefangene sei und nicht mehr heraus könne.' Despite an awareness of danger, she lacks the strength of will necessary to free herself. So she drifts on towards catastrophe. ' Das Verbotene, das Geheimnisvolle hatte seine Macht über sie', but not sufficiently to banish the qualms of conscience, and she freely admits in despair : ' Effi, du bist verloren '. That she is not indifferent to social convention is illustrated ironically by the moral lecture she delivers to Roswitha on the dangers of flirting with married men, having seen her in jocular mood with the coachman, Kruse—when she herself was on the way back from a stolen meeting with Crampas !

Internal conflicts of guilt and desire mirror themselves subtly in her outward appearance, displacing some of her former childlike characteristics. Even Innstetten, not always the most perceptive of men, is nevertheless quick to spot the change when he returns from Berlin, noticing first the new sparkle in her expression, then a slight pallor, and finally a not wholly displeasing trend towards maturity. Effi has the good grace to blush. Only the power of external forces can rescue her from the situation into which she has drifted, and her husband's news of the transfer to Berlin sounds like a heavenly intervention. Sensing freedom, like a trapped bird, she very nearly betrays herself when rescue is in sight, uttering a cry of thankfulness : ' Gott sei Dank !' which momentarily alerts even the trusting, somewhat complacent Innstetten.

Her inner conflict is an essential expression of her divided character. She is able to deceive skilfully, but at the same time she hates dissimulation. This is made clear by the persistence of her guilt-feelings after the move to Berlin. ' Ich habe die Schuld auf meiner Seele ', she admits to herself during a quiet evening at Hohen-Cremmen. Yet far more oppressive than her guilt is the secret fear, the sense of inevitable if belated discovery, and shame at the rôle she is still sometimes forced to play when the Kessin days are discussed. All this, moreover, for an affair with a man whom, as she admits in her later agony of loneliness, she did not even love.

Only in her last days does she finally resolve her conflicts and understand the motives which impelled both herself and others. Then only can she mention again the name of her husband and face death in a state of inner reconciliation and forgiveness ; ' Denn er hatte viel Gutes in seiner Natur and war so edel, wie jemand sein kann, der ohne rechte Liebe ist.' Exhausted both physically and emotionally by burdens and perplexities too heavy for young shoulders, she takes comfort from an old saying : ' Es hat nicht viel zu bedeuten, wenn man von der Tafel etwas früher abgerufen wird.' Her tragedy has rightly been summed up as that of ' die arme Effi Briest, die nicht das Talent besaß, eine Euphemia von Innstetten zu werden.'[8]

Effi dominates the story which bears her name, so that sometimes even her husband serves the primary purpose of illustrating and clarifying her personality for the reader. However, the secondary and minor characters are no mere ciphers but exist in their own right as fully rounded human personalities. Prominent amongst them are Effi's parents, from whose conversations we learn a great deal about their daughter. For a long time the reader may be misled as to the relative importance of this pair, for it is Frau von Briest who seems to be the dominant partner and who provides much of the background information, while her jovial husband, with his pet phrase, ' Ach, laß Luise, das ist ein zu weites Feld ', appears to be cast in a supporting rôle. In the long run, however, it becomes clear that Vater Briest, in his fumbling, slightly inarticulate way, has in fact a firmer grasp of the essentials and a far greater degree of insight into his daughter's tragedy than has his more self-assured spouse. He is the first to comment on an essential difference between his daughter and the newly-acquired son-in-law : ' Innstetten ist ein vorzüglicher Kerl, aber er hat so etwas von einem Kunstfex, und Effi, Gott, unsere arme Effi, ist ein Naturkind.' Significant also is his remark to Frau von Briest : ' Überhaupt hättest du besser zu Innstetten gepaßt als Effi.' This is echoed by Effi herself in chapter 9, when she confesses to a feeling of inadequacy in her new rôle as Frau Baronin von Innstetten : ' Ach, ich tauge doch gar nicht für eine große Dame. Die Mama, ja, die hätte hierher gepaßt . . . Aber ich—ich bin ein Kind und werd es auch wohl bleiben.'

During the earlier conversation in chapter 5, Frau von Briest analyses her daughter with remarkable objectivity, points out the contradictions in her character, and admits her to be ' überhaupt ein ganz eigenes Gemisch '. In her view Effi does not yet really understand the deeper meaning of love, in spite of her emotional nature. (One is inclined at this point to wonder just why, in such circumstances, she had not only permitted her teenage daughter to marry but even arranged the match.) The aspect of her nature which, according to the mother, is most developed, consists of ' Vergnügungssucht und Ehrgeiz '. The latter may well be satisfied by her husband's success in his career, but Frau von Briest is concerned about the former element, which she defines as ' ihr Hang nach Spiel und Abenteuer ', and fears that Innstetten may come to grief through failure to recognise and cater for it. (Again one wonders, why allow—let alone encourage—this union ?) Developing still further this element of ballad-like prescience, Effi's mother adds the dark warning : ' Dann weiß ich nicht, was geschieht. Denn so weich und nachgiebig sie ist, sie hat auch was Rabiates und läßt es auf alles ankommen.' As well as illustrating contemporary social attitudes towards marriage in ' Society ', Frau von Briest's practical, indeed business-like part in the promotion of this ' good match ' involves her in considerable moral responsibility for the outcome—that which H. H. Reuter calls : ' eine letzte menschliche Konsequenz des als Eheschließung getarnten unmenschlichen Kaufes.'[9]

During Effi's first holiday back in Hohen-Cremmen, it is her father, with his sympathetic understanding of animals and their ways, who notices his daughter's close attachment to her dog, Rollo. ' Immer Rollo ', lachte Briest, ' wenn man's nicht anders wüßte, so sollte man beinah glauben, Rollo sei dir mehr ans Herz gewachsen als Mann und Kind.' He is perturbed, too, that Innstetten has not applied for leave and accompanied his young wife. Later, in chapter 24, Briest again spots the danger-signals. He considers it strange that Effi should still regard Hohen-Cremmen as her real home and asks his wife whether there is any true love in the marriage ; ' Von Anfang an war mir's so, als ob sic ihn mehr schätze als liebe.' In her reply to him Effi's mother admits that her daughter is ' eine sehr schlaue, kleine Person ', but feels that the marriage has got on to a more even keel since their transfer to Berlin. At the same time womanly instincts warn her that her daughter is concealing something to which she would really like to confess, for ' Kampf und Widerstand sind nicht ihre Sache '.

What of the third party in the intrigue which develops at Kessin ? Major von Crampas, the new district commander of the local militia, is no dashing young hero in Effi's own age-group or even near it. He is forty-four, married to a difficult, unhappy woman who shuns social life (but whom, in the long run, he refuses to desert), and is the father of two children of ten and eight (who play no part in the story). Even before his arrival he is known by reputation to be a "ladies' man", one, moreover, who has been involved in a duel because of this proclivity and suffered permanent damage to his left arm. Yet in this atmosphere of stifling boredom at Kessin his coming represents an exciting novelty. The reader is never allowed to forget the danger associated with Crampas, despite his obvious charm. In chapter 15 it is linked with the weakness of Effi's character ; no sooner has Innstetten mentioned the coquettish element in his young wife, concluding: ' Du hast was Ver-führerisches ', than Crampas appears on the scene. In the talk that follows several points emerge which emphasise the reckless streak in Crampas, his longing for renewed military action, and his conviction (based on a gypsy prophecy) that he will die in a soldierly manner. The irony of this conversa-tion becomes apparent in retrospect ; the participants are Major von Crampas—doomed to be killed in a duel—, Baron von Innstetten—the man who is to kill him—, and Effi—the cause of the tragedy.

The October ride together by the sea provides further clues to the Major's character as well as that of Innstetten. On hearing Innstetten's legalistic reference to the harbour regula-tions, Crampas laughs at him, remarking : ' Muß denn alles so furchtbar gesetzlich sein ? Alle Gesetzlichkeiten sind langweilig.' Effi admires this and claps in approval, but her husband is irritated and reproves Crampas as an old soldier, used to discipline, for sneering at ' Zucht und Ordnung '. The latter, however, defends his frivolous attitude towards life, maintaining : ' Überhaupt ohne Leichtsinn ist das ganze Leben keinen Schuß Pulver wert', an ominous pointer to future events as well as to his past. Innstetten even warns him of the practical consequences of such a philosophy of life, indicating Crampas' injured left arm.

Chance (or is it fate ?) then favours Crampas' designs on Effi, for Innstetten is prevented from taking any further part in these rides together because of a sudden election campaign which requires his presence on duty elsewhere. The expeditions continue, however, accompanied in the distance by two servants. Crampas thus has Effi virtually alone with him, and their conversations become increasingly intimate in tone. Gradually he begins to analyse Innstetten for Effi, revealing (or at least claiming to reveal) that even in his army days he had been somewhat apart from his comrades, more respected than liked. He, too, likes to be thought 'different' (a point in common with Effi) and had cultivated or assumed an interest in the occult—but at this point Crampas tries (or pretends) to end the topic on the grounds that it is not proper to discuss a friend behind his back. Effi, thoroughly intrigued, urges him to continue and soon reveals the mysterious sounds and happenings in her house at Kessin, which have caused her so much distress, also the strange, unsatisfactory attitude of her husband towards the phenomenon. Asked for an explanation, Crampas suggests that living in a haunted house appeals to Innstetten as being ' interesting ', even distinguished. More subtly he adds that Effi's husband has another little weakness—a pedagogic streak—and hints vaguely at a connection between Effi's state of fear and Innstetten's desire to dominate and control her life . . . ' eine Art Angstapparat aus Kalkül ', as she later calls it. This gentle insinuation by Crampas is not without its effect ; gradually and unobtrusively he has won his way into her confidence, played on her fears, and quietly undermined her trust in her husband.

Another ride and picnic are planned during a brief spell of mild, sunny weather in mid-November, and again Innstetten is called away on duty at the last moment. Although he knows that Crampas is a notorious philanderer, he permits his wife to set off alone with him. The incident underlines not only Innstetten's folly but the contradictions in the character of Crampas, who appears to miss the company of his former regimental comrade in spite of the opportunty given him for furthering his designs on Effi ; ' denn so rücksichtslos er im Punkte chevaleresker Liebesabenteuer war, so sehr war er auch wieder guter Kamerad. Einem Freunde helfen, und fünf Minuten später ihn betrügen, waren Dinge, die sich mit seinem Ehrbegriffe sehr wohl vertrugen. Er tat das eine und das andere mit unglaublicher Bonhomie.' Entertaining and gallant as always, Crampas inserts, almost unnoticed, the occasional endearment into his speech, calls his companion ' teuerste Effi ' then pretends to correct this supposed slip of the tongue. He tells her a tale of a Spanish king, Pedro the Cruel, who revenged himself in gruesome manner on his wife's lover, and finally insists on keeping the glass from which Effi has drunk, openly mocking her pretended annoyance and assurance that she will tell her husband.

Danger also lurks in the amateur production by Crampas of the Wichert comedy, *Ein Schritt vom Wege*, with its symbolical title, in which Effi plays a leading part, but he takes no advantage of an all-too-conspicuous situation. He is content to await what seems to him, from past experience, the natural development of the affair. Still Innstetten takes no precautions against this experienced seducer ; ' Er ist überhaupt ein Damenmann, und nun gar Damen wie du, das ist seine besondere Passion ', he remarks casually to his teenage wife. Even Effi is distressed by the way in which Crampas manœuvres the invitation to Oberförster Ring's party so that his wife is not included, remarking that such conduct must inevitably lead to its own punishment. But Major von Crampas, as Innstetten points out, gives no thought to the future ; he is partly Polish and of unpredictable temperament : ' . . . kein rechter Verlaß, eigentlich in nichts, am wenigsten mit Frauen. Eine Spielernatur.' Effi promises to be cautious in her dealings with him but, on receiving from her husband a little lecture about ' Charakter und Festigkeit und . . . eine reine Seele ', suddenly recalls Crampas' description of him as an ' Erzieher '.

The chance/fate element then plays a further part in bringing about the catastrophe. The party at Oberförster Ring's home has passed off pleasantly and uneventfully, but an accident to one of the sleigh-drivers makes a redistribution of passengers necessary on the return journey so that Innstetten can take the reins of another sleigh. Husband and wife are thus divided. On the journey another complication occurs, which results in Crampas and Effi being left alone in one sleigh. It is, ironically, Innstetten who decides to lead the cavalcade along the shorter route through the woods which affords Crampas his opportunity. Only after the event does Innstetten seem to realise the danger involved and gives a belated warning to Effi : ' Sei auf deiner Hut. Er ist ein Mann der Rücksichts-losigkeiten und hat so seine Ansichten über junge Frauen. Ich kenne ihn von früher.' Again the reader will be tempted to ask why had he then allowed such risks to be taken previous-ly. Even the lack of firmness in his wife's character is, it now appears, known to him : ' Du bist eine reizende kleine Frau ', he says to her, ' aber Festigkeit ist nicht eben deine Spezialität.' This the experienced Crampas has also long since recognised.

When, six years later, Crampas is faced with the consequences of his actions, one again sees the contradictions in his person-ality. Although enjoying his life, he has long since recognised its emptiness, and the streak of superstitious fatalism in him already anticipates the outcome of the duel. After a moment of shock and fear he regains his composure, faces his lot and dies with courage.

Prominent among the minor characters during the Kessin chapters is the hunchback chemist, Alonzo Gieshübler, ill-favoured by nature but a man with a heart of gold and the strength to rise above his misfortune. He, almost alone in that bleak, cheerless phase of Effi's life, has the sensitivity to ap-preciate her dilemma and her loneliness. In a hundred differ-ent ways he tries to express his concern for her well-being without any of the personal motives actuating Crampas. After the daunting series of obligatory visits to the local nobility, with their glacial, unfriendly manners and limited outlook, Effi suddenly realises that Gieshübler is the only person in the whole of Kessin and the surrounding area with whom she can communicate. ' Ich steh und falle mit Gieshübler. Es klingt etwas komisch, aber er ist wirklich der einzige, mit dem sich ein Wort reden läßt, der einzige richtige Mensch hier.' The

friendship is swiftly established and soon becomes indispensable
to her, making up for much that is lacking in her relationship
with Innstetten.   One may perhaps also suspect that Gieshübler's sensitive awareness of human motivation has alerted
him to the danger represented by Crampas.   On the day
following the fateful sleigh-ride he includes in his note to her
the remarkable sentence : ' Ich weiß nur, daß Sie dem Schloon
glücklich entronnen sind : aber es blieb auch durch den Wald
hin immer noch Fährlichkeit genug.'

In a different way, consolation is also provided by two other
minor figures, one human and one canine—Roswitha and
Rollo.   The humble servant, devoted to Effi both before and
after her separation from Innstetten, is one of those simple
souls who, once having been shown kindness, never forget it.
Her loyalty in adversity provides a telling commentary on the
moralising attitudes of ' good ' society and the conformity of
those who had less to lose than Roswitha.   It is no mere co-
incidence that Rollo, the Newfoundland dog, should have
taken to her at their initial meeting, for his is also an even
simpler version of devotion which knows no flinching.

The smoothly-flowing prose of *Effi Briest* reflects the ease
with which it was written.   In spite of the apparent breadth of
the novel compared with many by Fontane, there is little
which could be pared away without detriment to the main
theme, for Fontane has conquered his long-persistent weakness
of indulging in irrelevant episodes or descriptions for the sake
of the interest they hold.   The speed of composition was offset
by the careful stylistic revision later devoted to the novel
which, in the opinion of many, is his finest.   Joseph Dresch has
claimed that this work, more than any other, earned for its
author the title of ' le classique du réalisme '.[10]   Most of the
familiar features are present, but are presented with delicate
skill.   The use of symbols and *Leitmotive* is restrained and effective.   The call back to childhood security, ' Effi, komm ! ' is
underlined by Innstetten's recollection of the incident shortly
afterwards and the almost superstitious importance he attaches
to it notwithstanding his rational principles.   Effective, too, is
the unconscious irony of Briest's telegram to his ailing, unhappy
daughter some years later, which likewise reads : ' Effi komm '.
There is subtle play on the concept of softness and yielding in

the conversation between Effi and Johanna (chapter 9), during which the servant admires her mistress's hair, ' . . . so lang und seidenweich '. ' Ja, es ist sehr weich ', replies Effi. ' Aber das ist nicht gut, Johanna. Wie das Haar ist, ist der Charakter.'

The *Leitmotiv* of anxiety figures prominently in the Kessin chapters. Indeed it runs like a scarlet thread throughout the entire work. ' Ich habe solche Sehnsucht und . . . ich habe solche Angst ', admits Effi to Johanna in the eerie old house when her husband first goes away on duty. Stylistically the figure of the Chinese servant who is supposed to haunt the Innstetten home may strike the modern reader as unconvincing, but, having once accepted the implied fact that the building has an uncanny quality and that Effi has the kind of temperament which makes her aware of it, one cannot but admire the effective use which is made of the ghost theme. It recurs at intervals throughout the period spent at Kessin, usually mirroring the insecurity in Effi's inner life, and it is an ominous sign when Johanna is found to have brought with her to the new home in Berlin a small picture of the Chinaman from the old house at Kessin. Even in the relaxed atmosphere of Gieshübler's party (chapter 11) there is a discussion of ghosts and haunted houses, while the story of the Chinaman and the supposed hauntings even makes its way prominently into Effi's long letters to the place she really regards as ' home ', her parents' house at Hohen-Cremmen. In the main these ghostly activities are confined to phenomena which could be explained away logically, and this Innstetten attempts to do, albeit with an unsatisfactory duality of purpose, leaving behind a residue of doubt and insecurity. For him ' Spuk ist ein Vorzug, wie Stammbaum und dergleichen.' In Effi's dreams, however, naked fear rises to the surface, and the link between the ghost-theme and her own sense of isolation becomes evident. Reinforcement of the uncanny atmosphere in the house is provided by the figure of the eccentric Frau Kruse, the coachman's wife, with her psychological abnormality and sinister appearance. In the background, too, there is always the threatening symbol of the lonely grave, where the Chinaman was laid to rest outside the Christian burial ground. Effi notices it, for example, at the end of chapter 16, following Crampas' insinuating analysis of her husband, which has had a considerable effect on her.

There are many unobtrusive minor symbols. One may think of the swing in the garden of Hohen-Cremmen and its associations with both Effi's childhood and her penchant for dangerous situations, her mingled fear and delight at the thought 'jetzt stürz ich '. Then there are the symbolic tales of the ' Gottesmauer ' and of Don Pedro's revenge in chapter 18. Dreams are used to reflect the hidden anxieties in the minds of both Effi and Innstetten ; nightmare mingles with reality in the former's nocturnal terrors described in chapter 9, while her husband's belated fears with regard to Crampas express themselves in dream-language in the opening lines of chapter 20.

Although not as prominent a feature as in previous works, the ' drastic ' generalisation still occurs as a familiar hallmark of Fontane's prose style. ' Ein Chinese . . . hat immer was Gruseliges ', the reader is told early in chapter 6 ; ' Andalu-sierinnen sind immer schön ', declares Effi in chapter 8 ; 'Alle alten Tanten sind neidisch ', she maintains in chapter 21. Again, in the twenty-third chapter, Frau von Briest cuts short her answer to the question about her health with the character-istic Fontane phrase : ' Krankheitsberichte sind immer lang-weilig '.

Traces of the ballad influence linger on, especially in the prefiguration of coming events—Crampas' anticipation of his soldierly end has already been mentioned ; Effi, at the tender age of 17, muses on the possibilities of her own death and longs to be buried in Hohen-Cremmen. Like a portent of future events, too, comes the innkeeper's unsuspecting recommenda-tion to Effi, during the Baltic trip, that she should seek accom-modation at a village outside Saßnitz—called ' Crampas '. She just cannot bury the past, even while on holiday, and the humorous reminiscences of life in Kessin conjured up by her husband for the delectation of their guests in Berlin represent for her an exhausting ordeal and a reminder that this unhappy era still dogged her footsteps ; ' Es war ihr zu Sinn, als ob ihr ein Schatten nachginge.'

The ability, of which the author himself was conscious, ' die Menschen so sprechen zu lassen, wie sie wirklich sprechen ',[11] here reaches its highest perfection, not only in the traditional ' festive ' settings of parties and dinners, seen to advantage particularly in the ninth chapter, but in the varying registers of private conversation between husband and wife, mistress and servant, parent and daughter. The Hohen-Cremmen discussions involving Effi, her parents and their friends are superbly presented, showing an infallible ear for every nuance of speech in an intimate circle. These brilliant passages are supplemented, as in many of this author's novels, by epistolatory exchanges. In this way the reader obtains all the information he needs in indirect and unobtrusive fashion. Only in the case of Effi's internal monologues does he resort to a more obvious device.

A skilful use is made of retrospective description, both of events occurring during the novel and those preceding it. We hear, for example, in the opening chapter about Frau von Briest's youthful romance with Geert von Innstetten twenty years earlier, and this is all the more intriguing since the version we have comes to us through her daughter. Effi goes on to supply the reader, as well as her three young friends, with much more information of a useful kind about Innstetten, his background and career, and the resort of Kessin. The marriage festivities are also dealt with retrospectively in a little over two pages, a technique which enables the author to give us the essence of the occasion without expanding it into a full chapter as happens elsewhere in his work but which here would have merely a retarding effect.

One constant feature of Fontane's work is the element of discretion, and in this respect *Effi Briest* is no exception. The reader is not regaled with salacious details of the affair with Crampas ; only its mild beginning during the sleigh ride is described. Similarly there are no gory details of the duel, only the briefest indications of what occurred : ' . . . alles erledigte sich rasch ; und die Schüsse fielen. Crampas stürzte.' Nor does Fontane even permit himself the last dramatic exchange of words between victor and vanquished that one is led to anticipate ; ' Innstetten trat an Crampas heran. " Wollen Sie . . . " das waren seine letzten Worte.'

As a social document, this novel is rich in contemporary comment, both explicit and implicit. Attention has been drawn to the Innstetten-Wüllersdorf conversations, which represent Fontane's most open denunciation of certain rigid conventions of his day. Even the servants discuss the ethics

of the duel within the current concept of honour, Johanna echo-
ing the phrases of the class by which she is employed, Roswitha
—simpler and more 'earthy' in character—expressing her
doubts as to its wisdom. Underlying the open discussion of
such controversial topics, however, is an uneasy questioning
of the soundness of the whole social structure and its ability to
endure much longer without rapid reform—a theme which is
to occupy the central position in Fontane's next and final
novel, *Der Stechlin*. The characters in *Effi Briest* tend to be
direct products of their environment. In their conformity with
the ethos of their caste they suggest analogies with primitive
tribal society and its multiplicity of taboos as well as its dire
retribution for all those who flout them. This factor and the
absence of real love and understanding (save for Vater Briest
and Roswitha) make it difficult at times for the modern reader
to feel a sense of close identification with the principal figures
in spite of the stylistic excellence of this work.

Der Stechlin

Assessments of Fontane's last completed novel have differed
radically and will no doubt continue to do so. They vary from
almost total rejection by critics such as Conrad Wandrey and
Harry Maync to the enthusiasm of Hans-Heinrich Reuter and
others who wish to upgrade its position in Fontane's work.
Wandrey speaks of ' das Versagen der Gestaltungskraft ' and
explains that ' die Menschenwelt des *Stechlin* bleibt nebulos '.
For him the famous ' Gesprächstechnik ' has now become an
end in itself rather than an artistic device ; ' Gespräche sind
der eigentliche Inhalt des Werkes, die Menschen haben keinen
Eigenwert mehr.' He maintains that it would even be possible
to transfer speeches from one character to another, something
which would have been unthinkable in the earlier novels, and
claims that—so little are the characters individualised—one
often has difficulty in remembering who is speaking during the
longer conversations.[12]

Reuter, by contrast, points to the teeming richness of ideas
and topics in this final work, which he feels could have given
rise to numerous fresh themes in novel form, had the author
been spared : ' Abermals also : nichts von greisenhafter
Verarmung, von Verkümmern.'[13]

Perhaps Fontane should be allowed to state his own view of
Der Stechlin. ' Einerseits auf einem altmodischen märkischen
Gut, andrerseits in einem neumodischen gräflichen Hause
(Berlin) treffen sich verschiedene Personen und sprechen da
Gott und die Welt durch. Alles Plauderei, Dialog, in dem
sich die Charaktere geben und mit ihnen die Geschichte.
Natürlich halte ich dies nicht nur für die richtige, sondern
sogar für die gebotene Art, einen Zeitroman zu schreiben.'[14]
To his publisher he describes the story with disarming candour
in these words : ' Zum Schluß stirbt ein Alter und zwei Junge
heiraten sich—das ist so ziemlich alles, was auf 500 Seiten
geschieht. Von Verwicklungen und Lösungen, von Herzens-
konflikten oder Konflikten überhaupt, von Spannungen und
Überraschungen findet sich nichts.'[15]

Der Stechlin is a very substantial novel of forty-six chapters
and with a wide variety of characters. In loosely-constructed
form the author offers his reflections, at the end of a long life,
on man and society, especially the society of Prussia at the turn
of the century. Although he modified his original plan of
writing a ' Bildungsroman ', in which the nobility of the Mark,
as it then was, would have been compared specifically with an
idealised aristocracy of the future, the reader does find strong
traces of this theme in his treatment of the two generations of
the Stechlin family.

The novel is built around the figure of the elderly Dubslav
von Stechlin, whose character and personality are presented
in great detail. Sometimes reminiscent of Berndt von Vitzewitz
in *Vor dem Sturm* and often also of Fontane himself, Dubslav is
characterised by his tolerance, good-humour and gentle irony.
Though intellectually of only average stature (as he himself is
well aware), he possesses a sincerity of feeling and goodness of
heart which lead him instinctively to the right decisions. As
Pastor Lorenzen says of him during the funeral oration : ' Er
hatte vielmehr das, . . . was immer gilt und immer gelten
wird : ein Herz.' This old Junker ' mit dem Stück Sozialdemokratie im Leibe ' has been described by Karl Frenzel as ' der
echte Märker und Fontanesche Mustermensch '.[16] In him
the limitations and weaknesses of his class are offset by solid
virtues and a humane tolerance which seem to point forward
to the possibility of a new and finer rôle in society for the

coming generation, symbolised by his son Woldemar. By up-
bringing and instinct Dubslav stands for the old Prussian
values of ' Königtum, Luthertum, Adel und Armee ', but in
the serenity of old age he opens his mind to new ideas and,
like Fontane, is prepared to question the validity of everything
in the world around him. A passage of his son's diary, in which
he compares his father with his new friend in Berlin, Graf
Barby, is illuminating :

> ' Und dazu der alte Graf! Wie ein Zwillingsbruder von Papa;
> derselbe Bismarckkopf, dasselbe humane Wesen, dieselbe
> Freundlichkeit, dieselbe gute Laune . . .   Aber was am ver-
> wandtesten ist, das ist doch die gesamte Hausatmosphäre, das
> Liberale. Papa selbst würde zwar darüber lachen—er lacht
> über nichts so sehr wie über Liberalismus—, und doch kenne
> ich keinen Menschen, der innerlich so frei wäre, wie gerade
> mein guter Alter. Zugeben wird er's freilich nie und wird in
> dem Glauben sterben: "Morgen tragen sie einen echten alten
> Junker zu Grabe." Das ist er auch, aber doch auch wieder
> das volle Gegenteil davon. Er hat keine Spur von Selbstsucht.'

In his relationship with his servants and other representatives of the humbler classes Dubslav is a paragon of natural
courtesy and good-will. With the elderly retainer Engelke he
is on terms of such intimacy that the old man is always the
first to hear the news from his master's letters, including
confidential family items, and his opinions are both sought and
respected, as may be seen especially towards the end of chapter
26. The same tolerance on principle is extended to other races
and confessions as well as to other classes. The unattractive
locum tenens, Dr. Moscheles, is repellent to him not on account
of his alien origins or his Jewish faith, but because of his
mannerisms and political ideas. As the strictly Lutheran
Superintendent Koseleger observes, not entirely in approval,
we may suspect : ' Und dann heißt es ja auch, der Major von
Stechlin habe mehr oder weniger einen philosemitischen Zug.'
This description is gladly accepted by Dubslav, ' weil er
Unchristlichkeiten nicht leiden kann und Prinzipienreitereien
erst recht nicht.' All the greater is the honest old man's disappointment, however, when he feels his open and unprejudiced
trust in all types of humanity betrayed—as in the case of his
business associate, Baruch Hirschfeld.

There is, however, a certain degree of inconsistency in Dubslav's character which makes him more convincing as a human being. Peaceful and tolerant though he may be in the major issues, in small matters he can exhibit remarkable irritability. It is Moscheles' red tie and odd way of holding his walking stick which lead to his rejection by Dubslav von Stechlin as much as his sympathy with the Social Democrats. Even the loss of Adelheid's company is regretted, following her hasty and skilfully contrived departure, for ' sie besaß doch nebenher einen guten Verstand, und in allem, was sie sagte, war etwas, worüber sich streiten und ein Feuerwerk von Anzüglichkeiten abbrennen ließ. Etwas, was ihm immer eine Hauptsache war.'

How close is Dubslav von Stechlin to his creator, Theodor Fontane ? Certainly not close enough for him to be represented as a self-portrait, although this was sometimes suggested in the past, but points of resemblance are unmistakable. Both tend to look at a question from two points of view and as a result sometimes fail to arrive at a clear and satisfying solution ; ' Paradoxen waren seine Passion ', we are told of Dubslav in the opening chapter. Both enjoy conversation, especially if it sparkles with humour as well as controversy. They have the same capacity to find happiness in the little pleasures of everyday life, to feel an almost disproportionate enjoyment in the well-told anecdote. Neither has any time for extremists in political, social or religious matters. Both are capable of irony at their own expense. It may be said with equal truth of Fontane as of Dubslav : ' Sein schönster Zug war eine tiefe, so recht aus dem Herzen kommende Humanität, und Dünkel und Überheblichkeit . . . waren so ziemlich die einzigen Dinge, die ihn empörten.' There are many echoes from Fontane's past life—his mixture of political enthusiasm and scepticism in 1848-9, his lengthy travels through the Mark of Brandenburg, his affection for and exasperation with the old country Junkers, his first visit to England while a serving soldier, like Woldemar, and his later protracted residence in that country, reflected in the London reminiscences of the Barbys. This is a novel of kindly old age and a gentle passing, completed and revised just before Fontane's own death came to him with equal mildness. It is as though the writer sensed the end was near while he wrote, and indeed he admitted as much in a letter to Ernst Heilborn on September 23, 1897 : he expressed both triumph and surprise at having completed this substantial work, concluding sadly : ' Aber nun ist es auch vorbei ; die Kräfte sind hin.'

To what extent is it a ' political ' novel, and how is this element distributed ? Fontane clearly felt it to be a political work when he wrote to Ernst Heilborn [17] : ' Ich stecke so drin im Abschluß eines großen, noch dazu politischen und natürlich märkischen Romans, daß ich gar keine anderen Gedanken habe und gegen alles andre auch gleichgültig bin.' Even more specific is his letter of 8 June, 1896, to C. R. Lessing : ' Im Winter habe ich einen politischen Roman geschrieben (Gegen-überstellung von Adel, wie er bei uns sein *sollte*, und wie er *ist*). Dieser Roman heißt : *Der Stechlin*.' Interpretations have varied widely from a supposed championing of the old order to a thinly-veiled anticipation of a Marxist society. At the centre of the novel's political discussions stands Pastor Lorenzen, the reformer, who nevertheless enjoys the confidence and indeed the friendship of the tolerant old Dubslav von Stechlin. The elderly Junker has even, in past years, entrusted the educa-tion of his son Woldemar to Lorenzen as house tutor. Pastor Lorenzen is no unbalanced revolutionary hothead, but an earnest practical Christian who seeks to redress the more flagrant wrongs in the life and society of his day. He conveys these ideals with such tact and skill that Woldemar may yet be successful in combining the best of the old ways with the noblest of the new ones. Acting as a kind of foil for Lorenzen is the newly-rich Gundermann, with his eternal complaint of ' Wasser auf die Mühlen der Sozialdemokratie '—a caricature of reaction, and described by Pastor Lorenzen as ' ein Bour-geois und ein Parvenu, also so ziemlich das Schlechteste, was einer sein kann.'

Surprising political opinions are revealed casually in the conversations between Lorenzen and Dubslav, the elderly squire with his hankering after the ' good old days ' of the alliance with Tsarist Russia. England, Fontane's second love and other source of despair after Prussia, receives a scolding through the voice of Pastor Lorenzen because of its hypocrisy and greed, ' weil der Kult vor dem goldenen Kalbe beständig wächst '. When the ailing Junker senses that his days are

numbered, he also feels an overwhelming desire to talk about
the future, for then Schloß Stechlin will be in the hands of his
son Woldemar, who has been educated and strongly influenced
by Lorenzen. In spite of his love for his son, Dubslav feels that
he is 'ein unsicherer Passagier', who might well be reconciled
to the new creed of social democracy and open the family
home to embittered, anti-establishment politicians, ' Katheder-
sozialisten ' and their kind.   Lorenzen, however, anticipates
quite a different future for Schloß Stechlin, suggesting that
Woldemar will find himself in the position of a liberally-minded
Crown Prince who, on coming to the throne, finds that many
of his plans were impracticable and is forced to compromise
with, if not wholly accept, the ways of the former king.

Necessarily cautious in his conversation with Dubslav,
Lorenzen discloses much more of his political and social views
in the long, frank talk with Melusine : ' Ich lebe darin und
empfind es als eine Gnade, da, wo das Alte versagt, ganz in
einem Neuen aufzugehn.'   More specifically he adds : ' In
unserer Obersphäre herrscht außerdem eine naive Neigung,
alles ' Preußische ' für eine höhere Kulturform zu halten ',
an assumption which may at one time have had its uses, but
which no longer serves any real purpose.   He believes in a more
fluid form of society, in which everyone has the right to find
his own natural level ; formerly one was either a castle owner
or a linen weaver by right of birth—' jetzt kann jeder Leinen-
weber eines Tages ein Schloßherr sein '.   Lorenzen points to
the outstanding epochs in Prussian and German history—
political, social and spiritual—and acknowledges their greatness, though adding : ' Was einmal Fortschritt war, ist längst
Rückschritt geworden.'   The modern era demands, in his view,
new values and new heroes.   When asked directly by Melusine
whether he is against the ' old families ' and nobility of Prussia,
he replies—very much in the voice of Theodor Fontane—
that he is not, at least not on a personal basis, that these old
families still retain many fine qualities, and remain popular,
but are squandering their opportunities through failure to
adapt themselves to a new age, through the misconception
that they are indispensable. ' Wohl möglich, daß aristokratische
Tage mal wiederkehren, vorläufig, wohin wir sehen, stehen
wir im Zeichen einer demokratischen Weltanschauung. Eine

neue Zeit bricht an. Ich glaube, eine bessere und eine glück-
lichere.' This long exchange of views between Lorenzen and
Melusine may appear to be more than a little contrived in
the context of the novel, but it is most important for the light
it sheds on both characters as well as serving as a mouthpiece
for much of Fontane's social and political thinking in the last
few years of his life.

Contrasting violently with this political parson, as well as
with the mild and tolerant outlook of Dubslav von Stechlin,
is the latter's sister Adelheid, Domina von Wutz, a caricature
of reaction and social snobbery. Her definition of ' freedom '
is at least noteworthy for its succinctness : ' Was heißt Freiheit?
Freiheit ist gar nichts ; Freiheit ist, wenn sie sich versammeln
und Bier trinken und ein Blatt gründen.' At the other end of
the scale is Dr. Moscheles, whom Dubslav instinctively distrusts.
' Einer ist wie der andre ', he says angrily of the aristocracy
after his snub by Herr von Stechlin ; ' Was wir brauchen ist
ein Generalkladderadatsch, Krach, tabula rasa.'

The cordial relationship which quickly springs up between
Dubslav von Stechlin and his counterpart in the Barby family,
following Woldemar's engagement, leads to some further
illuminating exchanges on political matters. Dubslav expresses
a surprising preference for the War of Liberation in 1813 rather
than the campaigns of Frederick the Great, ' weil alles, was
geschah, weniger den Befehlscharakter trug und mehr Freiheit
und Selbstentschließung hatte.' While he cannot support the
doctrinaire liberal concept of freedom, he believes in the same
ideal and claims that this viewpoint is spreading steadily
through the ranks of the nobility. Into these Dubslav-Barby
conversations Fontane strews his random thoughts about the
future and the new century just ahead, and some of these
visions of the twentieth century show astonishing prescience.
Dubslav wonders whether Japan will become a new power,
like Britain, in the Pacific Ocean, whether China with its
teeming millions will suddenly awaken to political conscious-
ness, and, above all, whether the ' fourth estate ', the working
class, will become a force with which the world will have to
reckon. During the steamer excursion on the Spree (reminiscent
of a similar trip made in *L'Adultera*), it is Graf Barby's elder
daughter, Melusine, who has a prophetic vision of great air

battles in future wars.

The Berlin interlude—one of the most satisfying parts of the whole novel—is valuable in addition for the insight it affords into the social conditions of the servant class during the 1890s, a theme already touched upon in *Frau Jenny Treibel*. This problem is discussed at some length in chapter 14 within the family circle of Barby's coachman, Imme. Through the young girl Hedwig, the reader learns something of the way in which servants lived in less enlightened households at the end of the nineteenth century in Berlin—the so-called ' Schlafgelegenheit', which is nothing but an alcove in the kitchen or a camp bed in the bathroom, the unwanted attentions from male members of the household, and the perpetual jealousy and suspicion of the wives.   Before the Berlin police intervened, conditions were apparently even worse, and the voice of Hedwig's uncle on the subject symbolises the deep rumblings of discontent that lay beneath the tranquil surface of the bustling, confident new capital city : ' Der Bourgeois tut nichts für die Menschheit. Und wer nichts für die Menschheit tut, der muß abgeschafft werden.'

The election motif, also prefigured in *Frau Jenny Treibel*, again shows a central character out of context and in danger of becoming ridiculous in the eyes of his associates.   From the solemn platitudes of the village political meeting at the Dorfkrug in chapter 17 to the carnival-like atmosphere of the election-day dinner at the ' Hotel zum Prinzregenten ' in chapter 20, the impression is given of a meaningless charade in progress, an alien novelty grafted on to a largely intact system of authoritarian, hierarchical society.   The defeated Conservative candidate, Dubslav von Stechlin, is secretly relieved by the result, while none of his landowning fellow squires seem to fear that the victory of the Social Democrats will make any real difference to their future rôle in the society around them.   As Woldemar's friend and fellow officer, Czako, says in an earlier context : ' Unsre Leute gefallen sich nun mal in der Idee, sie hingen mit dem Fortbestande der göttlichen Weltordnung aufs engste zusammen.   In Wahrheit liegt es so, daß wir sämtlich abkommen können.'   Barely twenty-one years after these words were written, the whole aristocratic society of Prussia and Germany, together with the Hohenzollern monarchy on which it depended, collapsed in revolution after the defeat of 1918.

After one has considered the political implications in this work, of which there can be varying interpretations as with so many of Fontane's Delphic utterances on such matters, one is left with a feeling that, in spite of the wide range of characters introduced in this novel, few of them remain vividly imprinted on the memory apart from old Dubslav himself. Even Pastor Lorenzen is memorable more for what he says than what he is. Woldemar, the future heir, is little more than a pallid sketch. One notes with awe that he, like Botho von Rienäcker, proposes to take his young bride straight from the train to the art galleries (this time at Dresden) as a honeymoon treat ; some light is also thrown on his personality by Melusine during her long talk with Lorenzen. She says of her brother-in-law : ' Er hat einen edeln Charakter, aber ich weiß nicht, ob er auch einen festen Charakter hat. Er ist feinen Sinnes, und wer fein ist, ist oft bestimmbar . . . Er bedarf der Stütze', and she appeals to Lorenzen to go on giving him the support he needs. He appears throughout the tale in a pleasant if nebulous light— correct, courteous, full of social graces and genuine kindness ; but what he will eventually stand for is not very clear, since he still lacks depth of personality. His engagement to Armgard at the end of chapter 25 must rank as one of the most improbable and unconvincing love-episodes in the history of literature ; ' Ich glaube fast, ich bin verlobt ', she says to her sister—on what appears to be the flimsiest of evidence—and her uncertainty is understandable. Woldemar had shown similar courtesy to both sisters and could equally well have chosen Melusine.

Melusine, the divorcée and ex-Countess Ghiberti, emerges as one of the few strong and highly individualised personalities in this novel. Dubslav von Stechlin (who, despite his years, retains a keen eye for an attractive woman) says admiringly of her when they first meet : ' Das ist eine Dame und ein Frauenzimmer dazu '. The discussion with Lorenzen in chapter 29 illustrates her intellectual grasp of human affairs and her astonishing independence for a woman of the 1890s. Here, too, Fontane seems to be pointing forward to the future, suggesting greater equality of the sexes, and in this one can see his appeal for the writers of the Naturalist movement. In *Melusine* the reader may find an intriguing mixture of qualities —intellect and sensuality, dignity and playfulness, agnosticism and belief, pride and humility. Crowning them all, however, is an unswerving honesty.

From amongst the very large group of secondary characters, two perhaps stand out because of their unique humorous appeal. They are the music-teacher, Dr. Wrschowitz, and the painter, Cujacius. Both are, in a sense, caricatures and remind the reader of the unconstrained humour of Fontane as expressed in such tales as *Onkel Dodo* or in his family correspondence. Neither plays an essential part in the story—but then, who does in this tale in which so much and yet so little happens ? Wrschowitz's endless references to ' Krittikk ' may pall after a while, but surely the thumbnail sketch in Czech accents of the Berlin ' Madamm ' (chapter 24) deserves its modest niche in the gallery of literary humour alongside the contribution of Lessing's Riccaut de la Marlinière ? Unforgettable also is the glorious climax of a long-smouldering enmity between these two vain, temperamental artists, when, all dignity forgotten, they resort to an exchange of gross insults.

The style of this novel is familiar in many respects. There is a tendency to go back to earlier idiosyncrasies which seemed to be disappearing in the major works of later years. A stylised use of the possessive adjective is again noticeable—the travellers in chapter 14 are referred to as ' unsere Reisenden '—and there are numerous echoes of both the *Wanderungen* and the first novel, *Vor dem Sturm*, with its digressions and anecdotes, as for example in the opening description of the Stechlin lake, the visit to its shores in chapter 28, or the exploration of the park at Rheinsberg, with its historical associations, in chapter 19. The nostalgic reminiscences of London and English life, especially in chapters 22 and 25, read almost like pages borrowed from *Ein Sommer in London*. Drastic and provocative generalisations appear with unusual frequency : ' Rokoko hat immer eine Geschichte ' and ' Rokoko ist doch immer unsittlich ', the reader is assured in the second chapter. ' Alle Lehrer sind nämlich verrückt ' and ' Alle Lehrer sind ein Schrecknis ', it is asserted in chapter 5. ' Alle Klosteruhren gehen nach ' is the contribution of chapter 6, and so it continues.

While many of the conversations contain material which is of considerable historical and social interest, few are really vital to the story itself or aid either characterisation or exposition. The same may be said of the many incidental characters introduced into the tale. There are occasional signs of careless revision as, for example, in chapter 36, where the day breaks twice. Chapter—or rather section—titles have suddenly re-appeared, each with its symbolical function.

The effective use of humour has been alluded to earlier in connection with Cujacius and Wrschowitz. These are the most obvious examples, but one should not forget Adelheid's priceless summary of England (which she had never visited) in chapter 27 or the incident of her sudden departure in chapter 39. Fontane had long been an admirer of the English and American style of humorous writing, with which certain of his short tales and much of his intimate correspondence show strong affinities.

It has been noted earlier that one of Fontane's favourite devices for character-revelation is to allow two groups of people to discuss each other separately, often just before or just after a social event. This is employed here, too, as early as the second chapter, where Rex and Czako talk about Woldemar and his father while they, in their turn, analyse the guests. In this way the reader acquires certain basic information about both groups. Similarly Rex and Czako discuss Woldemar a second time on the ride home, during which he leaves them temporarily, and the reader is informed of the link between Woldemar and the Barby family. The same technique is employed in chapter 21, when Rex and Czako walk home together and pool their impressions of the Barby family.

The familiar use of dinner parties is again in evidence. In chapter 3 the Berlin visitors—Czako, Rex and Woldemar—are brought together around the dinner table with various Stechlin notabilities, so that the reader may learn something about them all in relaxed social conversation. It is handled by Fontane with his usual virtuosity, though the reader is left on this occasion with an impression of elegant but somewhat futile chatter, as witness for instance the long and solemn discussion of rats in Berlin and Paris. The effect is reinforced by Frau Gundermann's empty generalisations on the subject of ' young people today '.

The well-known Fontane discretion in treating harrowing or highly personal situations is clearly illustrated in this novel. Nothing could be more discreet than the engagement between Woldemar and Armgard ; it is hardly noticeable. Likewise the death of old Dubslav von Stechlin is registered in a single sentence, even though foreshadowed throughout several chapters.

How is one to rank this final novel amongst the life's work of its author ? The range of critical attitudes has been indicated earlier, but at least a tentative judgement is called for. To the Fontane-lover, who is already familiar with the novelist's work, this tale offers much that is of interest and value for the understanding of Fontane as a stylist, an interpreter of Mark Brandenburg and its people, as a fireside philosopher and political thinker. In it one finds more open access to the author as a person than in any other work. Nevertheless, as a novel in its own right and taken without reference to all that has gone before or knowledge of the man writing it, *Der Stechlin* must be rated as a secondary work, one with much charm in places but containing serious defects in structure and an uneven mastery of characterisation. Its artistic appeal derives primarily from the sensitive and loving way in which Fontane has presented a milieu.

CONCLUSION

Some Distinctive Features of Fontane's Prose Style and Literary Technique ; a Summary of his Themes

QUESTIONS of style and technique have been reviewed in some detail as each work was presented and discussed. The purpose of this chapter is therefore to provide a summary and leave the student of Fontane with an impression of those features which are typical of his prose work as a whole.

Fontane was a conscious stylist, who wrote to one of his publishers : ' Ich bilde mir nämlich ein, unter uns gesagt, ein Stilist zu sein, nicht einer von den unerträglichen Glattschrei-bern, die für alles nur *einen* Ton und *eine* Form haben, sondern ein wirklicher.'[1] So skilfully has he achieved his object in the maturer works that it is frequently difficult, if not impossible, to appreciate the amount of careful revision which has taken place since the original draft was written. Sometimes this ' Pularbeit ', as he called it, took far longer than writing the entire first version of the tale. The result is, at its best, an example of German prose which displays an exquisite sense of creative workmanship even in the smallest details. It shows a striving after stylistic perfection rather than a spontaneous outpouring of unselfconscious genius, a steadily growing mastery of every subtle nuance in language, an ever-increasing precision of description and portraiture.

Outstandingly successful was his reproduction of conversa-tion. The spoken word is the reader's key to the characters and it is principally through their conversational exchanges that he comes to know them. Fontane consciously strove for dialogue that would be, if not total reality, at least an artistic quintessence of that reality. ' Meine ganze Aufmerksamkeit ist darauf gerichtet, die Menschen so sprechen zu lassen, wie sie wirklich sprechen,' he once wrote.[2] In pursuing this goal he has been remarkably successful. Though his characters range from the humblest classes of urban and rural society to the brilliant social circles of the Prussian aristocracy, he has reproduced for all of his personages a mode of speech which is both convincing and natural. So natural does it sound, indeed, that it is possible to overlook the fact that there has been a subtle process of editorial refinement, performed in a manner which differentiates Fontane sharply from his younger contemporaries of the Naturalist movement. The result of his discreet stylistic intervention is an impressive *illusion* of reality.

The speech of his aristocrats is frequently characterised by a witty, intellectual quality, in which the author excelled and which is an integral part of the ' Fontaneton ' in his novels. Fashionable Berlin of the late nineteenth century was inclined to make liberal use of ' Fremdwörter ', of quotations in English, French or Italian, of maxims and proverbs, and a surprisingly large number of rhetorical questions. The jargon of the officers' mess was a specialised version of this cult, and Fontane mastered its nuances with especial virtuosity.

The language of the lower classes is often a blend of 'Hochdeutsch ' and dialect, the latter varying from the localised version of Berlin German to degrees of genuine regional dialect or even out-and-out ' Plattdeutsch '. Of all these people, the Berliners make the most lively and distinctive impression, with their haphazard stringing together of endless co-ordinate clauses, their frequent exclamations such as ' Na ', ' Nu ', ' Jott ', their hackneyed but apt folk-wisdom, their floods of questions, constant naming of the other conversational partner and their confused if picturesque use of long or unfamiliar words.

The speech of Fontane's characters is sufficiently sharply differentiated for the reader to sense not only to which social class a man or woman belongs but even to hazard a reasonably accurate guess at sub-divisions within that class. Few of his people are taciturn (though his gardeners tend to be an exception), and most express themselves easily, whether in company or in solitary reflection. Many are endowed with verbal mannerisms or stock phrases, which also aid the process of characterisation ; Legationsrat Duquede for instance in *L'Adultera* finds most things ' überschätzt ', Herr von Briest evades disagreeable topics with the invariable response : ' Das ist ein zu weites Feld ', and in *Der Stechlin*, Gendarm Uncke considers many remarks to be 'zweideutig', while Dr. Wrschowitz talks incessantly of ' Krittikk '.

The process of speech-differentiation becomes increasingly effective as the series of Fontane's novels and ' Novellen ' progresses. An early tendency for the characters to converse in rather stilted, ' bookish ' German is soon overcome. As the author's skill in the presentation of conversation increases, together with its use as a means of revealing personality, it is also noticeable that the proportion of actual narration decreases, since many of its functions are taken over by lively, dramatic dialogue which usually becomes the centre of interest in the work. In the case of the last novel, *Der Stechlin*, conversation forms the whole basis of the story, but in others, too, it is frequently the mainstay of the reader's attention, since plot and action are on a very modest scale. Events are mainly of an everyday character : people travel, meet friends and relatives, go on excursions to country restaurants, give dinner-parties and attend those of their acquaintances, and join in family reunions. When, out of these simple, harmless beginnings, great psychological complications result, sometimes even culminating in tragedy and grief, the reader may be taken unawares.

One sphere in which Fontane's mastery of conversation is seen to the greatest advantage is in the presentation of dinner-parties and similar social gatherings. They serve a double purpose for the present-day reader. Firstly they help him to understand the principal characters of the work, who reveal a great deal about themselves in their relaxed conversation at the dinner table or over coffee and liqueurs. This understanding is aided by the comments of the other guests, not only in the hearing of the company at large but also in subtle private exchanges on which the reader is allowed to eavesdrop. Secondly, the views expressed on current affairs, famous personalities and so forth help to illuminate what is now a bygone historical era. In addition, the range of secondary characters thus introduced enables Fontane to indulge his skill at human portraiture without any danger of obscuring the principal theme. As a master at presenting affluent nineteenth century society on convivial occasions, Theodor Fontane rivals Anthony Trollope in English letters, and, by his example, has encouraged a similar use of such scenes in the work of Thomas Mann.

Turning now from the conversation of the novel characters to more general considerations of prose style, the reader soon observes that Fontane himself has a number of favourite forms of expression which appear again and again in his works. One of these is his way of making a sweeping generalisation, some-times—though by no means always—adding a modifying afterthought. The habit is distributed widely among the characters, and instances (e.g. ' Palme paßt immer ', ' Alle Portiersleute sind eitel ') have been noted throughout this examination of his works.

There is scarcely ever any attempt to highlight dramatic moments. Joseph Dresch has pointed out that, far from ex-ploiting his crises, Fontane appears to be trying to avoid them altogether.[3] After a lengthy period of psychological preparation the turning-point finally arrives, only to slip past almost unnoticed. It is not until the end of the novel, when the reader looks back, that it can be seen how important one particular incident was for the whole development of the story. Often the real crisis lies not in outward events at all, but in the realisation of some previously hidden truth by one of the principal characters. ' C'est un moment psychologique important, brusquement dévoilé dans l'âme d'un personnage', states Joseph Dresch.[4] It is not so much the external event constituting the crisis of the novel or *Novelle* which interests Fontane, as the effect it has on the minds of his characters. ' Die eigentliche Welt ist ihm stets die der Seele ', Maync has observed.[5] The emphasis in these prose stories is thus on ' Innenhandlung ', and to illustrate this effectively the author sometimes continues the tale beyond the point where one might have assumed that it would end. The crisis, if represented by one outward occurrence, is described sparingly and with dis-cretion, as for example the duel between Innstetten and Crampas in *Effi Briest*, or that of St. Arnaud and von Gordon (*Cécile*), which is related merely through a brief newspaper report. Perhaps the most striking case in which discretion is triumphant in circumstances where sensation might seem to be mandatory is that of *Unterm Birnbaum*. The discussions and plans leading to the murder of the Polish traveller are kept from the reader altogether, and he remains in the dark through-out, except for vague suspicions, until the criminal is revealed by chance. Tension arises only from the delay in establishing the guilt of Hradschek.

Such deliberate avoidance of dramatic tension extends also into the field of the erotic. Here Fontane's artistic delicacy leads him to omit all scenes of physical intimacy in works such as *Irrungen, Wirrungen* or *Effi Briest*, where they play such a major though hidden part in the story. This kind of omission was partly through deference to prevailing literary convention and a desire to spare the Wilhelminian family readers' susceptibilities. It included not only situations likely to provoke moral indignation, such as an irregular sexual union or an act of marital infidelity, but also, by extension of the same principle, the detailed depiction of violence or harrowing death-bed scenes. Even the discovery of Effi Briest's long-forgotten love-letters from Crampas takes place while Effi is away, thus precluding any sort of violent confrontation between husband and wife. Another reason for this discretion of approach was that Fontane eschewed scenes of sustained high emotion in real life as well as in his art. As a writer he felt unable to portray them adequately and preferred the sparing indications of the ballad-poet. In the words of Paul Schlenther : ' Fontane ist kein Ausmaler, sondern ein Andeuter.'[6] The reader's curiosity is often aroused in this way, for a good deal is left to his imagination. Why, for example, did Cécile react so peculiarly to a number of remarks made during various excursions in the Harz ? Why did the high-ranking army officer greet both Cécile and St. Arnaud on the station platform in Potsdam without coming over to speak to them ? As Otto Pniower said of the author : ' Sein Ideal ist eine diskrete, verhüllende, aufs Erratenlassen gestellte Kunst.'[7]

One characteristic feature of Fontane's way of telling a story is the obvious pleasure he derives from lingering over minor features and the little things of everyday life. ' Ich behandle das Kleine mit derselben Liebe wie das Große ', he wrote in 1883.[8] In such features he discovered what he felt to be the characteristic quality of people, places and events, and consequently both style and technique were considerably modified. ' Was heißt großer Stil ?' he asks through the voice of Ebba in *Unwiederbringlich*, and immediately gives the answer : 'Großer Stil heißt soviel, wie vorbeigehen an allem, was die Menschen eigentlich interessiert.'[9] The definition might equally well have been found in one of Fontane's letters to a friend or publisher, for it is this principle which appears to guide his selection of material and distribution of emphasis. People take precedence over the plot, while everyday problems predominate over sensational events. Whenever circumstances permit—and indeed sometimes when, strictly speaking, they do not—Fontane prefers to linger in the quiet by-ways of life and leave the bustling main roads to others. The artistic effect is a varied one. It can provide an interesting and valuable contribution to the work as a whole; at other times, especially in the earlier works, it can be exasperating. In *Vor dem Sturm*, for instance, there are several chapters on matters which have no real bearing on the main theme and which could have been left out. On the other hand, one of them—' Bei Frau Hulen '—is a future Berlin novel in miniature which no one would want to miss, whatever its degree of irrelevance. This tendency—digression from the theme and the insertion of superfluous material—was potentially a threat to Fontane's development as a novelist and a weakness which he clearly found hard to overcome. The great discipline of the *Novelle* form in the two works immediately after the lengthy novel, *Vor dem Sturm*, helped him considerably to rectify this stylistic fault, though unfortunately it was to recur at intervals throughout his life's work and finally to triumph openly, though with the author's sanction, in his last and most discursive novel, *Der Stechlin*. Some of his digressions have acquired a new historical interest since their day, while others remain either interesting or otherwise as anecdotes, but seem misplaced. Excursions were often the excuse for introducing irrelevant material, as for example the story of the Präzeptor von Altenbrak in *Cécile*, while Baedeker-style descriptions of old churches, museums and art galleries remind us of Fontane, the ' Wanderer '. Karl Frenzel sums it up by saying : ' Plaudern ist sein eigentliches Talent . . . man empfängt schließlich den Eindruck einer frei vorgetragenen, nicht den einer niedergeschriebenen Geschichte.'[10] The free use of anecdotes, as also of letters and diary excerpts, can sometimes give Fontane's novels an episodic character. He tends also in some works to concentrate on the individual chapter as a stylistic unit, treating the novel as a whole and the relationship of its chapters to one another in freer fashion.

One cannot imagine Fontane's prose without its essential

ingredient of gentle humour. It was a quality which he appreciated in other writers and on which he laid particular stress in his own work. He did not write ' humorous ' novels as such, although in *Frau Jenny Treibel* humour plays an exceptionally large part. His was the quiet brand of humour which provokes an appreciative smile rather than loud laughter. Something of its robust sources, however, may be seen in a study of his private correspondence, where it plays an important part in freeing him from distress, even despair, when things are going badly. It has a remarkably modern touch in places, as does the boisterous humour of the short tale *Onkel Dodo*, in which he satirises a fresh-air fiend. Genuine humour implies the ability to laugh at one's own expense, and this Fontane frequently does in his letters. He relates, for example, how he ran the gauntlet of cruel witticisms from cabmen in London while wearing an old-fashioned, German-style fur coat—all he could then afford—or how he allowed his hair to grow long during the damp and dismal English winter until the advent of what appeared to be a sunny, spring morning, on which he betook himself and his ' lange Mähne ' to the barber, emerging like a shorn sheep from this ' Verschönerungsakt ' to find himself in a howling gale. His audience with the King of Bavaria is treated in similar ironical, self-deprecating fashion, as he confesses that his ageing, cracked patent-leather shoes were kept in shape only by dint of wearing three pairs of socks. There are numerous examples of this kind of approach in his letters, and the humour one encounters in the novels and *Novellen* is a subtle and more delicate distillation of this wholesome brew. Fontane is a master at employing humour as a means of relieving a tragic theme or a tragic interpretation of life, and his gently ironical tone often conceals a streak of profound pessimism in the author himself. He cannot alter the laws of life, which sometimes maltreat his novel-characters, but he does offer the reader a form of relief, since ' der beste Weg ist der des Humors '.[11]

Fontane's way of depicting a natural background is interesting. As a ' wanderer through the Mark of Brandenburg ' he was familiar in some detail with its countryside as well as its historic buildings, so that he was able to draw on this experience with great advantage in his prose fiction. Usually, however, it is not the whole scene which he presents, but the elements which distinguish that landscape or view from all others. Normally, too, nature-description has a double rôle to play ; the observant reader will notice that it is subtly linked to the psychological mood of the characters and serves to bring about some revelation of importance or to contribute to a spiritual crisis of some kind. ' Die Landschaftsschilderung hat nur noch Wert, wenn sie als künstlerische Folie für einen Stein auftritt, der dadurch doppelt leuchtend wird ', the novelist wrote in 1873.[12] In other words, human nature takes precedence over external nature. Less subtle than this interplay between man and nature are occasional examples where the natural background assumes an almost dramatic significance, such as the storm on the night of the murder in *Unterm Birnbaum* or the ominous stillness of the forest immediately before the shooting of Förster Opitz in *Quitt*.

Use is sometimes made of autumnal scenes to foreshadow the coming winter of human hopes, while the motif of the sunset also takes on symbolic significance. Just before Christine's suicide in *Unwiederbringlich*, for instance, the feeling of autumn is stressed, and the deserted husband in *L'Adultera*, van der Straaten, finds the late-October day in harmony with his own bleak mood. The setting sun, glimpsed through the window of Stine's apartment, has obvious significance for the love without a future between herself and Waldemar. The earlier ' balladesque ' *Novellen*, *Grete Minde* and *Ellernklipp*, are rich in scenes of this kind.

One of the principal ways in which outdoor settings play a part in influencing the fate of the characters is through the skilful use made of country excursions. These outings nearly always have consequences of importance, since people, once removed from their normal urban surroundings and constraints, talk and behave more freely and naturally : things are thus said and done which hasten on the crisis of the novel. Such turning-points are : the trip to the Stralauer Wiese in *L'Adultera*, during which Melanie and Rubehn become aware of their love for each other, the visit by Botho and Lene to Hankels Ablage (*Irrungen, Wirrungen*), which brings their greatest joy but is also the beginning of the end. In *Frau Jenny Treibel*, too, it is an excursion to Halensee which provokes the engagement of Corinna and Leopold, which has such dramatic consequences.

Although his description of background scenes is normally linked closely to the characters and their fate, Fontane nevertheless shows great skill in the evocation of atmosphere, especially when dealing with the Mark of Brandenburg that he knew so well. Other areas, such as Silesia and the Harz, in which he spent frequent and prolonged holidays, are also successfully exploited as the background of his stories or parts of them. It is when he attempts to portray areas not personally known to him that the author's magic fails. Compare, for instance, the two parts of *Quitt*, or consider the depiction of Hungary in *Graf Petöfy*. No amount of careful research could replace personal experience, and Fontane came to realise this. ' Das Büchermachen aus Büchern ist nicht meine Sache ', he once admitted in a letter to his wife.[13]

It is, however, in his portrayal of the urban backcloth of Berlin that he excels most brilliantly. To his contemporaries it must have been fascinating in a different sense, for he not only introduces familiar street-names, parks, public buildings, cafés and restaurants, excursion resorts and so forth, but also succeeds in evoking the whole spirit of the thriving new capital city, complete with topical allusions. So vivid was the background for some of his more pedantic readers that they felt it should be possible to plot all the movements of his characters on a street-map of the city and occasionally took him to task about some topographical slip or other, rather to the elderly writer's irritation.

Not only is the external appearance of streets and buildings used in order to provide a *milieu* for his characters, but the interior furnishings of their homes frequently give a useful indication of their tastes and interests, telling their own story of the inhabitants and the various influences on their lives. It is especially noticeable in the introductory description of Pauline Pittelkow's flat in *Stine*. Hobbies are likewise used to characterise the person concerned ; van der Straaten and his art collection, for example, or Lehrer Krippenstapel and his bees. This, of course, suggests a link with the technique of the young Naturalist authors who were writing during the same period. Can he be in any way classed as one of them ? Many of them looked up to him with respect and affection ; some, after the publication of *L'Adultera*, would have liked to claim him as a kind of literary patron. Fontane himself, however, was in no doubt about the gulf which divided them. While he shared their dislike of social hypocrisy, he did not express this view in a direct, frontal attack but rather by subtle implication. Though he also evoked a convincing atmosphere of reality, it was not the photographic reality of the Naturalists but a selective, artistic presentation. Nor was his subject-matter taken from the same kind of background, for he hardly knew the industrial proletariat and complained bitterly of ' lauter Schnapstragödien '[14] produced by the Naturalist authors. He saw that one of their main services was an infusion of a new element of realism into literature which had been out of touch with the many changes in late nineteenth century Germany. He felt, however, that this was only a beginning : ' Will dieser erste Schritt auch schon das Ziel sein . . ., so hört alle Kunst auf, und der Polizeibericht wird der Weisheit letzter Schluß.'[15] The extreme manifestations of Naturalism might be necessary in order to end an era of literary complacency and pallid imitations of bygone styles, but it was not a lasting heritage. To admit previously unacknowledged social classes and social problems into literature was, in his view, to perform a signal service. It was their exclusive concentration on the sordid aspects of life which caused Fontane to reject the Naturalists. He believed that a work of art should contain a judicious blend of elements, as in real life, and that the whole should undergo a discreet process of artistic transfiguration ; ' Ohne diese Verklärung gibt es aber keine eigentliche Kunst', he felt.[16]

For him, perhaps the greatest contribution of the Naturalist writers was their influence on dialogue, into which they had introduced the recognisable tone of everyday reality, albeit without that process of selection and refinement which he felt to be aesthetically essential in all forms of art. A point of difference, however, lay in their respective attitudes towards social conventions. Characters in Naturalist works flout the social laws in defiance and on principle ; Fontane's people only do so when there is a specific personal reason or through the working of natural laws which lead to an inevitable collision.

It is difficult, too, to see the average young adherent of Naturalism sharing Fontane's keen aesthetic interest in the life-style of
the Prussian aristocracy. One may perhaps regard him as an
intellectual bridge between the old and new values in literature,
a conciliatory rôle for which he was temperamentally well
suited.

If the Naturalists operated effectively only within certain
limits, the same can be said of Fontane, and he was well
aware of this. At first one may be dazzled by the wealth and
variety of his characters, which include not only those typical
figures, the Berliner and the rural *Märker*, but representatives
of many other German-speaking regions (including the ' fringe '
areas, where German and Slav populations mingled), as well
as a fair sprinkling of foreigners, especially English. From this
profusion it may not be evident that he feels conscious of any
kind of restriction, but basically the problems presented and
the central characters involved in them are all closely akin.
The themes which predominate are those of love and marriage,
while the representative figures are mainly drawn from the
minor aristocracy and wealthy upper-middle classes.

In some respects his pre-occupation with problems connected
with love-affairs and marriage is surprising, since in his personal
life such matters appear to have caused few complications.
There is a revealing observation in a letter of 1883, written
during a trip to Norderney: 'Die alte Dame war sehr verbind-
lich gegen mich. Was früher die jungen Damen an mir
versäumt haben—worüber ich jetzt sehr milde und beinahe
dankbar denke—holen die alten nach.' Debating the reasons
for this, he concludes : ' Die jungen fühlten . . . daß Liebe
nicht meine Force war.'[17] Similarly, when discussing with his
wife the motivation of *Graf Petöfy*, he admits frankly : ' Im
übrigen weiß ich sehr wohl, daß ich kein Meister der Liebes-
geschichte bin ; keine Kunst kann ersetzen, was einem von
Grund aus fehlt.'[18] Compare this, however, with a panegyric
on the sublimity of love contained in a letter of 1876 to his
wife : ' Ich könnte ein hohes Lied schreiben über die Erhaben-
heit, die Herrlichkeit, die Wonne, die Wunderkraft der Liebe,
und zwar nicht Phrasen, die ich hasse, sondern Empfundenes.'[19]
It hardly seems possible that the same writer is making this
statement. The following lines, however, resolve the apparent

contradiction : ' Ich liebe Liebe, aber ich gucke sie mir an und prüfe sie auf ihre Echtheit.'[20] Sham sentimentality that passes for love, he deplores, and this is reflected in his work. Deep and genuine feelings are also present, but these are indicated with discretion.

In the novels and *Novellen*, problems of love and marriage tend to fall into certain recognisable categories. The marriages which break down usually do so because of gross inequality between the ages of the partners or because of a fundamental difference in temperament. The love-relationships outside marriage are of two kinds : the affair of convenience between a nobleman and a girl from the people, and genuine love between two persons of widely different social origins who cannot marry on account of class barriers. In the former case, the relationship causes no social problem and is tacitly ignored. In the latter case, however, society, as constituted in the last years of the nineteenth century, shows its disapproval by ostracism or worse, and, unless the lovers are strong and independent enough to emigrate, the bonds have to be broken either by renunciation or suicide. One breach has nevertheless been made in the age-old wall of social prejudice. If the young woman is from the newly-rich industrial upper-middle class, an exception may be made, for the wealthy new bourgeoisie possessed what so many of the nobility lacked, namely money with which to maintain their estates and town houses, their servants and horses, while in return they could offer the *cachet* of a title and a respected old family name. Women from the lower-middle or working classes, on the other hand, could provide no such form of ' social compensation ', and, however worthy in character, remained unacceptable. In a few instances the partners recognise the hopelessness of their situation and submit in time to the will of society. Those who do, rescue their social standing but at a great cost to their inner emotional life. In many cases, however, the realisation that they have reached an impasse comes too late, and they either perish or spend the rest of their lives in great unhappiness. Despite Fontane's own reasonably happy marriage (as far as one can judge from the correspondence), there is a surprising lack of normal, stable marriage-relationships in his tales, at any rate amongst the principal younger characters.

Although Fontane did not specify his social criticisms in detail or draw any rigid conclusions, they are there by implication—his usual way of making important points about people and society. There are no flaming protests in the Naturalist style or direct frontal attacks on the strongholds of social prejudice ; Fontane turned away from the storming of barricades as early as 1848. He uses subtler weapons, among them delicate irony of tone and an outlook characterised by scepticism. The reader is left in little doubt concerning his views on the generally tolerated affair of convenience between different social classes ; it lacks dignity, trust, understanding and all those qualities which ennoble human relationships. Ironically, society sees very little wrong with it, while at the same time frowning on a supposed *mésalliance* in marriage because of diverse social origins. It is obvious that, for Fontane, the real *mésalliance* is a marriage contracted for the wrong reasons, such as the acquisition of wealth or a title, thus reducing a human being to the level of an object to be bartered. At the same time he recognised that a new moral order could not be achieved overnight and that meanwhile compromises with contemporary society would sometimes be necessary ; open flouting of its rules would lead to disaster in the majority of cases. Ideally, too, marriage partners should look for similarities in outlook, values and temperament rather than complementary characteristics. Writing to his son Theo, Fontane expressed it thus : ' Das Richtige ist : verbleib innerhalb der eignen Sphäre, dieselbe Nationalität, dieselbe Religion, dieselbe Lebensstellung. Nur aus dieser Gleichheit ergibt sich auch die Gleichheit der Anschauungen, die Übereinstimmung in den entscheidenden Dingen, ohne die kein rechtes Glück und keine rechte Freude möglich ist.' [21]

One of the ' solutions ' frequently encountered in his prose tales is that of suicide, but it is again clear by implication that, in the novelist's view, it represented no real solution at all but was a form of moral cowardice. Similarly the duel between ' men of honour ' is shown both implicitly and, in *Effi Briest*, explicitly to be an act of senseless folly. At the same time Fontane never blames his guilty, erring or unhappy characters; his attitude is one of detachment, his conclusions marked by tolerance and understanding of human frailty. The reader senses rather than sees the tragic inevitability of the disaster towards which his characters are marching, but these are merely the 'natürlichen Konsequenzen, die mitunter sehr hart sind.'[22]

By presenting a limited number of carefully selected characters, who are personalities in their own right and at the same time symbols of a social class, a cultural background and a geographical area, Fontane succeeds in evoking the spirit of an entire historical age. In most cases it is the late nineteenth century in Prussia, but this is not invariably so ; some of the earlier works go back to the beginning of that century, while *Grete Minde* is set in the early seventeenth century, before the outbreak of the Thirty Years War. The reader is concerned not only with the outward events of the characters' lives but also with their psychological motivation and the part played by society in forming or modifying their attitudes. As a means of providing the necessary inner illumination, the long internal monologue is used, revealing in some detail the individual's most private thoughts. Alternatively there is the device of the letter or a page from a diary.

Inevitably there is a fair amount of repetition or at least similarity in themes and situations, but it is by no means true to assume from this that Fontane's works are basically static. Not only in the depiction of the characters themselves does Fontane show constant progress, but in his manner of introducing them. Compare, for example, the clumsy formality of his introduction in *Vor dem Sturm* with the effortless ease in the major social novels, culminating in *Effi Briest*. The entire series of his works shows a process of increasing structural integration, which lapses again only in his last and most discursive novel, *Der Stechlin*, and that deliberately.

With his gentle humour, his tone of genial *causerie*, the brilliance of his dialogue and occasional evocation of mild, autumnal melancholy, Theodor Fontane has gradually appealed to a wider circle of readers. His fame has spread from his fellow-citizens of Berlin and Prussia to all the German-speaking lands, and it now also finds an echo in the English-speaking world.

It is difficult to lay down precisely the qualities which distinguish a good novelist, but one may reasonably expect some proof of mastery in at least one of the following spheres : characterisation, plot, social background. Fontane could claim distinction in the first and last of these, his plots usually playing a secondary rôle. In some of the prose tales—*Irrungen, Wirrungen* for instance—the characterisation is of a very high order and suggestive of Jane Austen or Chekhov. Above all else he shows a superb skill at depicting the social background of his own day. In presenting it, he records facts and incidents, laws (both written and unwritten) which govern the conduct of men and shape their destinies, but he does not attempt to censure or moralise, still less to clamour for reform as did, for example, Dickens. In tone, therefore, he is more akin to Trollope. His plots are seldom more than a framework for his characterisation and social portraiture. He thus falls short in any comparison with Tolstoy, whose skill extended to all three spheres.

Fontane's prose style has provided a model and an inspiration for a worthy successor in the field of the novel, Thomas Mann, who openly acknowledged his debt. The work of both authors shows the same cool detachment and gentle irony, a similar objectivity in the treatment of people and events. Both men possess a keen eye for the significant detail and each is a master of dialogue, the easy flow of which may sometimes conceal from the reader the endless care which has gone into their search for the precise word or the telling phrase.

Theodor Fontane was a product of his age, inasmuch as he could not have written in the way he did except against that particular background and in that prevailing social climate. Though a child of his own era, he rose above it. His detachment lent his work a quality which is in some respects more easily appreciated today than it was during his lifetime, and not merely in his own country. There is a ' European ' as well as a ' regional ' quality which differentiates him from his outstanding contemporaries, Storm and Keller. They have remained, in spite of undoubted stylistic merit and thematic interest, essentially German regional novelists in the widest sense, whereas the mild, unassuming Theodor Fontane has achieved recognition among the major European social novelists of the nineteenth century, and is worthy to join the company of Thackeray, Meredith, Trollope and Dickens from

England, Zola and Flaubert from France, or Chekhov from
Russia. In the words of a distinguished Fontane scholar, the
late Kurt Schreinert: 'Er wurde der Begründer des Berliner
Gesellschaftsromans, der niemals wieder eine solche Kunsthöhe
erreicht hat.'[23]

NOTES

Unless otherwise specified, page references to Fontane's works are from the following edition : Theodor Fontane, *Sämtliche Werke*, München, 1959—.

CHAPTER ONE
1. *Meine Kinderjahre*, Chapter 2, p. 28.
2. Ibid, Chapter 3ff.
3. Ibid, Chapter 6, pp. 56-58.
4. Ibid, Chapter 6, p. 52.
5. Ibid., Chapter 3, p. 33.
6. Ibid., Chapter 15, pp. 154-7.
7. Ibid., Chapter 2, pp. 17-18.
8. Ibid., Chapter 13, pp. 125-6.
9. Ibid., Chapter 13, pp. 124-5.
10. Ibid., Chapter 13, p. 126.
11. Ibid., Chapter 13, p. 126.
12. Ibid., Chapter 10, p. 91.
13. Ibid., Chapter 9, p. 84.
14. Ibid., Chapter 9, p. 84.
15. *Von Zwanzig bis Dreißig*, Section 2, Chapter 6, p. 107.
16. Letter of 1.12.1857 to Wilhelm von Merckel.
17. *Meine Kinderjahre*, Chapter 9, p. 83.
18. Ibid., Chapter 16, p. 167.
19. Ibid., Chapter 13, p. 130.
20. Ibid., Chapter 13, p. 130.
21. Ibid., Chapter 18, pp. 183-4.
22. *Die Grafschaft Ruppin*, p. 176.
23. *Meine Kinderjahre*, Chapter 18, p. 185.
24. *Von Zwanzig bis Dreißig*, Section 2, Chapter 6, p. 117.
25. Ibid., Chapter 6, p. 118.
26. *Meine Kinderjahre*, Chapter 14, p. 139.

CHAPTER TWO
1. *Von Zwanzig bis Dreißig*, Section 1, Chapter 1, p. 14.
2. Ibid., p. 15.
3. Ibid., Section 2, Chapter 1, p. 66.
4. Ibid., Chapter 2, p. 77.
5. Ibid., p. 79.
6. *Shakespeares Strumpf*, 1841.
7. *Von Zwanzig bis Dreißig*, Section 2, Chapter 4, p. 90.
8. Ibid., Chapter 7, p. 120.
9. Ibid., Section 3, Chapter 2, p. 134.
10. Ibid., p. 140.
11. Ibid., p. 142.
12. Ibid., Section 4, Chapter 1, p. 156.
13. Ibid., Chapter 2, p. 162.
14. Ibid., Section 5, Chapter 1, pp. 308-9.
15. Ibid., Chapter 3, p. 317.
16. Ibid., Section 6, Chapter 1, p. 328.
17. Ibid., p. 334.
18. Ibid., p. 334.
19. Ibid., Section 6, Chapter 1, p. 338.
20. Ibid., p. 342.
21. Ibid., p. 343.
22. Ibid., Chapter 2, p. 344.
23. Ibid., p. 346.
24. Ibid., p. 346.

²⁵ Ibid., Chapter 3, p. 354.
²⁶ Ibid., Section 7, Chapter 2, p. 368.
²⁷ Ibid., Section 8, Chapter 1, p. 377.

CHAPTER THREE
¹ Letter of 18.9.1857 to his mother.
² Letter of 7.8.1876 to his wife.
³ Letter of 17.6.1876 to Mathilde von Rohr.
⁴ Letter of 14.7.1875 to Wilhelm Hertz.
⁵ Letter of 9.12.1894 to Georg Friedlaender.

CHAPTER FOUR
¹ Letter of 18.8.1885 to Emilie Zöllner.
² Paul Schlenther on p. xxxviii of his Introduction to the *Gesamtausgabe der erzählenden Schriften*, S. Fischer, Berlin, 1925.
³ *Der alte Derffling* (or *Der alte Derfflinger*), 1846.
⁴ *Der alte Zieten*, 1847.
⁵ Franz Servaes, *Theodor Fontane* : (*Die Dichtung*, vol. 24), 1900 ; p. 33.
⁶ Gustav Roethe, 'Zum Gedächtnis Theodor Fontanes,' *Deutsche Rundschau* 182, 1920, p. 110.
⁷ Harry Maync, 'Theodor Fontane, 1819-1919' : *Zeitschrift für den deutschen Unterricht*, 15. *Ergänzungsheft*, p. 7, Leipzig and Berlin, 1920.
⁸ Paul Schlenther on p. xxix of his Introduction to the *Gesamtausgabe der erzählenden Schriften*, S. Fischer, Berlin, 1925.
⁹ *Vorwort zur ersten Auflage, Wanderungen durch die Mark Brandenburg*, Berlin, 1861.
¹⁰ *Vorwort zur zweiten Auflage, Wanderungen durch die Mark Brandenburg*, Berlin, 1864.
¹¹ See Hinweise, p. 410, *Fontanes Werke in zwei Bänden*, ed. Werner Lincke, Bergland Verlag, Salzburg and Stuttgart, 1961.
¹² Ibid.

CHAPTER FIVE
¹ Letter of 1.11.1876 to Mathilde von Rohr.
² Ibid.
³ Letter of 17.6.1866 to Wilhelm Hertz.
⁴ Ibid.
⁵ Else Croner, *Fontanes Frauengestalten*, Langensalza, 1931, p. 10.
⁶ Hans-Heinrich Reuter, *Fontane*, München 1968, p. 550.
⁷ Further details will be found on p. xxv of *Grete Minde*, ed. A. R. Robinson, Methuen, London, 1955. Pages 69—75 of the present study are adapted from the author's introduction to that edition.
⁸ Letter of 24.8.1882 to his daughter Mete.
⁹ Letter of 14.3.1880 to Gustav Karpeles.

CHAPTER SIX
¹ Edgar Groß, Nachwort, Bd. 2, *Theodor Fontane, Sämtliche Werke*, München 1959, p. 395.
² Conrad Wandrey, *Theodor Fontane*, München 1919, p. 190.
³ Hans-Heinrich Reuter, *Fontane*, München, 1968, pp. 654-6.

CHAPTER SEVEN
¹ See Conrad Wandrey, *Theodor Fontane*, München 1919, p. 213.
² Letter of 8.9.1887 to his son Theo.
³ Conrad Wandrey, *Theodor Fontane*, München 1919, p. 232.
⁴ Letter of 14.7.1887 to Emil Dominik.
⁵ Hans-Heinrich Reuter, *Fontane*, München 1968, pp. 667-8.
⁶ Conrad Wandrey, *Theodor Fontane*, München 1919, p. 320.

7 Hans-Heinrich Reuter, *Fontane*, München, 1968, p. 696.
8 Ibid., p. 700.
9 Ibid., p. 826.
10 Conrad Wandrey, *Theodor Fontane*, München 1919, p. 299.
11 Letter to Paul Schlenther, 8.11.1896.

CHAPTER EIGHT
1 Joseph Ettlinger, *Theodor Fontane* (*Die Literatur*, Bd. 18), Berlin 1904, p. 46.
2 Conrad Wandrey, *Theodor Fontane*, München 1919, p. 252.
3 Ibid., p. 267.
4 Letter of 2.3.1895 to Hans Hertz.
5 Erich Schmidt, *Charakteristiken* II, Berlin, 1901, p. 244.
6 *Effi Briest*, Chapter 4, p. 195.
7 Ibid., Chapter 13, p. 256.
8 Paul Schlenther on p. lxiv of his Introduction to the *Gesamtausgabe der erzählenden Schriften*, S. Fischer, Berlin, 1925.
9 Hans-Heinrich Reuter, *Fontane*, München, 1968, p. 683.
10 Joseph Dresch, *Le Roman Social en Allemagne*, Paris, 1913, p. 337.
11 Letter of 24.8.1882 to his daughter Mete.
12 Conrad Wandrey, *Theodor Fontane*, München, 1919, p. 301.
13 Hans-Heinrich Reuter, *Fontane*, München, 1968, p. 837.
14 Letter to the editor of the Stuttgart periodical, *Über Land und Meer*, 1897.
15 Ibid.
16 Karl Frenzel, 'Theodor Fontane als Erzähler,' *Deutsche Rundschau* 129, Berlin 1906, p. 157.
17 Letter of 12.5.1897 to Ernst Heilborn.

CONCLUSION
1 Letter of 3.3.1881 to Gustav Karpeles.
2 See Chapter 8, note 11.
3 See Joseph Dresch, *Le Roman Social en Allemagne*, Paris, 1913, p. 308.
4 Ibid., p. 308.
5 Harry Maync, 'Theodor Fontane, 1819-1919,' *Zeitschrift für den deutschen Unterricht*, 15. *Ergänzungsheft*, 1920, p. 18.
6 Paul Schlenther, on pp. xliii-iv of his Introduction to the *Gesamtausgabe der erzählenden Schriften*, S. Fischer, Berlin, 1925.
7 Otto Pniower, 'Theodor Fontanes Effi Briest,' *Deutsche Literaturzeitung*, 1896, p. 244.
8 Letter of 8.8.1883 to his wife.
9 *Unwiederbringlich*, Chapter 22, p. 150.
10 Karl Frenzel, 'Theodor Fontane als Erzähler,' *Deutsche Rundschau* 129, 1906, p. 154.
11 Letter of 10.10.1889 to Friedrich Stephany.
12 See vol. 9 of *Gesammelte Werke*, Berlin, 1905-10, II. Serie, p. 211.
13 Letter of 12.4.1871 to his wife.
14 Letter of 10.10.1889 to Friedrich Stephany.
15 *Literarische Essays und Studien*, 1. Teil, p. 473 (Vol. XXI/1 of the collected works), München, 1963.
16 Letter of 24.6.1881 to his wife.
17 Letter of 19.7.1883 to his wife.
18 Letter of 15.6.1883 to his wife.
19 Letter of 31.7.1876 to his wife.
20 Ibid.
21 Letter of 15.3.1886 to his son Theo.
22 Letter of 8.9.1887 to his son Theo.
23 Kurt Schreinert, *Einführung* p. 20, in *Theodor Fontane, Gesammelte Werke in vier Bänden*, Sigbert Mohn Verlag, Gütersloh, 1960.

A SELECT BIBLIOGRAPHY

1. Editions of Fontane's collected works :
   Gesammelte Werke (21 vols.), F. Fontane & Co., Berlin, 1905-10.
   Gesamtausgabe der erzählenden Schriften (9 vols.), S. Fischer, Berlin, 1925.
   Sämtliche Werke (28 vols.), Nymphenburger Verlagshandlung, München, 1959—.
   Sämtliche Werke (18 vols.), Hanser Verlag, München, 1962-66.

2. Annotated editions of individual works for the English-speaking reader :
   Grete Minde, ed. A. R. Robinson, Methuen, London, 1955.
   Die Poggenpuhls, ed. D. Barlow, Blackwell, Oxford, 1957.
   Irrungen, Wirrungen, ed. G. W. Field, Macmillan, London, 1967.
   Frau Jenny Treibel, ed. H. B. Garland, Macmillan, London, 1968.

3. English Translations of Fontane's works :
   (a) Fiction
   Beyond Recall (*Unwiederbringlich*) by Douglas Parmée, London, 1964.
   Effi Briest, by Douglas Parmée, London, 1967.
   (b) Travel
   Across the Tweed (*Jenseits des Tweed*), by Brian Battershaw, London, 1965.

4. Autobiographical Works and Correspondence :
   Meine Kinderjahre ; *Von Zwanzig bis Dreißig*, ed. C. Coler, Berlin, 1961.
   Theodor Fontanes Briefwechsel mit Wilhelm Wolfsohn, ed. W. Wolters, Berlin 1910.
   Theodor Fontane, Briefe an seine Familie, ed. K. E. O. Fritsch, Berlin, 1924.
   Theodor Fontane, Briefe an seine Freunde, O. Pniower & P. Schlenther, Berlin, 1925.
   Theodor Fontane u. Bernhard von Lepel, ed. J. Petersen, München, 1940.
   Storm—Fontane : *Briefe der Dichter*, ed. E. Gülzow, Hamburg, 1948.
   Briefe an Georg Friedlaender, ed. K. Schreinert, Heidelberg, 1954.
   Theodor Fontane, Briefe an Wilhelm u. Hans Hertz, 1859-98 : ed. K. Schreinert & G. Hay, Stuttgart, 1972.
   Dichter über ihre Dichtungen : *Theodor Fontane*, I, II, ed. R. Hirsch, W. Vordtriede, R. Brinkmann, W. Wiethölter, München, 1973.

5. Works of Criticism :
   (a) Principal Studies
   Servaes, F., *Theodor Fontane*, Berlin, 1900 (Vol. 24 of *Die Dichtung*, ed. P. Remer.)
   Ettlinger, J., *Theodor Fontane*, Berlin, 1904 (Bd. 18, *Die Literatur*, ed. G. Brandes.)
   Kricker, G., *Theodor Fontane* ; *Von seiner Art u. epischen Technik*, Berlin, 1912.
   Wandrey, C., *Theodor Fontane*, München, 1919.
   Krammer, M., *Theodor Fontane*, Berlin, 1922.
   Spiero, H., *Fontane*, Wittenberg, 1928.
   Seidel, H. W., *Theodor Fontane*, Stuttgart, 1940.
   Reuter, H. H., *Fontane*, München, 1968.
   Müller-Seidel, W., *Theodor Fontane*, Stuttgart, 1975.

   (b) Other Studies and Articles :
   (N.B.—The following titles are a selection. An almost complete bibliography has been provided by J. Schobeß in *Literatur von und über Theodor Fontane*, Potsdam, 2nd ed., 1965, which lists the extensive holdings of the Fontane-Archiv in Potsdam. It is augmented by R. Koester, 'Theodor Fontane Bibliography—A Supplement', *German Quarterly*, Vol. XLI, No. 4, Nov. 1968. There is also a detailed bibliography at the end of vol. 2 in H. H. Reuter's 1968 study, *Fontane*.)

   Brahm, O., 'Theodor Fontane, Literarisches und Persönliches,' *Neue Deutsche Rundschau* X, 1898.

Frenzel, K., 'Theodor Fontane als Erzähler', *Deutsche Rundschau*, 129, Berlin, 1906.
Amann, P., 'Theodor Fontane und sein französisches Erbe,' *Euphorion*, Bd. 21, Berlin, 1914.
Schönemann, F., 'Theodor Fontane als Märker,' *Zeitschrift für den deutschen Unterricht*, 28, Berlin, 1914.
Schönemann, F., 'Theodor Fontane und England,' *PMLA*, Vol. 30, Baltimore, 1915.
Mann, T., 'Der alte Fontane' in *Das Fontane-Buch*, ed. E. Heilborn, Berlin, 1919.
Maync, H., 'Theodor Fontane 1819-1919,' *Zeitschrift für den deutschen Unterricht*, 15. Ergänzungsheft, Leipzig & Berlin, 1920.
Roethe, G., 'Zum Gedächtnis Theodor Fontanes,' *Deutsche Rundschau* 182, Berlin, 1920.
Hayens, K., *Theodor Fontane; a Critical Study*, London, 1920.
Shears, L. A., *The Influence of Walter Scott on the Novels of Theodor Fontane*, New York, 1922.
Shears, L. A., 'Theodor Fontane as a Critic of the Novel,' *PMLA*, Vol. 38, Baltimore, 1923.
Soergel, A., 'Theodor Fontane' in *Dichtung und Dichter der Zeit*, Leipzig, 1928.
Petersen, J., 'Fontanes Altersroman', *Euphorion* XXIX, Stuttgart, 1928.
Behrend, E., *Theodor Fontanes Roman 'Der Stechlin'*, Beiträge zur deutschen Literaturwissenschaft XXXIV, Marburg, 1929.
Sieper, C., *Der historische Roman und die historische Novelle bei Raabe und Fontane*, Forschungen zur neueren Literaturgeschichte LXII, Weimar, 1930.
Gilbert, M. E., 'Das Gespräch in Fontanes Gesellschaftsromanen', *Palaestra* 174, Leipzig, 1930.
Croner, E., *Fontanes Frauengestalten*, Pädagogisches Magazin, Heft 1337 Langensalza, 1931.
Davis, A. L., 'Fontane as a Political Thinker', *Germanic Review*, Vol. VIII, pp. 183-194, New York, 1933.
Sauer, A. K., *Das aphoristische Element bei Theodor Fontane*, Germanische Studien, 170, Berlin, 1935.
Downs, B. W., 'Meredith and Fontane', *German Life and Letters*, Oxford, 1937-8.
Wegner, H. G., 'Theodor Fontane und der Roman vom märkischen Junker', *Palaestra* 214, Leipzig, 1938.
Wandel, C., *Die typische Menschendarstellung in Theodor Fontanes Erzählungen*, Berlin, 1938.
Wiskott, U., 'Französische Wesenzüge in Theodor Fontanes Persönlichkeit und Werk,' *Palaestra* 213, Leipzig, 1938.
Kohn-Bramstedt, E., 'Marriage and Misalliance in Thackeray and Fontane', *German Life and Letters*, 1938-39, pp. 285-97, Oxford, 1939.
Park, R., 'Theodor Fontane's Unheroic Heroes,' *Germanic Review*, Vol. XIV, pp. 32-44, New York, 1939.
Fürstenau, J., 'Fontane und die märkische Heimat', *Germanische Studien* 232, Berlin, 1941.
Genschmer, F., 'Theodor Fontane; a Study in Restraint', *Monatshefte* XXXIII, pp. 265-74, Wisconsin, 1941.
Rose, E., 'Theodor Fontane's Novels and the Spirit of Old Age,' *Germanic Review*, pp. 254-62, New York, 1948.
Schrader, I., *Das Geschichtsbild Fontanes*, Limburg/Lahn, 1950.
Robinson, A. R., 'Problems of Love and Marriage in Fontane's Novels', *German Life and Letters*, Oxford, 1951-2, pp. 279-85.
Barlow, D., 'Fontane's English Journeys', *German Life and Letters*, Oxford, 1952-3, pp. 169-177.
Ritscher, H., *Fontane—Seine politische Gedankenwelt*, Göttingen, 1953.
Radbruch, G., *Theodor Fontane, oder Skepsis und Glaube*, Leipzig, 1948.
Barlow, D., 'Fontane and the Aristocracy,' *German Life and Letters*, Oxford, 1954-55, pp. 182-191.

Carter, T. E., 'A Leitmotif in Fontane's "Effi Briest",' *German Life and Letters*, Oxford, 1956-7, pp. 38-42.
Robinson, A. R., 'A Report on the Present-Day Distribution of the Fontane Manuscripts', *Modern Language Review* 51, London, 1956, pp. 572-75.
Stern, J. P. M., 'Effi Briest: Madame Bovary: Anna Karenina,' *Modern Language Review*, London, 1957, pp. 363-75.
Bosshart, A., *Theodor Fontanes historische Romane*, Winterthur, 1957.
Barlow, D., 'Symbolism in Fontane's "Der Stechlin",' *German Life and Letters*, Oxford, 1958-9, pp. 282-6.
Furst, L. R., 'The Autobiography of an Extrovert: Fontane's "Von Zwanzig bis Dreißig",' *German Life and Letters*, Oxford, 1958-9, pp. 287-94.
Raddatz, F. J., 'Gedanken um den alten Fontane,' *Neue Deutsche Literatur*, Berlin, 1956, pp. 112-22.
Schillemeit, J., *Theodor Fontane, Geist und Kunst seines Alterswerkes*, Zürich, 1961.
Rowley, B. A., 'Theodor Fontane: a German Novelist in the European Tradition?' *German Life and Letters*, Oxford, 1961-2, pp. 71-88.
Demetz, P., *Formen des Realismus: Theodor Fontane*, München, 1964.
Remak, J., *The Gentle Critic: Theodor Fontane and German Politics*, 1848-98, Syracuse, N.Y., 1964.
Samuel, R. H., 'Theodor Fontane', in *Selected Writings*, Melbourne, 1965, pp. 112-22.
Robinson, A. R., 'Schoolmasters and Scholars in Fontane's Prose Works,' *Modern Languages* 47, London, 1966, pp. 18-21.
Koester, R., 'Death by Miscalculation: Some Notes on Suicide in Fontane's Prose', *German Life and Letters*, Oxford, October 1966, pp. 34-42.
Sasse, H-C., 'The Unknown Fontane: Sketches, Fragments, Plans,' *German Life and Letters*, Oxford, October 1966, pp. 25-33.
Richter, K., *Resignation. Eine Studie zum Werk Theodor Fontanes*, Stuttgart, 1966.
Günther, V. J., *Das Symbol im erzählerischen Werk Fontanes*, Bonn, 1967.
Thanner, J., *Die Stilistik Theodor Fontanes*, Hague, 1967.
Nürnberger, H., *Theodor Fontane in Selbstzeugnissen und Bilddokumenten*, Hamburg, 1968.
Mittenzwei, I., *Die Sprache als Thema. Untersuchungen zu Fontanes Gesellschaftsromanen*, Bad Homburg, 1970.
Attwood, K., *Fontane und das Preußentum*, Berlin, 1970.
Strech, H., *Theodor Fontane : Die Synthese von Alt und Neu*, Berlin, 1970.
Jolles, C., *Theodor Fontane*, Stuttgart, 1972.
Kahrmann, C., *Idyll im Roman : Theodor Fontane*, München, 1973.
Moser, H. & Wiese, Benno von, 'Theodor Fontane,' Sonderheft, *Zeitschrift für deutsche Philologie*, Bd. 92, Berlin, 1973.
Preisendanz, W., *Theodor Fontane*, Darmstadt, 1973.
Bange, P., *Ironie et Dialogisme dans les romans de Theodor Fontane*, Grenoble, 1974.
Aust, H., *Theodor Fontane: 'Verklärung'. Eine Untersuchung zum Ideengehalt seiner Werke*, Bonn, 1974.
Robinson, A. R., 'Recollections in Tranquillity: an Examination of Fontane's Autobiographical Novel'. In *Festschrift for C. P. Magill*, Cardiff, 1974.

6. Wider Critical Studies containing significant contributions on Fontane :
Schmidt, E., *Charakteristiken* II, p. 233 ff., Berlin, 1901.
Meyer, R. M., *Gestalten und Probleme*, pp. 203-14, Berlin, 1905.
Dresch, J., *Le Roman social en Allemagne*, Paris, 1913.
Pascal, R., *The German Novel*, pp. 178-214, Manchester, 1956.
Garland, H. B., 'Theodor Fontane', in *German Men of Letters*, ed. Natan, London, 1961.

INDEX